14 Days

W9-AXC-031

HUNTING IN AFRICA

By FRANK C. HIBBEN

Frank C. Hibben, who has made four trips to Africa and has hunted on four continents, writes of his safaris through jungles, deserts, plains, and mountains, hunting the rarest and most dangerous animals in the world.

In these eighteen true stories, the author takes us with him as he tracks lions in the brush and a herd of dangerous Cape buffalo; baits the vicious leopard; dodges the stupid rhino and barely escapes an elephant stampede. We follow the difficult paths of rare gazelles and antelopes—the forest sitatunga, called "the ghost of the forest"; the dibitag, which inhabits the arid stretches of East Africa; the Nile lechwe, which lives in inaccessible swamps; and we also venture into the treacherous Sahara for the addax.

Mr. Hibben introduces us to the customs and life of the natives, the work of the white hunters, the problems of wild game conservation, and the history of hunting.

Through story and thirty-two pages of photographs taken by the author and his wife, including a rare sequence of five pictures of a lioness killing a wildebeest, we travel with Mr. Hibben, reliving his exciting tales of hunting in Africa.

Hu

Books by Frank C. Hibben

Hunting in Africa

- by FRANK C. HIBBEN

HILL AND WANG · NEW YORK

FIRST EDITION SEPTEMBER 1962

The author and the publisher acknowledge permission to collect
in book form pieces first published in the following magazines:
Field and Stream ("Walk Around a Rhino," "Africa's Rarest and
Most Beautiful Animal"); *Sports Afield* ("Hunting the Country
of Beau Geste"—published in this volume as "Hunting the Sahara
of Beau Geste"); *Outdoor Life* ("Rare African Trophy").

Manufactured in the United States of America

To my wife, Brownie,
who has hunted these same regions
with notebook and camera

Contents

Illustrations

The illustrations appear following pages 44 and 172.

ix

Introduction

THE URGE to hunt is latent in all of us, dating, perhaps, from that ancient age when our ancestors hunted to live. In my own case, the hunting fever appeared at an early age and in a very strong form.

From the time I was first able to read, I liked hunting stories. My earliest idol was Teddy Roosevelt, whose sporting adventures in North America I determined to emulate. Teddy's book on his African trip came out in 1909, the year before I was born. When I read of this great adventure, I was ten years old, and people were still talking of the best-selling book. From Theodore Roosevelt, hunter and founder of the United States Park System, I derived two driving ambitions: one, to become an outdoor sportsman like Teddy, the other, to become a great conservationist. I wanted to preserve our wildlife heritage. I can vividly recall worrying night after night as I fell asleep about the extinction of the American buffalo herds after the great slaughter of 1883.

With these twin drives, I started on an early career of hunting, love of the outdoors, and conservation. In my native Ohio, in the early 1920's, there was no such thing as big game hunting, and even small game was scarce. Nevertheless I tramped the fields with my father, and we counted it a lucky day when we brought back a rabbit. On these expeditions I wore a favorite hat, which looked like the slouched sombrero of the hero of San Juan Hill; I carried a cartridge box on a bandoleer over my shoulder, and held my single shot .22 rifle at the ready as we stalked through rabbit country. As far as I was concerned, we were on safari.

For even greater thrills, I haunted the Cleveland Museum of Natural History, and worked there as an assistant preparator of small mammals. While we were making up scientific skins of rats and bats, Phil Moulthrop, the other assistant, and I listened open-mouthed to the tales of great hunters who visited the museum. Carl Akeley, Osa and Martin Johnson, Harold Clark, and others who had known Teddy Roosevelt and had been to Africa, sat down among the skins and smells of the museum workroom to talk of adventure in far places.

Very early, I had decided that hunting alone would be an uncertain career, so I determined to become an archaeologist, as the two seemed to complement each other. And indeed they did. At the age of twelve, I had already excavated an ancient site on my own, and gone on my first big game hunt. For the latter, I had acquired an old Winchester .32 special rifle. A friend of mine, whose parents were wealthy, had acquired the gun. He had taken it apart but could not reassemble it. He told me that if I could put it back together, I could have it. It was many years before I realized that the old Winchester was a very inadequate weapon. In the meantime, I used it to kill deer and elk, and I bagged a grizzly bear with it when I was fifteen years old. One adventure led to another. I wanted to know and to hunt all the kinds of American game that Teddy Roosevelt had written about.

Upon graduation from Princeton in 1933, I was offered a job by the American Nature Association, studying and hunting the mountain lion in the American Southwest. I spent a year at it. Later, when archaeological expeditions took me to Alaska, Canada, and Mexico, I studied and hunted all of the North American big game mammals.

By choice, or perhaps by sheer good fortune, I married Brownie (her maiden name was Brown), who is as avid about the outdoors as I, and an expert photographer as well. As Brownie and I covered each phase of American wildlife, from

the jaguars of Central America to the polar bears of the arc-
tic, we constantly talked of the greatest adventure of them
all—Africa.

Our chance came in 1956, when we mounted an expedition
to Greece and the Near East, to study antiquities. On this
trip, we hunted in Europe, Egypt, Turkey, Iraq, and Iran.
On a shikar in India, we bagged a man-eating tigress, a couple of other tiger and a leopard, as well as buffalo, gaur (the
Indian bison), and a scattering of deer and antelope. In Iran
we hunted on the royal preserves with the brother of the
Shah, Prince Abdorreza. But the real adventure was Africa.

As we stepped off the plane at Nairobi, capital of Kenya,
we felt almost as though we had been there before. Our white
hunter was Andrew Holmberg, at that time a member of the
famous Ker and Downey Safari Company. Andrew had taken
Ernest Hemingway on safari, as well as a long list of other
notables, ranging from Asiatic potentates to American industrial tycoons. Andrew was then (and still is) one of the
leading white hunters of East Africa.

On that first hunt, Brownie and I were on safari two
months. It seemed like less than a week. We hunted virtually
all of the game animals to be found in Kenya and Tanganyika
. . . and we worked hard at it. Andrew is the kind of white
hunter who won't let you shoot unless the animal is a trophy
specimen. As for dangerous game, Andrew believes in taking
the client close and letting the client do his own shooting.
During this whole trip, Andrew shot his double rifle only
once, and that was when a charging elephant was only thirty
feet away—and my gun was empty.

They say in Kenya that the stranger who watches an African sunset will come back to Kenya to look again. It is true.

No one can argue that an African safari is not expensive.
But at least they are within financial reach of the ordinary
man, that is, if the ordinary man, like any good American,
buys everything on time and spends more than he can afford.

After licking our financial wounds for a couple of years,

and again on an archaeological expedition, Brownie and I returned to Africa in February of 1959. I had been asked by the State Department to be a consultant on certain African problems. We spent our first two months in the Sudan, doing some archaeological digging and Sate Department traveling. We were able to hunt most of the major game animals in the Sudan.

From there we moved westward to French Equatorial Africa, which is now broken up into several republics. In what is now the Central African Republic, we were joined by Tom Bolack and his beautiful wife. Tom is an oil man, and also lieutenant governor of the State of New Mexico. Like myself, Tom is an avid hunter, and had always wanted to try the Big League of big game hunting—a safari in Africa. For our trip, we had acquired a French white hunter, Jean Bepoix. Jean knows the country well—especially the spots where the game animals are to be found—and he speaks the languages of the native tribes.

Hunting and photographing, Brownie and I moved through the Congo and Uganda, sometimes with native guides, such as the Pygmies, sometimes with professional white hunters like Nick Swan, a young white hunter just starting on his career, and Stan Lawrence-Brown, an old elephant hunter. With Nick Swan we again went on safari in Kenya and Tanganyika, as we were especially anxious to get a really big bull elephant and to bag trophy specimens of certain antelope to improve our collection. We also went on safari to the Northern Frontier of Kenya with David Ommanney, who had only just recovered from a mauling by a leopard. With David, who seemed to be more nervy than ever after his leopard experience, we survived a charge by a mountain rhino on Mount Kenya.

The African bug had bitten us badly, both literally and figuratively. On our last safari I had picked up tick fever, and Brownie fell victim to malaria. But these difficulties seemed to stimulate our desire to go back to the Dark Continent, particularly to the areas in which we had not hunted before.

In 1960 we returned once more. We went on safari in Portuguese East Africa (Mozambique). There we hunted a number of varieties of rare antelope with Gilberto Barros, a young Portuguese white hunter who, as it turned out, had different methods of hunting than any of the other white hunters whom we had known.

Again we went on safari in Kenya, this time with a young white hunter named Theo Potgieter. We tried again for the elusive bongo in the mountain areas of Kenya, and again made an attempt to bag a very large elephant. After Kenya, we went on safari in Somalia, which had achieved its independence only two months before. I was the first American to hunt Somalia and to explore the game possibilities of the new republic.

In Somalia, our white hunter was Guliano Belli dell'Isca, an Italian. As with other white hunters, we found that Guliano had his own way of doing things, both as to the safari itself and to hunting dangerous game. For example, in Kenya, with Andrew Holmberg, we baited lion; in Mozambique, with Barros, we called up lion by imitating their roar; and in Somalia, with Belli, we tracked lion, found them asleep, (or, as it turned out, almost asleep,) and shot them at the range of a dozen feet. With our safari in Somalia we also shot a number of rare antelope found only in that arid country.

In 1962 we traveled to Southwest Africa, to hunt the fabled gemsbok and other kinds of game found only in that corner of the continent. Hunting out of Windhoek, our white hunter was Basie Martens, of Boer extraction. In 1962 also, we returned to our first love, Kenya, and our first white hunter, Andrew Holmberg, who had by this time recovered from a shot through the foot by an elephant gun.

Our greatest ambition had been realized. We had hunted Ice Age animals, and we had hunted as Teddy Roosevelt did. The following stories depict only a few of the highlights of

these safaris, some of the adventures that we had, and some of
the animals that we saw. Is the adventure over? Not at all.
Brownie and I have seen many African sunsets. I hope that we
will see many more.

Hunting in Africa

1 · African Hunting Past and Present

FOLLOWING THE GREAT Ice Age, primitive man began the process that has come to be known as civilization. In other parts of the world changes were taking place, as centuries-old ways of life began to be obliterated in favor of new ways. Africa, however, remained unaffected by these changes. It continued in its dreamlike existence for centuries. While the peoples of Asia, Europe, and later, the Americas were evolving new civilizations, Africa persisted in a way of life that had long been outmoded.

One might wonder why the great culture of Egypt and the Valley of the Nile did not extend into Africa. The Egyptian civilization had flourished and flowered very early. It is likely, however, that the drying up of the Sahara, occurring as it did after the great glacial age, effectively isolated Egypt from all but negligible contact with the rest of the world. In any event, it is certain that even if a part of that great civilization was communicated to Africa, it did not take hold. Some tribes did introduce innovations: agriculture was begun, and the raising of cattle was adopted. But such changes had little effect on Africa's primitive life. When, at last, European explorers rediscovered Africa, they called it the Dark Continent. Dark it was—not so much in the color of the people's skins as in their primitive status.

The first European explorers who penetrated Africa did

not do so for sport. It is true that a number of these early frontiersmen hunted on a grand scale; but they hunted for commercial reasons. The earliest European colonists—the Portuguese, the Dutch, the French, the Germans, and the British —reported rich lands populated by primitive people, but they also mentioned vast herds of game. These early explorers described hundreds of species and tens of millions of animals. They did not realize, however, that they were looking at a world which was obsolete. The Dark Continent had somehow been forgotten in the passage of time.

But once civilization had entered Africa, it began to take hold quickly. In the nineteenth century, Europeans of a dozen nationalities penetrated Africa from the east, south, and west. The Arab conquest had overrun Egypt and North Africa centuries before. Arabic speech, Arabic dress and customs, and the Mohammedan religion had penetrated the northern third of Africa and left its mark. Following the establishment of a port by the Dutch East India Company at Capetown, Dutch colonists penetrated the fertile lands of South Africa to settle and farm, bringing with them guns which they would use with great effectiveness. They killed literally millions of animals, some for meat, many wantonly. Whole herds were destroyed at a time to clear the land for farming and ranching.

In West Africa, the nineteenth century slave trade had already penetrated deeply. Most of the slaves who were brought to the United States, to the West Indies, and especially to Brazil came from West Africa and the Gulf of Guinea. With the slave traders came guns. Native chieftains who gathered slaves for the "blackbirders" were rewarded with firearms. Some of these chieftains formed small armies which they supplied with rifles. These armed bands collected many slaves and they also hunted ivory. The country now called the Ivory Coast was a gathering point for this trade. In less than a century, every elephant—and many other animals as well—had been killed. Today, much of West Africa is virtually without game.

But the vast majority of the Ice Age fauna of Africa lies in the eastern portion of the continent. Here, rich volcanic uplands form a vast plateau. Much of this highland is open grasslands and savannas. The grass-eating animals and the predators which live upon them have flourished for the last million years. When the Europeans landed on the East African coast and then penetrated inland, they were amazed at the countless animals that they saw. Even the hard-bitten explorers who came to found colonies and to get ivory and gold were impressed by this ancient world which had been so long untouched.

Portuguese and Arab traders had, of course, seen some of these sights since the fifteenth century. But the western world did not really become conscious of the game of Africa until the memorable trips of Stanley and Livingstone. Livingstone attempted to find the source of the Nile by penetrating inland from the east coast—and disappeared. When he had been missing for two years, Stanley, a newspaper man, went to look for him. They finally met at the spot which is now called Ujiji on Lake Tanganyika, and their memorable exchange of greetings was widely publicized. Prior to this time, most Europeans and Americans had scarcely thought of Africa, and certainly had never heard of the teeming game herds there.

Strangely, the early explorers, most of whom were looking for the sources of the Nile, were little impressed with either the panorama of the animal herds or the spectacular African scenery. Englishmen such as Burton and Speke, and the Scot, Joseph Thomson, seemed to take the wonders of the Ice Age fauna for granted, even though some of the most beautiful animals, such as Thomson's gazelle and Speke's antelope, were later to be named after them. Obsessed by the drive for exploration and harassed by disease and hostile native tribes, the Europeans used game animals for food and regarded the more dangerous ones as merely another hazard of the trip.

African hunting started with the ivory trade. Before the days of plastics, ivory was a vital African commodity, second in its importance only to slaves. Ivory had, from earliest times, been a major trade item in ancient Egypt (it was traded from Nubia along the Upper Nile, and the land of Punt, which is modern Somalia), China, India, and Arabia. As Asiatic elephants carry small tusks, however, the virtual disappearance of elephants in China and most of southeast Asia was inevitable, and traders turned to Africa in their search for ivory. (Arab traders had been shipping tusks out of Africa since the early Arab invasions of North Africa.)

The ivory trade in East Africa was initiated on a large scale by an Arab named Hammed ben Muhammed, widely known as Tiboo Tib. In his better moments, Tiboo Tib guided such explorers as Livingstone and Stanley and Dr. Wilhelm Junker. Tiboo Tib brought with him improved European-made firearms. The flintlocks and muzzle-loading guns of the early Arab traders had made little impression upon the African game herds. New guns of heavy caliber, shooting brass cartridges with improved powder loads, were more effective. Tiboo Tib turned these guns against the elephant herds of East Africa. There is no count of how many elephants he killed. It is certain that Tiboo Tib and his men, at the height of their activities, brought in over 30,000 pairs of tusks. But this great destruction by Tiboo Tib in the 1860's still left millions of elephants in East Africa. But Tiboo Tib had shown the way. Dozens of hunters followed his trails, used his guides, and took up ivory hunting as a profession. Armed with the same improved elephant guns, such famous hunters as Martinez Schwarz, Henry Hartley, Karamojo Bell, and Frederick Selous marched into various districts and killed thousands of elephants for their ivory.

The romantic stories which the ivory hunters brought back were spread to other would-be hunters of Europe and America. Even at the close of the nineteenth century, some enthusiastic sportsmen made the arduous trip to Africa to hunt game. The trip to Africa around the turn of the century was a difficult and time-consuming business. Most of these early sportsmen sailed down the Red Sea and landed at some port on the eastern coast, such as Zanzibar. As the Boer colonists had killed most of the game in South Africa, and the slavers had virtually wiped out the animals of the west, the eastern portion of the continent was the logical point of penetration. The earliest sportsmen followed in the steps of the ivory hunters, who had learned the routes and ways of traveling from the preceding Portuguese and Arabs.

On the east coast, the adventuresome sportsmen picked up a hundred or more porters, bearers, and interpreters. Usually these were from the Naswahili tribe. The Naswahilis had become accustomed in the nineteenth century to performing these offices, and they now made a business of it. As the Naswahili moved in all directions through East Africa at the behest of these hunters, the Naswahili language became known to nearly all the tribes in what is now Kenya and Tanganyika. Naswahili, or as it is now usually called, "Swahili," is the lingua franca of East Africa and the trading language.

In Swahili, "safari" means a trip. The trip, for these early hunters, was inevitably on foot. Sometimes they were able to penetrate some distance into the continent by means of a boat; but most of the distance, especially up onto the East African plateau, had to be done on foot. The image of a long line of porters, each carrying a bundle on his head, and the hunter with his pith helmet, was automatically evoked by the word "safari," and cartoonists still depict an African safari in these terms.

In 1896 the British began building the Mombasa and Uganda railroad. The building of this railroad, which was delayed for several weeks by the famous family of man-eating lion at Tsavo, opened up the interior of the East African plateau. It also introduced to the East African scene large numbers of Hindus, some of whom were brought in to work on the railroad, and some of whom came as merchants. The Hindus, however, are not hunters, having very little of the hunting tradition in their background.

For the European hunter, the Mombasa railroad meant that

the very heart of the game country had been penetrated, and
a walk of three or four hundred miles was no longer necessary.
A way station on the Athi Plains of Kenya became the starting
point of safaris. This place was called Nairobi. Nairobi has
developed into a modern city, the capital of Kenya; and to
this day safaris usually start out from Nairobi.

But even with the railroad to Nairobi and beyond, East
African hunting was still impossible for any hunter other than
a European industrial tycoon or a British lord with unlimited
time and money. Safaris starting from Nairobi before World
War I were still walking safaris. Months of preparation were
necessary, not to mention the long duration of the hunting
trip itself. There were still dangerous tribes to be dealt with.
The country was virtually unmapped. And then, of course,
the dangerous animals themselves presented a constant hazard.

Perhaps the greatest dangers of all in Africa are not those
one can see or touch. Every mosquito probably carries malaria.
Tsetse flies, with a bite like a branding iron, are not only pain-
ful, but those of certain districts may inject encephalitis or
sleeping sickness into humans. Ticks carry tick fever. Many
of the waters are affected by belhartzia. Leprosy, fungus diseases, and a dozen other forms of creeping, horrible death may
come from the grass, the trees, or the water. And early hunters
dreaded the hot African sun, with its threat of sunstroke. To
combat these hidden dangers, the hunters dosed themselves
with quinine, and dressed themselves in pith helmets and spine
pads. Many of them died of the dreaded black water fever
(the last stages of malaria), or of some other unknown malady.
But in spite of the dangers, the difficulties, and the death, to
Africa they came just the same.

Modern hunting in Africa probably began with the safari
of President Theodore Roosevelt in 1908. Teddy was the idol
of American sportsmen of the time, and greatly admired in
Europe. His book, *Adventures of an American Sportsman*,
was widely read in the western world. African hunting became known to every member of modern civilization who

felt within himself the spark of the ancient hunting fever. "Safari" became synonymous with the unknown, the romantic, and the dangerous. Every one of the millions of would-be hunters dreamed that some day he might go on safari.

At first, very few of them actually did. The costs of getting to Africa and of fitting out a safari were almost insurmountable. The invention which did most to popularize the modern safari is certainly the motor car. Wheeled vehicles, especially those with special gears and 4-wheel drives that enable them to move across country, soon made the walking safari obsolete. A walking safari might cover twenty miles in a single day; a motorized safari can cover five times that distance—and hunt on the way.

The advent of the motorized safari brought with it a new set of rules. A motor car with a hunter inside could go across country and reach areas which the foot safari could never attain, or which, at best, the foot safari could hunt only after a trek of several months. But the greatest advantage—or, perhaps, disadvantage—of motorized hunting was that most of the game animals seemed unafraid of a motor car. Furthermore, the smell of gasoline seemed to cover the human scent, so that the game could not even detect the nearness of the enemy by his human smell. Most animals seemed to think a safari car was some kind of lumbering rhino or other animal; they would either stare dumbly at the metal monster, or ignore it entirely.

The first hunters out of Nairobi who went on safari in trucks found that they could shoot almost any animal from them with no trouble or danger whatsoever. Ivory hunters quickly took advantage of this situation, which enabled them to bring in truckloads of tusks. Unfortunately, the market for ivory in India and southern Asia remained as strong as ever. Artificial substances, such as plastic, had replaced ivory in many parts of the world, but in India ivory is a sacred substance for religious objects and especially for ornaments in connection with Hindu weddings. Ivory hunters with trucks obligingly

fed some thousands of pounds of tusks into the trade channels
to India.

But the sportsmen saved the situation. Just when the motor
car and the modern rifle seemed to be bringing about the extinction of African game, the hunters passed new laws to con-
serve the herds. Most important of these new regulations was
that no animal of any kind may be shot from any vehicle.
Furthermore, the hunter must be a hundred steps from his car
when he shoots at anything. Thus the hunters, by these rules,
put the hazard back into hunting, and developed again a sport
which requires skill and perseverence. Most hunters agreed
that when their sport became too easy, and presented no danger at all, it was not worth the candle. At the same time, the
sportsmen undoubtedly saved the game herds from complete
annihilation.

But in spite of rules and regulations, the decimation of the
Ice Age animals of Africa continued at an alarming pace. Relatively little of the destruction was carried on by hunters on
safari. With the advent of the motor car, the South Africans
virtually completed the annihilation of the game in the southern third of the continent. There the ranchers and the farmers
were kings. Game was regarded as the natural enemy of the
man who wanted to raise stock or plow the rich grasslands and
plant crops. Under the leadership of the Imperial East Africa
Company, colonists began to pour into the East African highlands to establish farms and ranches. Laws were soon passed
favoring the colonists at the expense of the game animals. A
settler might buy land from the Crown, fence it, and then
shoot every game animal within its boundaries. Furthermore,
any animal which crossed those boundaries after the farm was
established could be shot with impunity.

In the period between the two world wars, the colonization of South Africa was completed, and the settlement of
East Africa by European colonists progressed rapidly. On the
farms and ranches thus created, large numbers of native labor-
ers were necessary to clear the land and work the soil. These

natives had to be fed; and the cheapest food for the plantation workers was meat—usually dried meat, which is called "biltong." To keep an adequate supply of bilthong coming into the farming communities, there grew up a class of professional hunters known as market men. These sold bilthong by the ton to the settlers as the cheapest form of food. The bilthong hunters did not hunt for sport, so they ignored such "petty rules" as not shooting from a motor car, and not killing females of a species. The bilthong hunters killed as much and as often as they could. In a few short years these commercial hunters had cleared whole districts of every kind of game animal. As the evils of commercial hunting became more evident, the practice was outlawed.

The market for cheap protein food remained, however, and illegal market hunters soon replaced the original bilthong men. Whole tribes of natives, with their original ways of life displaced or changed by the importation of European civilization, turned to poaching game as a method of livelihood. As the laws of most of the European governments of Africa denied the use of guns to the natives, they used more primitive weapons for killing. The bow and arrow, usually tipped with poison, was used on a large scale. The wire noose became the deadliest and the cruelest method for the taking of many animals.

To this day these illicit methods are used. Poachers such as the Ikomas of northern Tanganyika make rude fences across the game country by chopping down thorn trees and piling them in a long line. At gaps in these thorn tree barriers, they set wire nooses, which they purchase by the thousands from illicit traders. Herds of game are then stampeded through the barrier openings. As each animal becomes ensnared, the hunters hamstring the hapless beast, leaving it hanging in the noose, struggling and crippled but not yet dead. As poachers often catch several hundred animals at a time, this cruel method serves to keep the carcass fresh in the hot African sun until the poachers can get around to dressing each animal and making the meat into bilthong.

Tribes, such as the Wakambas of eastern Kenya, which have always had a hunting tradition, now turn more and more to poaching as a livelihood. Small groups of hunters, armed with bows and poison-tipped arrows, track a herd of elephants until they can approach very close. An audacious hunter then sinks a poisoned arrow into the belly of the elephant, just forward of the hind leg, where the skin is thin. In two or three days, the elephant will die. The poachers follow the dying animal closely, hoping to find the carcass. Sometimes, however, the tracks are lost in a welter of other elephant tracks, or, as often happens, the arrow is poorly placed or the poison a little old, and the elephant dies a lingering death extending over several months. Often elephants wounded with poison arrows go berserk, and kill the first human they see. The elephant poacher, if he manages to find his quarry, uses the meat and sells the tusks. The trafficking in this illegal ivory is forbidden, but it goes on at a lively rate nonetheless. Unscrupulous merchants with small boats are constantly waiting on the East African coast to carry a cargo of contraband tusks to India.

Meat hunting is still legal in certain parts of Africa, such as Angola and Mozambique. In Mozambique a market hunter may buy a license allowing him to shoot and preserve twenty-five tons of bilthong. The expenses of fitting out a truck and of hiring a number of native meat cutters, however, are so great that a commercial hunter, even thus licensed, must shoot fifty or seventy-five tons of dried meat to make a profit. Even though Mozambique is reducing the number of legal meat hunters with each passing year, the number of illegal and unlicensed bilthong hunters is increasing.

In the midst of this destruction, many men also wished to preserve. Although some species have become extinct, these vanished animals serve as a lesson. The curious anomaly is that it is invariably the hunters themselves who are the greatest conservationists. Most of the concepts of conservation and game laws came from Europe, where the overpopulation and the pressures of civilization had already made necessary sets of rules under which some game could survive. Fortunately, by the time of the advent of modern firearms, rules of conservation and the code of sportsmanship which went with them were already well established.

It was the hunter, Theodore Roosevelt, who was foremost on the scene in establishing parks and preserves in America. It has been the hunting groups in Africa who have been foremost in establishing sanctuaries where remnants of the once-teeming African game herds might be preserved. It was the hunters also who prescribed the sportsmanlike use of the same weapons which they themselves had developed. Who would shoot a sitting bird? Yet if you are out for meat, the squatting partridge is a far easier target than a bird on the wing. The hunters also forbade the shooting of females, except when the number of females of that particular animal overran the food supply of the area.

The tradition of the hunting of the biggest, fiercest, most heavily-horned males was encouraged until it became the very point of hunting. Among modern sportsmen, the term "meat hunter" is usually considered an epithet of contempt. Hunting is a royal sport. It now has a set of rules which cannot be violated. Most of these rules were established by the hunters themselves to make the chase more difficult, to preserve the animal in question, and to make certain that once the trophy is won, it is a feat worth boasting about. Even so the element of danger is preserved. Animals which might "fight back" are those most highly honored by the modern sportsman. The present day hunter might easily annihilate a charging buffalo with a hand grenade, but this would not be according to the rules.

In spite of sporadic attempts at conservation and sportsman-like rules for the safari hunter, by the end of World War II, well over ninety per cent of all African game had been destroyed. Those remnants which were left were preserved mostly in a series of parks and reserves which had been set aside for this purpose. Most of these reserves were established almost too late to save the game. Efforts to establish these parks and reserves came primarily from the sporting hunters, who wanted to preserve at least a part of the game herds for future generations, and from conservation agencies, who wanted to save the animals for their own sake. Not a few of the African colonists began to realize that the game which they were destroying so rapidly was one of their most valuable assets. In 1960, in Kenya Colony alone, the tourist business brought in by hunting and photographing in the game areas amounted to over fifteen million dollars. With the exception of coffee exports, this was Kenya's most valuable commodity.

Almost too late, the National Park System saved the remnants of African game. Just before the wave of independence swept Africa in the 1960's, some sixty-five national parks or preserves had been established on the whole continent. Fewer than half of these, or only thirty-one parks and reserves, yet contained any sizable game herds. In the others, the animals were already dead. The largest national park is Kafue National Park in Northern Rhodesia, comprising an area of 8,650 square miles. The second largest, Southern National Park in South Sudan, covers an area of some 7,800 square miles. Well known to European and American tourists are such parks as the Kruger Park of South Africa, Amboseli National Park in Kenya, Tsavo National Park in eastern Kenya, Queen Elizabeth and Murchison Falls National Parks in Uganda, and Prince Albert Park in the Congo.

With the establishment of these parks and preserves, some of them of tremendous size, it would seem that the conservationists and hunters alike might breathe a sigh of relief. But the situation was not saved. The poachers could operate in a national park with greater impunity than in open territory, and they did so. In the Serengeti National Park in northern Tanganyika, poaching has annually accounted for the loss of twenty thousand game animals. Elephant poachers in the

Tsavo National Park have killed over three thousand elephants: their carcasses have been found since the park was established. With the rising wave of African nationalism, much of the good work which was done was quickly undone. The Congolese, in their first surge of independence, swept over Prince Albert Park in the Congo in an orgy of killing. In other parts of the Congo, the animal herds were decimated or killed off entirely. The Sudan has also suffered this same fate. Before some of the newly-independent people realized the value of their game animals, they had shot them all.

But not all of the calamitous destruction of the animals that had found refuge in the national parks came at the hands of poachers and newly liberated African nationals. The fate of Ngorongoro crater perhaps is a forewarning of the end of all game in all of Africa. Ngorongoro Reserve was a victim of politics.

Ngorongoro was first created as a preserve by the Germans in 1914, when Tanganyika was German East Africa. West of famous Mount Kilimanjaro, it was first called "Land of the Giant Craters." Ngorongoro itself is a single crater of an extinct volcano; the crater measures eighteen miles across and looks like a section of the surface of the moon. The edge of the crater is covered with a dense jungle growth, which serves as a home for several elephant herds and groups of buffalo. The floor of the crater, with a lake in its center, furnishes grazing ground for about 100,000 plains animals, and the many lion and leopard which live upon them. Even as early as World War I, this picturesque segment of ancient Africa was threatened with destruction. An enterprising German, Ziedentop, conceived a plan for building a factory in the Ngorongoro crater, and canning the meat of the wildebeest and hartebeest which lived there. Fortunately, the collapse of the German African empire brought an end to Herr Ziedentop's plan. In 1940, the Serengeti Plains, just north of Ngorongoro, were declared a national park. Some tens of thousands of game animals migrate annually from Ngorongoro across the Serengeti Plains and back again. In 1951, Ngorongoro itself was included in the Serengeti National Park, and the animal herds seemed safe.

But what man can do, man can undo. On July 1, 1959, under tremendous pressure from London and Washington to turn the control of all parts of Africa to Africans themselves, the park board excluded Ngorongoro crater from the lands of the park. Masai tribesmen, who wanted more grazing land for their cattle (which, incidentally, they require as a matter of social prominence, and not as meat), moved into the crater. Although the Masai never owned this area of Tanganyika in ancient times, they were not reluctant to gain the new grazing grounds for their cattle herds. In the first flush of enthusiasm, the Masai, who have a warlike tradition and carry long slender-bladed spears, killed all of the rhino in the crater, and speared all of the lion that might bother their flocks. Now the Masai cattle keep the wild game from the water, and soon will eat all of the forage on the rim of the crater, which is the home of the animals there. With the poachers and their wire nooses exacting a terrific toll of the Serengeti herds, soon this whole segment of African wild life will disappear.

The establishment of Prince Albert Park in the Congo was an even greater struggle, and it ended, too, in tragedy. This park was established on July 9, 1929 by Prince Albert of Belgium after his American visit, during which he had examined and become enthusiastic about the United States park system. An American naturalist, Carl E. Akeley, was instrumental in setting up the park, and especially in establishing the Gorilla Sanctuary as part of the park. Akeley made two expeditions into this area of the eastern Congo. He collected a group of gorillas for the American Museum of Natural History, and was one of the first to study the life habits of these primates. Akeley found that most of the mountain gorillas lived on three extinct volcanoes, called the Verunga Mountains. He recommended that this area be made a gorilla sanctuary. On his second expedition to the area, Akeley died; he is buried at the foot of Mount Mikeno. Through Akeley's efforts, the Belgian government added this region to Parc Albert as the Mikeno Gorilla Sanctuary. With further additions in 1934 and 1935, the size of the park increased to some two million acres, with a north and south length of 180 miles.

Meanwhile, population pressures and racial tensions were building up in the Congo. Much of the rich game area where Akeley, Selous, and other early pioneers had hunted had now become heavily populated and cultivated areas. Tribesmen pushed up on Mount Mikeno to find more grazing land for their cattle. The rich valleys of Parc Albert also attracted them. But cattle and people alike were excluded by the Belgian government.

On June 30, 1960, the Congo was suddenly declared independent. Parc Albert was one of the first places to feel the wild surge of enthusiasm of the liberated (and now armed) natives, who swept over the park. Large numbers of gorillas were killed. The tame elephants around park headquarters, that had never been shot with anything more lethal than a tourist camera, were now shot by Congolese military rifles. In a few short days, Parc Albert was a shambles, and the remnants of the game herds there fled to the heavy cover, hiding and running to preserve their very existence, just as other remnants of African wild life had been forced to do in other corners of the continent.

The system of parks and reserves had come into existence almost too late to save some segments of African game. The spread of nationalism in the 1960's threatened to wipe out even this respite in the march of destruction. Many of the park officials in Kenya, Tanganyika, Uganda, and the Congo gave up the losing struggle. Their attitude was expressed by one official, who bluntly said, "The blacks are going to kill them all soon anyway. Why should we try to save them now?"

Conservationists struggled hard to stem the inevitable tide. But again it was the hunters who produced the most telling results in a series of new laws and regulations. Hunting groups

sought to persuade the new governments that the game was
their most valuable resource. New countries, such as the Sudan
and Somalia, set up game and fisheries departments patterned
after those run by the former colonial powers. The Sudan,
which, during its first period of independence from Britain in
1956, had allowed its parks and reserves to be overrun and the
game slaughtered, now established "Sudanese Tours and Safaris," a government-run organization. In Somalia, also, the
transition to independence was fairly peaceful, as hunting
groups from Europe and America persuaded the new government to establish an agency to watch over the game, to issue
licenses, and to make regulations. The Somalia government
also established a park and several sanctuaries. Tanganyika,
with independence, wisely kept hunting laws and closed areas
much as before.

The republics which were formerly part of French Equatorial Africa have also established game and fish agencies, and
hunting regulations patterned after the laws passed by the
former French government. In many cases, the modern hunter
will find that the natives of these areas seem more interested
in the paper work than they are in the game which the paper
work is supposed to protect. But progress is being made, and
at least in a few spots the forces of destruction are held in
check.

One of the recent innovations is that instituted by the British
in Kenya, Tanganyika, and Uganda. This is the block system,
which divides all of the hunting lands into areas for control.
Hunting safaris are each assigned to a block, for which they
must sign up in advance. No two safaris may hunt in the same
block at the same time. In the block system, strict control is
maintained over the various kinds of game animals which may
be taken. Thus, the hunting of leopard and lion may be forbidden in certain blocks if these animals are becoming scarce. If
a particular kind of animal is desired by every safari, the Game
Department may decree that only a certain number of that
animal may be taken from a given block in any one year. If

poaching, drought, native cattle, or simply the spread of civilization depletes the game herds in any block, hunting in that area may be sharply curtailed, or forbidden altogether.

With the block system, the British Government also instituted a rule by which a portion of the money which is derived from hunters and their licenses is returned to the natives who live in a particular block or group of blocks. In this way, the government is trying to bring home to the natives the monetary value of game, and the importance of preserving it.

In most cases, the new governments have taken over the block system and its various regulations. In Tanganyika, the new government is continuing the block regulations patterned very closely after those of the preceding British Protectorate. The shooting of rhinos is closed in Tanganyika for an indefinite period. Lion, which are becoming scarce, are also forbidden in the northern blocks, where they were formerly very plentiful. With the precedents of the British regime, these new regulations are going fairly well.

The pessimistic part of the picture is that the new governments are unable to stop large scale poaching. It should be noted, though, that the former colonial powers also seemed unable to cope with this major problem. With independence, natives who previously had been forbidden to have guns, now were armed, and they began to use these new weapons. In many parts of Africa, the colonial powers, rather than denying the inhabitants firearms altogether, had issued licenses for a limited number of very primitive weapons such as cap and ball rifles. In north central Africa, flintlock guns and other types of muzzle-loaders were allowed by the colonial governments, whereas modern breech-loading weapons were strictly prohibited. It is only natural that, with independence, each native armed with a cap and ball musket should want to exchange it for a modern rifle. Most of them have done so. Game animals which could escape the short range and inaccuracy of muzzle-loading guns, cannot survive indiscriminate shooting by superior modern weapons. Even when the new native-dominated governments decreed hunting regulations patterned on the former ones, most native hunters ignored these new rules. They were sick of rules. They shot what they wanted.

As we view African game now, there are some places left where the modern hunter and the modern safari can still go. There are a few spots where the human eye can still see a thousand animals at a glance. The modern rifleman may still feel, in these places, that he is a man among men. The hunting rules of the new governments may yet hold back the spread of populations and the forces of destruction. Every hunter still hopes that he can go on safari in Africa.

2 · The White Hunter and His Animals

AFTER THE Boer War, a small number of sportsmen, mostly British, went to South Africa to hunt the animals of the veldt. The story of the last of the South African game herds is told in such books as *A Hunter's Wanderings in South Africa* by Frederick Selous. Other hunters turned to places more difficult to reach, such as the Sudan, Abyssinia, and Somalia.

The majority of sportsmen, however, turned to East Africa, where the game herds were relatively untouched even into the twentieth century. The increase in numbers of American hunters going to Africa began with the classic hunt of Theodore Roosevelt. The beloved Teddy, following a lifelong desire to see and hunt African game, refused the nomination for another term as President of the United States in 1908. Four months later, Teddy was on his way to Africa, where he stayed a full year. He took with him a retinue of sportsmen and naturalists, for he wanted to record the flora and fauna of this last segment of unspoiled Africa, as well as hunt, before it was too late. Following Roosevelt was the great hunter and naturalist, Carl E. Akeley. It was Akeley who created the greatest monument to the hunter, Roosevelt, by founding and designing the Roosevelt African Hall of the American Museum of Natural History in New York.

With the arrival of sportsmen avid to go on safari but lack-

ing any knowledge of the country, the animals, or the dangers
of both, what has come to be a typical African institution
gradually came into being. This was the white hunter.

At first, the white hunters were ivory shooters or settlers
who took European and American hunters on safari as a matter of convenience or personal obligation. Early in the twentieth century, however, a regular class of professional hunters
developed—men who organized safaris as a business and guided
sportsmen as a profession. Probably nowhere else in the world
today is a professional hunter more necessary than in Africa.

In the old days of the foot safari, the white hunter acted
more as a guide than in any other capacity. If the would-be
sportsman did not have a resistance to malaria—and a considerable amount of common sense and instinct for self preser-
vation as well—he probably did not survive. With the
development of the motorized safari, however, the white
hunter came into his own. Without the offices of the white
hunter, the whole safari could not function, and the hunt
would be a dismal failure, if not a complete disaster. Realizing
that hunters from Europe and the States were willing to pay
fat prices to enjoy the "big league" hunting in Africa, a number of men in East Africa proclaimed themselves white hunters, and began to organize safaris. Some of these—ex-elephant
hunters, or simply colonials who had done a bit of hunting on
their own—were dismal failures in the role of white hunters.
These men were capable enough hunters by themselves, but
they often lacked the organizational ability to get together a
complicated safari and make it work. Many of these early
white hunters found that they couldn't stomach some of their
clients. A few of the "sportsmen" wanted to shoot animals by
the hundreds; others proved themselves cowardly when faced
by dangerous game.

Out of these early attempts to make safaris and African
hunting a real business, there emerged a class of white hunters
with the requisite qualifications for success. As one sportsman
put it, his white hunter had to be a "businessman, leader,

psychologist, linguist, hero, and a nice fellow, all rolled into one."

As most African safaris move cross-country with little regard for the few roads or settlements, the white hunter has to know the terrain. If a client wants a top specimen of a particular kind of game, his white hunter must know the place to get the trophy. Knowledge of where to go to get particular trophies is the stock in trade of the white hunter.

The successful white hunter has an organized band of "safari boys": gun bearers, trackers, skinners, camp boys, cook, and assistants. This crew, although they are called boys, may include veterans of sixty years or more of hunting and tracking. They answer to the white hunter; they are paid by him; and their loyalty belongs to him. Without them, a safari would never be able to leave camp.

Of course, the wild animals themselves are the major reason for the presence of the white hunter. A novice, even though he might be an accomplished hunter in his home terrain, might not know what to do in the midst of a herd of rampaging buffalo. Perhaps the nimrod hunter would be uncertain whether it is wiser to fire or to fall back when an elephant sticks out his ears or thrusts up his trunk. The white hunter, a man who has spent years among these animals, is able to admonish his client to stand firm, or to cover his retreat if it becomes necessary to retire. In the last resort, the white hunter must have nerves of iron and an excellent aim. With his double rifle, he must back up the client's play. When clients, overly nervous or careless in their shooting, wound a dangerous animal, the white hunter must go into heavy cover after the game, to see that it is killed quickly and painlessly before it becomes a menace to the next person to pass that way.

Important for many clients is the white hunter who has a knowledge of trophy-sized animals. With a tremendous amount of money spent on a safari and on the necessary licenses, the white hunter must be able to judge at a glance whether an elephant's tusks will weigh one hundred pounds each or only seventy-five. The successful white hunter must be able to tell, by looking through his binoculars, whether an eland has twenty-eight-inch horns and is an ordinary specimen, or thirty-inch horns and an excellent trophy. All of these judgments and decisions require years of practice, and must be made under field conditions, through heat haze, and at great distances. The results of these judgments makes the difference between a very successful safari and a satisfied client, and a mediocre trip and a hunter who will never return.

At times, the greatest headaches for the white hunter are not the dangerous animals, but the clients themselves. A man and his wife may come on safari together; trouble develops, and the white hunter finds himself the mediator of their quarrels. Several hunting partners may organize a safari. Although these men may have hunted many years together back in the States, in Africa the situation is different. An elephant charges, and one of the partners proves himself a coward. Or one of the men bags an outstanding trophy and boasts about it. If friction develops, the white hunter must diplomatically hold the group together.

Not the least of the offices of the successful white hunter is keeping his clients healthy. The early explorers, with poor knowledge of tropical diseases and an inadequate supply of medicines, often died. Stanley lost both of his companions; most of the early explorers ultimately became victims of incurable malaria. With modern prophylactics for malaria, and a medicine chest well stocked for eventualities, however, the modern safari client need have no fear. But the white hunter must be vigilant. Much of the water in Africa contains belhartzia, a nasty organism that enters the body and finally develops into flukes or worms. There are other more visible dangers, such as poisonous snakes: cobras, puff adders, and mambas are common in the game country. A white hunter can steer his client clear of most of these snakes, and there are seldom casualties from this direction.

Sunstroke was once greatly feared by the early explorers.

Even Teddy Roosevelt wore a pith helmet and a spine pad to protect himself from the dangerous rays of the African sun. Modern white hunters, however, have found that, with ordinary precautions, the African sun is no more dangerous than a bright day at Coney Island.

Not the least concern of the white hunter is the food on a safari. In the early walking safaris, the hunters carried hardtack, and lived on the meat of the animals they shot as they moved. In the modern motorized cavalcade, the successful white hunter trains a native cook to make everything from filet mignon of gazelle to crepes suzette.

Only a few white hunters of the early days had all of the qualifications for success. Those who did not soon dropped the business, or went back to ivory hunting. Those who succeeded, however, achieved fame. Such names as George Lucy, John Hunter, and George Cuninghame are remembered from the days of Teddy Roosevelt. White hunters such as Alexander Dugmore and Syd Downey earned the gratitude of hundreds of clients, who rate these men as the finest individuals they have ever met. As increasing numbers of sportsmen poured money into the hunting safari, some of the successful white hunters formed safari companies. Perhaps the best-known of these were Ker and Downey, White Hunters Limited, Safariland, Lawrence-Brown Safaris, and Selby and Holmberg. During the keenly competitive days after World War II, some of these companies were forced to close. Safariland dissolved, and the various white hunters in its company went out on their own or joined other groups. Andrew Holmberg and Harry Selby, two of the outstandingly successful white hunters of our time, dissolved their partnership, each continuing his work alone.

With the tremendous post-war increase of the safari business, it was inevitable that a number of men who were in no way qualified for the job should declare themselves white hunters. Many of these newcomers lacked some or all of the qualifications of the successful white hunter. Clients unfortunate enough to go on safari with these unqualified individuals invariably returned from their trips bitterly disappointed and without the trophies they had anticipated. Partly to guard against these upstart agents, the white hunters of East Africa organized an association to which they admitted only those who had proved themselves in the field. The East African Professional Hunters Association, consisting of some thirty members, includes most of the men who can truly call themselves white hunters.

Not all of the professional white hunters who appeared in the Congo, French Equatorial Africa, Southwest Africa, Angola, Rhodesia, Mozambique, and Somalia were of the high caliber of those of the Association. Some outside of East Africa proved to have all of the qualifications of the white hunters of East Africa. Others had much to learn and learned it the hard way. Practically none of the white hunters in the various countries of Africa were able to copy the plush safaris of Kenya. The well-trained safari boys, and the smooth-running organization of the safaris which leave Nairobi year after year, are without equal on the Dark Continent. Safari agents in other countries may charge as much, but they do not put on as good a trip.

For those on safari in various parts of Africa, there are over one hundred species of game animals from which to choose. These range all the way from the tiny dik-dik (an antelope which weighs no more than eight pounds) to the African elephant (which may weigh as much as eight tons).

All animals which are hunted are divided into various classes of big game. Many of the antelope and gazelle are classed as "plains game." These animals, such as the wildebeest, hartebeest, oryx, impala, eland, Grant's gazelle, and a host of smaller gazelles, are found in herds and habitually occupy open country. The plains game of South and East Africa were the first to feel the brunt of the colonization of the open grasslands, for that is where these animals graze. To the hunter, plains game is interesting in its variety and beauty, but seldom is it a major objective. Plains-dwelling antelope and gazelle are often a source of meat for the hunter, or are used for bait for the capture of lion or leopard. The chief interest of the modern sportsman in plains game is in the thrill of seeing them, and in bagging a large male specimen of each species, carrying a trophy-sized head of horns.

Quite in another class are the rare antelope and gazelle that live in special habitats, such as swamps, deserts, arid brushland, or dense jungle. Some of these animals are fairly common in their own type of terrain, and therefore are less coveted trophies to the sportsman. The waterbuck, for example, is normally not found in open grasslands or very far from water. In cover along streams, or near lakes or marshes, waterbuck are numerous, and, in some places, one of the commonest animals on the continent. The waterbuck, because of an oily secretion under his skin, is one of the very few animals in the African repertoire which makes poor eating.

Such animals as the gerenuk, or giraffe gazelle, which normally inhabits dry brushy country, such as the Northern Frontier district of Kenya or the dry washes of Somalia, live in a totally different environment. In their chosen habitat, gerenuk are common. The sportsmen hunting in this kind of country may shoot gerenuk for meat supply, and they are very good eating. Usually a sportsman in gerenuk country will try conscientiously to find a very large bull carrying a set of heavy, long horns. Even more specialized are the true desert-dwelling antelope and gazelle. These animals are adapted (in some cases) to living in terrain with little or no water or cover. Some species, such as the addax of the Sahara Desert, may never drink at all! They derive their supply of moisture from the scant vegetation of their desert home. The pursuit of such desert dwellers as the gemsbok of Southwest Africa, or the white oryx and the addax of the Sahara, challenges the sportsman who wants to add hardship to the list of difficulties of attaining a trophy. Even when the hunter has managed to get into the difficult places where these animals live, he may have to settle for any specimen of one of these animals, with no thought of trying to find a large bull of the species.

A few of the African antelope live in such difficult terrain that it is virtually impossible for the hunter, even armed with a modern rifle, to get a specimen. The lechwe and sitatunga fall into this category, and very few modern sportsmen can boast of having a specimen in their collection. Both the lechwe and sitatunga are swamp-dwelling antelope. These animals have elongated hoofs, which enable them to walk on treacherous floating swamp vegetation, too thick for a boat to penetrate, too thin to support the weight of a man. The lechwe, such as the red and black lechwe of Rhodesia and the Nile lechwe of the Sudan, are fairly numerous in the few places where the swamplands are to their liking. Because of their singular adaptation to these wet lands, the lechwe are one of the rarest game animals sought by the African hunter. The sitatunga, of several varieties, are equally difficult to find, and equally coveted by the sportsman looking for a really rare trophy.

Perhaps the most difficult of all are the okapi and the bongo. Both of these are forest-dwelling animals whose normal habitat is either the deep jungle of the Congo basin or one of the other spots in Africa with similar rain forest vegetation. The okapi, a relative of the giraffe, and, like his cousin, possessing very short, fur-covered horns, is little sought after by sportsmen as a trophy. Generally, hunters covet horned animals, and the bigger and more spectacular the horns, the better. Furthermore, the okapi is so furtive and rare in the rain forest where it lives, even the Pygmies who occupy this same jungle terrain have difficulty catching one with their pits and snares.

More popular with sportsmen is the equally furtive and rare bongo; in this species, both the males and the females have lyrate horns which make a spectacular trophy. The bongo, more widespread than the okapi, lives in heavy jungle growth from Mount Kenya in East Africa westward through the

Congo basin, wherever dense-growing rain forests are found. The difficulty of approaching a bongo in this type of cover, and of getting a good specimen, makes the bongo one of the most desirable sporting trophies in Africa.

Some African antelope and gazelle live in a very limited area and, because of this circumstance, make a desirable trophy. The Hunter's hartebeest is not a particularly handsome animal, nor does it have spectacular horns, but it occupies only a very small area in northeastern Kenya and southern Somalia. Similarly, the dibitag, a smallish gazelle with forward-curving horns of no great size, is one of the great prizes of Africa, because it inhabits only a limited area in northern Somalia and adjacent Ethiopia.

The nyala is an animal with limited distribution. The "common" nyala, an animal about the size of an American white-tailed deer, with lyrate horns, is found in heavy cover in southeast Africa, from Zululand north to Nyasaland. The spectacular mountain nyala, or "Queen of Sheba's antelope," lives among giant heather only in one small spot on the Orusi Plateau of Ethiopia.

A few African antelope, although not particularly rare or of limited distribution, are of such beauty and carry such spectacular horns that they are favorites with African hunters. The two outstanding animals in this class are certainly the greater kudu and the sable antelope. The male greater kudu, an animal which may weigh eight hundred pounds, carries spiraling horns which often reach a length of over sixty inches. The white face markings and the white body stripes of the gray-colored kudu, coupled with his spectacular horns, make a big bull kudu just about the most breathtaking sight in all of Africa; yet the kudu is neither rare nor of limited distribution. In earlier years, the greater kudu extended practically all over Africa. Even today, the greater kudu, in a spotty distribution, extends all the way from the Sudan in the north to South Africa. Some African hunters have made safari after safari just to bag trophy-sized greater kudu.

In the same class as the greater kudu, and even surpassing it in the estimation of many hunters, is the sable antelope. Although less widespread than the greater kudu, sable antelope are plentiful in southern Tanganyika, Mozambique, the Rhodesias, and Angola. The beautiful sable color and the backward-sweeping, scimitar-shaped horns of the bull sable make him a spectacular animal. Even a mediocre sable makes a beautiful trophy.

Horned animals will usually achieve the greatest growth of horn in only one part of their range. This is true with most greater kudu and the sable antelope. The keen sportsman will soon determine the area in which he has the best chance of getting a record-size bull. Greater kudu grow the finest and longest horns in the southern portion of their range, especially in Mozambique. The sable, in a very small area of eastern Angola, grow fantastic horns, half again as long as in other places. So marked is this difference that this animal has been called the "giant sable," and is rated as one of the top trophies in all Africa.

There are many antelope which fall between these various classifications, yet which are fine game and greatly desired by the avid hunter. The lesser kudu, for example, is smaller in size, and has correspondingly less horn development, than his flamboyant cousin; he lives in arid brush country where he is keen sighted and furtive, and very difficult to approach. Many a safari which has tried very hard to get a lesser kudu has left Africa without one. And yet the lesser kudu is widespread, and a very common animal. The roan antelope also falls in this category, although again fairly common and ranging in brush and scattered forest areas from West Africa southward through Rhodesia. With a body as big as a mule, the roan antelope is obviously related to the sable, although his color, as the name would imply, is reddish. But the horns of the roan are short and stubby compared with the long graceful scimitars of the sable.

Common and with wide distribution is the eland, the largest

of the antelope, an animal that looks like a Jersey bull with twisted, stubby horns. The eland is a plains animal, but prefers brush and scattered trees. The common (or Cape) eland is found from Capetown north to Kenya and Angola. Far more spectacular is the Lord Derby or giant eland, found only in a small area in the Sudan extending westward into French Equatorial Africa (in the region now called Central African Republic). The giant eland, which may weigh 2,800 pounds is, in spite of his size, shy and difficult to approach. Because of his rarity and limited range, the giant eland is rated high on the list of Africa's greatest trophies by sportsmen.

Some of the grass eaters seem to fall into no category at all. Such an animal is the giraffe. The giraffe is certainly spectacular in appearance, and there are many kinds, some of them occupying a very limited terrain. The giraffe, although easy to see, is very difficult to approach. A big bull giraffe may stand eighteen feet high. From this altitude he can see everything— his eyesight is excellent. Native hunters rate the giraffe as one of the most difficult animals to kill, and they often try, as giraffe meat is excellent eating. Most modern sportsmen, however, pass up the giraffe, possibly because of its lack of horn development. In some areas, such as Kenya, the giraffe is classed as royal game and may not be shot.

Not rated as rare or spectacular by most hunters are such animals as the hippopotamus, hyena, wild dog, and cheetah. Nonetheless, these animals are exciting in their way, and are rated by some sportsmen as trophy game. The hippo can be dangerous, especially to a man in a boat or to a hunter who gets between a feeding hippo and the water which is his natural sanctuary. Hyenas, of both the spotted and striped varieties, are usually considered scavengers and vermin, and therefore not game animals. And yet a hyena may be dangerous—and he is certainly intelligent. For his size, about one hundred pounds, the hyena has the most powerful jaws of all the African animals, and he can break the leg bones of a buffalo.

The African wild dog, which looks like a canine version of a three-color alley cat with long ears, travels in packs of a dozen or more, and, in spite of his small size and benign appearance, is a vicious killer. Making peculiar cries (which sound more like a flock of owls than a pack of killers), the wild dogs will run down a gazelle until it is exhausted, and then eat it alive. African hunters in the past who encountered a pack of wild dogs usually shot all they could, in the interests of good sportsmanship; and the wild dog, never really abundant, has now become quite rare.

The cheetah, whose range extends into Mesopotamia and southern Asia, has been known since Biblical times as a courser and hunter capable of being trained to help the human hunter. The Queen of Sheba is supposed to have had trained cheetahs. Perhaps the fastest animal on four legs, the cheetah displays a combination of canine and feline characteristics. The cheetah's feet have non-retractible claws and look like the paws of a dog. The cheetah's body, however, is much like a leopard's, although the cheetah has dark brown spots on a yellowish background instead of the rosettes of the leopard's hide. As the cheetah hunts by day and in the open, he is usually not difficult to see, and he is unwary of men; for these reasons most sportsmen consider the cheetah poor game. In the days between the two world wars, tens of thousands of cheetah skins were brought in by native hunters to sell on the market for pocketbooks, jackets, and novelties. Because of this slaughter, the cheetah is now rare in most parts of East and Central Africa. In many areas, such as Kenya, Tanganyika and Uganda, the cheetah is now classed as royal game and may not be shot.

In spite of the wide variety of plains antelope with spectacular horns, swamp dwellers, and jungle trophies, the greatest attraction in Africa by far is the "Big Five." These are the dangerous animals, the ones that bite back. The Big Five are the elephant, rhino, buffalo, lion, and leopard.

Hunters differ as to which is the most dangerous animal.

Under different conditions and at different times each has been considered the "most dangerous." Which truly deserves that reputation depends mostly on which hunter you ask.

Although the lion is traditionally considered the king of beasts, certainly the elephant should occupy the regal position. In size, intelligence, and in the hazard which he presents for the hunter, the elephant is probably the most thrilling game on earth.

Elephants have certainly been hunted from the Ice Age down to the present. Our earliest ancestors killed elephants for meat; later hunters killed elephants for their teeth.

In spite of the thousands of years of slaughter, African elephants are still fairly abundant. In East Africa, the Congo, Somalia, Sudan, and a few other spots on the continent, elephant herds are still large. One reason for this certainly is that the early ivory hunters usually shot bull elephants, as the cows carry relatively small tusks. Furthermore, the ivory hunters, if they had any choice, shot old bulls with the heaviest tusks. The old bulls, past breeding age, did not decrease the productiveness of an elephant herd. The period of gestation of an African elephant is thirteen months. Young elephants often stay with their mothers until they are ten years old. In spite of this slow rate of productivity, elephant herds continue to increase in certain parts of Africa, and will survive, perhaps, as long as any animal on the Dark Continent. The major reason is certainly their very great intelligence and adaptability.

The African elephant is larger than his Indian cousin, being of greater bulk and having longer and heavier tusks. The African elephant has a slanting forehead and very large ears. (The typical Indian, or Ceylonese, elephant possesses a domed forehead and relatively small ears.) A big African bull may weigh seven and a half tons, though a very large Indian bull might reach a weight of only five tons. The African elephant is found in several varieties which differ in size, coloring, and length and weight of ivory. The forest elephant of Africa, which lives in jungle terrain such as the Congo, is smaller, has long black hair on his body, and possesses tusks that are usually small in diameter and that extend straight downward, with only a slight curve. The bush elephant of Africa lives in open, often arid, country; he is the largest of all, with a slate gray hide, and practically no hair on his body. The bush elephant grows tusks which extend in front of his face, usually with a considerable curve and an upward swing. The largest ivory has been collected from the bush elephant. The world's record was killed in Uganda; his tusks weighed two hundred twenty pounds each and were over ten feet long. Another variety recognized by most sportsmen is the desert elephant, which has a very light colored hide which is thickened and cracked, especially on his back, almost like the epidermis of a crocodile. The desert elephant may water once every several days, often going many miles to get a drink. He is somewhat smaller in size than other elephants and only occasionally carries big ivory. All of these varieties of elephant undoubtedly will interbreed. The African elephant is undoubtedly a very dangerous antagonist for the sportsman, even though the modern hunter is equipped with the most recently developed elephant gun.

But most white hunters and sportsmen who have lost their lives in the pursuit of the Big Five have fallen before a charging buffalo. The African buffalo has also probably accounted for more deaths among native tribesmen than all of the other Big Five put together.

An African buffalo bull weighs about two thousand pounds. He is built heavily and close to the ground, and both males and females carry heavy horns which cover the whole top of the head in a "boss," sometimes attaining a spread of over fifty inches. The buffalo is intelligent. What makes him so dangerous is that buffalo are very common in most of the hunting areas. Many an African hunter, stalking some other kind of game, has suddenly been confronted by an irascible buffalo bull. As the white hunter Andrew Holmberg observed, "A buffalo would rather charge than run away." The natural inclination of a wounded buffalo, even though he is badly hurt, is to go into heavy cover, pick a good spot, and wait for his pursuers. The cemetery at Nairobi now holds the remains of a number of white hunters who died following wounded buffalo.

African buffalo are usually divided into two major varieties. In East Africa, and formerly numerous in South Africa, is the Cape buffalo. This is a dark gray or black animal, with an enormous boss on his head, and very wide-spread horns. From Uganda westward one finds the woodland buffalo, sometimes called the "bush cow." This is a smaller animal, reddish in color, and with much smaller horns. However, the bush cow's disposition is just as nasty as that of his larger cousin, the Cape buffalo.

Many hunters rate the rhinoceros as the most fascinating of the Big Five. The African rhino is found in three varieties, all of which carry two horns on the snout. (The Indian, or Asiatic, rhino is smaller, and has only one horn.) The largest African rhino is the square-lipped, or "white," rhino, which formerly was distributed from South Africa north to the Sudan. The white rhino may weigh three tons or more, and occasionally carries a very large horn. The pointed-lipped rhino, with two variations, is usually called the black rhino, and is by far the most common of these animals in Africa. Variations of the black rhino were formerly found all over the Dark Continent except in truly arid regions. The black rhino of the variety called the "bush rhino" is inclined to be darker colored; he has a short, blunt fore horn of about twenty inches in length, and usually inhabits savanna or brush country. Many hunters recognize a variety called the "mountain rhino." This animal habitually lives in mountainous terrain with very thick cover, sometimes in extremely wet and cold areas. The mountain rhino is somewhat larger in size, lighter in color than the black rhino, and usually carries a long, slender fore horn which occasionally reaches a length of fifty inches.

All three varieties of African rhinos are now becoming scarce. The white rhino is preserved only in a few protected spots in Natal, South Africa, Uganda, and the Sudan. The black rhino has been almost shot out in French Africa, Somalia, Angola, Mozambique, and the Sudan, and rhino hunting is now prohibited entirely in Tanganyika. A few spots in Kenya still have plenty of rhinos, but the number is diminishing yearly. Certainly the rhino will be the first of the Big Five to become extinct.

The rhinoceros has been described as "a dangerous idiot." With his two or three ton bulk and his horned snout, a charging rhinoceros is about as deadly and destructive a force as a hunter can imagine. But the rhino has a low saddle in the top of his head where his brain should be. No hunter would describe the rhino as intelligent or cunning, though every hunter would agree that the rhino has an evil temper. At the slightest noise, smell, or disturbance, a rhino will charge. Usually, however, if the hunter can avoid the first rush, he is safe. Natives usually have little difficulty spearing or snaring rhinos. Rhino meat is tough but good. Native poachers also kill the rhino for his horn—which is not true horn at all, but consolidated hair. Rhino horn is in tremendous demand in southern Asia and China as a material from which to make medicine, especially a concoction valued as an aphrodisiac.

The African lion is judged by some hunters to be the most thrilling of the Big Five. Frederick Selous, who killed more than three hundred during his hunting career, rated the lion as the most dangerous animal in Africa, and the rhino least. The African lion, larger and more sturdily built than his Asiatic cousin, formerly ranged all over the Dark Continent (except in the densest tropical rain forest and the true desert). Several variations of the African lion are recognized, ranging from the "desert lion," which inhabits the semi-arid bush country of Somalia and Ethiopia, to the "plains lion," which lives in the comparatively lush grasslands inhabited by plains game. Lion have been known to kill every other living thing in Africa, including elephants and humans. Some lion make a specialty of feeding on buffalo, and can kill a full-grown Cape bull. Other lion concentrate on the killing of giraffes, catching these ungainly animals at a disadvantage when they are drinking or resting. In any case, the African lion can kill what he can catch, and he is not above eating carrion if necessary.

The lion has been variously described by different sportsmen as everything from a lazy and stupid dolt of a beast to a cunning, vicious, and dangerous adversary, according to the circumstances. Depending upon the terrain and the kind of game the lion are feeding on, these big cats will hunt singly or in large "prides." In the open grass country, a pride of lion may consist of thirty or more, all living and hunting together. In more arid regions, lion habitually live in small family groups, or are solitary. But however he hunts, the African lion is a carnivore, and killing is his business. If a lion develops the habit of killing humans, he quickly becomes adept at it, and is as intelligent and cunning as any animal in the world. Teddy Roosevelt was very much impressed by the African lion, regarding these big cats as the most dangerous antagonists in Africa. Teddy's book, *African Game Trails*, is full of such statements as "We were shown where the settlers Messrs. Lucas and Goldfinch had been one killed and one crippled by a lion." Teddy was also very much impressed by African tribesmen, like the Nandi, who speared and killed lions with no more protection than a buffalo-hide shield.

In areas where lion have been little hunted or harassed by humans, they seem to have no fear of man, and do not seem to regard a man with a gun as a natural enemy. However, where they have been hunted extensively, they become shy and nocturnal. By nature, the lion does most of his hunting and prowling in the twilight hours, lying at rest during the heat of the day. If hunted extensively, the lion will lie up in heavy cover during the day, and he is very skillful in keeping hidden. In parks or preserves where lion are not disturbed, they will lie in the open and pay little attention to humans or motor cars.

The particular sportsman hunts for a large male lion bearing a heavy, long mane. A really good specimen will have a dark mane up to eighteen inches long, extending from the middle of the lion's back over the whole neck and shoulders down onto the forelegs. Most African male lion, however, do not have manes, or at best have only a small scruff along the back of the neck. Desert lion practically never have manes. The enthusiastic sportsman covets a very black maned lion, but these are scarce, and found only in a few areas of the game country. A few strains of lion in certain places seem to develop thick and dark-colored manes. Northern Tanganyika, southern Kenya, and certain spots in Uganda are especially famous for trophy lion.

Lion are hunted in many ways in the various parts of Africa where there are still any lion to hunt. In areas of heavy cover or high grass, such as Uganda, lion may be flushed out by a line of beaters, a method similar to the conventional type of tiger hunt in India. In Somalia and Ethiopia, where lion usually travel in small groups or singly, they are usually tracked. Tracking a soft-footed lion, especially in hard desert terrain, is difficult, but the Somalis are very good at it. In Mozambique, Rhodesia, and Angola, lion are called. A skillful caller, imitating the coughing grunt of a hunting lion, can call up the game within shooting distance. Calling is always done in the evening or at night when the lion are moving; the lion may be called close to a fire, so that their eyes shine, or an artificial light may be used to give the shooter a chance to aim. Most sportsmen, however, believe that the use of a light at night to take any kind of game violates sporting principles, even though it may be legal.

In the Sudan, French Africa, and British East Africa, lion are usually baited. Typical lion prey, such as zebra or plains antelope, are killed by the hunter, and then dragged behind a car, with the stomach of the carcass cut open so as to produce a maximum amount of smell. Usually the bait is dragged across a path that a pride would normally use when going to water. The bait is then hoisted by a rope into a tree. In Uganda, baits are usually left on the ground, and covered with thorn brush to keep away the hyenas, jackals, and vultures. The lion, if he finds the bait by following the drag trail, can scatter this protective covering with one blow of his forepaw. The baiting of lion, because it destroys so many animals simply for use as baits, is now limited or forbidden in many parts of Africa. Even in those areas where it is still legal, it is not as easy a method as it was in years past, when the big cats were less wary. Under normal circumstances, the African lion is lazy, and will appropriate a kill if he finds one. However, if the lion has been shot at or otherwise molested, he becomes extremely wary of a bait and will kill his own meat.

All white hunters will attest that following a wounded lion into heavy cover is the most dangerous task of the professional hunter. The lion, if he is not killed outright, will go into high grass or heavy brush and wait for his pursuers. The only saving grace, as the white hunter Syd Downey put it, is that "the lion is a gentleman even when wounded. He roars, and *then* charges." The reason that white hunters fear a wounded lion so much is that a charging lion, attacking with lightning speed in arching bounds, presents practically no target at all from the front. Many a hardened hunter who had shot all of the Big Five previously has frozen in terror when a wounded lion roared and came at him with mouth open and eyes blazing. Under these circumstances, even if he does not freeze, a hunter will only get in one shot. If the lion gets to the man, that man is almost surely dead. The fangs of the lion are so long, and his jaws so powerful, that a single bite is enough.

The leopard, rated by most sportsmen as the least dangerous of the Big Five, is only so judged because a leopard practically never attacks a human without provocation; moreover, he is small in body size. However, all white hunters agree that a wounded leopard is the most ferocious of any of the dangerous animals of Africa and, for his size, the most deadly of all.

The African leopard is almost identical with the Indian or Asiatic leopard, both in size and appearance. Both of these spotted cats average from about one hundred pounds for a female to two hundred fifty pounds for a very large male. The leopard, like the lion, is a carnivore and a killer. Both the lion and the leopard kill their prey by getting as close to the victim as possible and then making a dash. In this short burst of speed, the leopard is the fastest animal on four feet, not excepting even the cheetah. The hunting leopard, when he makes his kill, can cover forty or fifty yards in two seconds. When this lightning speed is directed against a human, it comes so fast that a hunter often cannot even get his gun to his shoulder before the spotted death is in the air before his face.

Leopard are normally hunted by baiting them along the stream where they water or along the game trail a hunting leopard is likely to pass. Leopard habitually feed on smaller game than lion, but a hunting leopard will often kill a zebra, wildebeest, or even occasionally a buffalo. Normal leopard food consists of such animals as Grant's gazelle, lesser kudu, and bush buck. As leopard often kill baboons, a baboon carcass makes good leopard bait. The hunter usually establishes three to six baits at a time, using the same method of killing and dragging the bait animal as in baiting a lion. However, leopard bait must be placed much more cautiously and carefully than lion bait, paying particular attention to obliterating all traces of human smell by rubbing the stomach contents of the bait animal on any spot on the ground or tree which the hunter might touch. Normally, a leopard, when he makes a kill, will hoist his victim into a fork of a tree, where he can eat it at his leisure away from the hyenas and vultures. A leopard can drive off one or two hyenas on the ground, but four or five will rob him of his kill. A leopard weighing one hundred fifty pounds can seize a lesser kudu weighing two hundred pounds in his teeth, and jump with the carcass up into a tree to cache the meat on a limb safely above the ground. The human hunter tries to place the bait exactly as a leopard would do it. The leopard is far more suspicious than the lion, and, before appropriating a bait, will prowl the vicinity for several hours to see if any danger is near. Usually the leopard hunter will make an artificial blind some distance away from the bait, or will choose natural cover, in a spot which gives a clear view of the bait tree, especially in dim light.

The sportsman after leopard usually checks his various baits from a distance with binoculars, to see if the meat has been eaten or the carcass shifted in the tree. If a bait has been appropriated by a leopard, the hunter must get into his blind or place of concealment with extreme care, as the leopard will lie nearby to guard his newly found kill. If he sees the human hunter, the chances are that he will leave and never come back.

The leopard is normally nocturnal and cautious. Many a hunter has had leopard in his bait trees and never seen them, as the cats would come only during complete darkness. But if the leopard is timid and retiring under normal circumstances, he is nothing of the sort when wounded. If a hunter shoots a leopard and does not make a swift kill, he or his white hunter has plenty of trouble. The leopard will always go into heavy cover, turn, and wait. Furthermore, unlike the lion, the leopard is no gentleman, and does not give a warning roar just before he charges. The leopard may utter a coughing growl, but only when he is already in the air in his leap to kill. Undoubtedly, if the leopard were of the same body weight, and his teeth were as long as those of the lion, there would be many a white hunter dead from the charge of a leopard. As it is, almost half of the members of the Professional White Hunters Association have been mauled by leopard. Some wounded leopard have displayed a ferocity and tenacity shown by no other animals of the Big Five. For this reason, if for no other, the leopard is a legitimate member of the select quintet rated as the most dangerous animals of Africa.

Any white hunter or veteran sportsman who judged that he could predict what each of the African animals would do in a given circumstance would be a foolish man indeed. Animals are like people. Most of them seem to conform; some of them do not. There is the timid lion who is the exception. There is the ferocious sable antelope which, instead of running, charges a man and runs him through with his sabre horns. Any one of the Big Five will occasionally attack unprovoked. Human hunters have been killed by baboons, not even rated as game under most circumstances. So, in the dark world of Africa, the modern hunter is surrounded by different kinds of life. He meets the expected and the unexpected. In each instance, he must rely on his hunter's instinct. Perhaps he goes to Africa to find out just how keen that instinct is.

3 · *Two Out of Three*

DEATH COMES in many sizes. This one was as big as life itself. The great head moved over us like a gray cloud. The two tusks seemed to shut off escape at either side.

No one knows just what he will do when faced by death. Will he react quickly and do the right thing? Or will his muscles freeze? This can be a pleasant question to debate in front of an open fire back home. If a man sees a big deer and reacts with buck fever, what will he do when a fighting mad bull elephant is charging from forty feet away?

I hadn't wanted to shoot an African elephant in the first place. "I sort of like elephants," I had told our white hunter, Andrew Holmberg, when he first asked me the question. "I like the peanut-eating variety of elephant, anyway."

"The African elephant is a totally different beast from his Indian cousin," Andrew had replied. "The African will weigh two tons more, and he has tusks four or five times the size of the Indian variety. And," added Andrew, as though clinching the argument, "these African beasts have a nasty disposition to go with their bulk."

"I still like elephants," I remember answering.

"You'll change your mind," replied Andrew decisively.

I did, too, although it wasn't Andrew that changed it. It was the elephants themselves. For one thing, as our two months safari progressed, we saw quite a lot of elephants. As we hunted in southern Kenya for lion, leopard, buffalo, and rhino, and farther south in Tanganyika for hippo, and the

41

spectacular antelope such as the greater kudu, sable, and roan, we came across herds of elephants.

Andrew, one of the foremost elephant hunters in East Africa, had carefully explained to my wife Brownie and me that the elephants in the southern Tanganyika country seldom, if ever, carried big tusks. I just as carefully explained to Andrew on a dozen such occasions that I *still* didn't want to shoot an elephant, whether he had big tusks or little ones. I could get awfully mad at a rhino; I had no love at all for Cape buffalo, one of which had come very near to killing us. But when it came to elephants, the answer was "No."

What changed my mind occurred one night at the foot of the Eyasi Escarpment. It was dark when we made camp. The place which we picked out was not a particularly good spot, but we had had little choice. The narrow band of junglelike country between Lake Eyasi and the foot of the escarpment was veined with rhino and elephant trails. We pitched one tent in a cleared space where two of these animal avenues crossed. Andrew directed the safari boys to light a big fire and to keep it going all night, so that the animals would know we were there. We wearily turned in, listening to the cries of thousands of flamingos on the lake, and the sound of a herd of baboons settling down in a fringe of fig trees above us.

A few hours later we were suddenly wakened by the crash of a great tree which splintered the ground right at the edge of camp. To our dismay, we saw that the fire had gone out. Somewhere an elephant squealed, and as though in answer, others trumpeted all around us. A whole herd had apparently marched into our camp before they realized anyone was there. The safari boys rolled out from under the truck where they had been sleeping. The beam of a flashlight cut through the noisy darkness. A vague gray body dragging the remnants of a tent behind it, thundered by in the shadows. The earth trembled, as though a dozen freight trains were roaring past.

In a moment, the stampede was over. Nobody had been stepped on, which was a miracle; in the morning the elephant tracks seemed to be through us, around us, and on top of us. A chocolate pudding which Abdullah, our cook, had set by the fire the evening before, had received a direct hit. When an elephant steps on a chocolate pudding, that's it!

"Pretty good herd bull with that bunch," Andrew commented quietly at the breakfast table next morning. "Looked like his ivory might go sixty pounds or more." He seemed to be watching me as he talked.

"I was willing to leave the elephants alone," I answered shortly. "But I was looking forward to that chocolate pudding. How big did you say that bull elephant was?"

And so it was decided, as all along Andrew had known it would, I suppose. On our return through Kenya, we got an elephant license at Nairobi, and headed for the Northern Frontier.

We went north for two reasons. In the first place, safari parties after elephants usually head in that direction because the biggest ivory is to be found in the Northern Frontier. The more pressing reason that we went to the far north, though, was that Andrew knew of a particular bull elephant in that vast country which he had determined to hunt. He told the story as we drove over the dusty road to the frontier town of Garissa on the Tana River.

Two years before, Andrew had been on the lower Tana when a lion had badly mauled five Somali tribesmen who were trying to protect their herd of cattle from the big cat. Andrew had taken the five Somalis all the way back to Nairobi to have them treated. In gratitude for all of this trouble, the Somalis had told him of a big bull elephant on the edge of the Emboni country, to the east and toward the coast. Andrew had felt that, even allowing for the usual exaggeration, this would prove to be an elephant among elephants.

When we checked into the office of the district governor at Garissa, I made the mistake of asking the official in charge about elephants in the vicinity.

"Five of the bloody beasts went through my garden last

night," the man answered bitterly. "Took the fruit trees and the fence with them, they did. Don't ask *me* about elephants!"

Most elephant hunters hunt along the Tana River, either above or below Garissa, or farther south along the Galana. We passed by these usual haunts, moving in a southeasterly direction past the trading post of Bura, and finally to the seacoast town of Lamu. Lamu is an old Arab and Portuguese port where many thousands of pounds of poached ivory have been smuggled out in past years. We picked up some fresh vegetables and supplies at Lamu, then doubled back up the coast into the Emboni country.

The road which we followed was little more than a faint pair of ruts which curved through open savannas with dom palms round about. This track, according to our maps, eventually went north into Italian Somaliland. The country was beautiful. As we slanted north away from the coast, we entered a wide belt of jungle which is called the Emboni Forest. Actually it is a forest only in spots. Magnificent tree ferns, tropical lianas, and creepers form patches of jungle-like growth which are as exotic as the plants which grew in past ages to form the beds of present-day coal. As the land rose gradually to the northward, we saw more and more game in the savanna glades. Lesser kudu and topi were common. There were waterbuck and the coastal variety of oribi. Dik-diks scuttled everywhere.

As we penetrated more deeply into the forest, we could see ahead the curious houses of the local tribesmen. The Embonis live in dome-shaped houses of bark, and are a hunting tribe. For many years they have made their living poaching elephants to sell to the Arab traders along the coast. The present government has had the greatest difficulty in trying to stamp out this illegal trade in stolen tusks. At the Emboni village, in the very middle of the forest, we sought out the chief.

The chief wore a fez on his head, and displayed some other mannerisms of the Arab traders. Perhaps the reason that he told us where the great bull elephant lived was because his

Plate 1. This old rogue, who lived in the forest at the foot of Kilimanjaro, charged the moment he saw us.

Plate 2. A bull elephant, in Uganda. Of no great size but with a nasty temper, he shook his head, stuck out his ears, and charged.

Plate 3. The largest bull we have ever seen in Africa carries well over one hundred pounds of ivory in each tusk. Murchison Falls Game Preserve.

Plate 4. Brownie and I by the bull we shot during the stampede in the Samburu country of eastern Kenya. His tusks were thick but short.

Plate 5. Cutting up an elephant for meat in Mozambique.

Plate 6. A Samburu poacher cuts the tail from our bull. Possession of the tail is a sign of ownership.

Plate 7. Ndege, our skinner, taking a large nerve from a tusk. A large nerve means a light tusk.

Plate 8. Our safari camp in Kenya.

Plate 9. This rhino from western Kenya has a 30-inch horn. Ngoro shows the thickness of the hide on the cape.

Plate 10. A bush rhino with a tick bird on his back. The bird's excited cries precipitated a charge but the rhino missed us.

Plate 11. Buffalo bulls grazing on a lush plain in Uganda. The Virunga Mountains in the background are the home of the mountain gorilla.

Plate 12. A herd of Cape buffalo on an open plain in Uganda. The big bulls advance toward us to protect the cows and calves.

Plate 13. A large Cape buffalo stares stupidly as he decides whether to charge or run.

Plate 14. A herd of woodland buffalo. The woodland or western buffalo is reddish in color and has smaller horns than his cousin the black or Cape buffalo.

Plate 15. The big bull we had trailed so far. He dropped just where he had turned for his last charge.

Plate 16. A red woodland buffalo in the Central African Republic.

Plate 17. A male lion crouches ready to make a kill as he watches a herd of zebra come down to water.

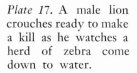

Plates 18–22. A lioness kills a large bull wildebeest. The lioness charged as he came to water. She reared up and grasped the bull's horns as a rodeo performer would bulldogging a steer. The lioness made the kill certain by biting his neck. She then dragged the carcass into the reeds where she had cached her three kittens.

Plate 23. Brownie inspects the placing of a wildebeest bait for lion. Ngoro makes certain that the carcass is high enough so that hyenas cannot drag it down.

Plate 24. The Ikoma tribal warriors dance the lion dance in honor of the death of our maned lion. Each man wears a headdress made of a lion's mane which he has killed with a spear. Their belts are made of cowrie shells which are used as money. Bracelets are made of elephant tusk.

Plate 25. Two lioness have pulled down half the wildebeest bait and are stuffing themselves.

Plate 26. The blond maned lion of Ikoma was considerably longer than I.

Plate 27. The Masai brother and sister of our gun bearer, Ngoro.

Plate 28. A large male leopard lies on a branch guarding his kill in the limbs above him. (Photo by David Good-now.)

Plate 29. The cheetah brought down the young wildebeest with a single slashing bite through the neck. No sooner had he done so than the vultures gathered and a pair of jackals came up to share in the feast.

Plate 30. The safari boys finally pulled the hippo around and rolled him onto the gravel bar. Tanganyika.

Plate 31. A bull and cow hippo in the Central African Republic. Cattle egrets usually accompany hippos, buffalo, and other big game.

Plate 32. Tom Bolack and the beautiful dama gazelle. Central African Republic

Plate 33. Our three addax. The one on the left is high in the world's records. Sahara.

Plate 34. Jean Bepoix and my big tiang bull. The tiang is the western version of the East African topi.

Plate 35. Our world's record white (or scimitar horned) oryx in the Sahara.

Plate 36. Jean Bepoix and guides Mamadu and Sobo with my first giant eland

Plate 37. Tom Bolack and his first giant eland.

own hunters, with their bows and arrows, could not go so far. The Embonis habitually kill elephants with bows and arrows. They cover themselves with elephant dung to disguise their human scent, crawl among the unsuspecting beasts, and then shoot them through the belly with iron-tipped arrows smeared with a poison made from the juice of a grass.

The big bull which we sought was one of three bulls, the chief told us. These three generally stayed on the edge of the Emboni Forest, near a water hole where Somali nomads sometimes camped. The spot was remote—a hundred miles from the Tana River and other usual elephant haunts.

Bulls which carry the biggest ivory are seldom breeding bulls with a herd. The big-tusked elephants are those which early in life have been whipped out of the herd of cows and young bulls, to go off by themselves. Usually such a venerable old bull has a younger bull with him as a guard or "askari." The bull which we sought had two such askaris. The big elephant himself was very, very large, the Emboni chief said. He carried tusks "as big around as a man's body, and so long"—here the chief indicated on the haft of his spear that the bull's tusks must be at least ten feet long.

We left the Emboni village and proceeded in a northeasterly direction toward the border of Somaliland. Any semblance of a road soon disappeared. We began to pioneer with our laboring safari car and truck by following elephant trails which led in the desired direction.

The water hole, as it turned out, consisted of five depressions located within a few hundred yards of each other. Each of these was the center of tracks leading in to the precious water, like spokes to the hub of a wheel. Of the water itself, there was practically none. As this was well along in the dry season, toward the end of August, the little water that remained in these shallow depressions was more nearly liquid mud. But apparently even this was enough for the elephants, several hundred buffalo, innumerable gerenuk, and Hunter's hartebeest, all of which hovered around the watering place.

During the next two weeks in this isolated area, we saw over two hundred elephants. The only water which they had during that time was the soupy, slime-coated mess in the five pools.

We had picked up four Somali trackers and one Emboni guide. Not only could they follow elephant tracks, but they could also tell which elephant they were following. Even with this, however, we made half a dozen false starts. We followed one particular bull over twenty miles until we were satisfied he was not the one we were after.

It was by accident that we came across the three bulls which were our mission in this remote country. We had taken a wide swing in the safari car to the north. There were many elephants that were feeding on sanseveria, which looks like the yucca plant of the American Southwest. Apparently they were getting enough moisture from the plant so that they did not have to come in to the water holes. The trackers saw the corrugated oval imprints where three bulls had crossed a dry wash twenty miles from the water holes. As we jumped down from the safari car, we heard the crash of a splintering tree in the distance. We were close behind them. Quickly our two gun bearers, Ngoro and Sungura, loaded the .470 double rifles. We carried three of these. Andrew carried one, I carried another, and Ngoro carried the third as a spare. Sungura brought up the rear with binoculars and cameras. When at close quarters with elephants, Andrew much preferred the old-fashioned double rifle with its 500 grain bullet to any lighter or single action guns.

As we approached the elephants, the trackers fell back. They had done their work well. Andrew pointed to the three slate gray hulks that moved diagonally away from us through the scattered trees. The three bulls were about the same body size as each other. We knew, however, that only one of them carried a mighty set of tusks. The other two were askaris with only mediocre ivory. It was one of the askaris which detected us first. The elephant whirled around and stuck his trunk up into the air. His great ears went out on both sides. The other bulls, too, turned in alarm, and began moving toward us, walking slowly.

"Look at that tusk!" Andrew whispered in amazement.

The first elephant carried tusks only three or four feet long at the most. The one behind, too, I could see was nothing extraordinary. But the great bull in the middle had a tusk which reached clear to the ground. At its base, it was as big around as a large man's thigh.

"There's only one," I said in amazement. "He has only one tusk."

"That's the biggest piece of ivory I've ever seen," Andrew muttered. "A hundred and fifty pounds if it's an ounce."

The three elephants stood perhaps seventy-five feet from us. I raised the heavy double rifle. Andrew had said to shoot him in the shoulder. So be it. A weight seemed to press the barrel of the gun down. It was Andrew's hand.

"Not a one-tusker, old boy," he said quietly.

"But, Andrew, you said it's the biggest piece of ivory you ever—"

"We never shoot a one-tusker," he said with quiet finality.

I had run into the code of the white hunters of East Africa before, but this was a new wrinkle. It did not matter that this one tusk would weigh more than two tusks of an ordinary trophy elephant. One-tuskers are simply not shot.

We photographed the three bulls as they circled to take our wind. Finally the one-tusked monarch himself walked right up to us. He was chewing a long trailing root, like a farm boy sucking a straw. He flapped his ears at us, trumpeted, then walked past in front of us as if daring us to shoot.

Our trackers were very apologetic. They felt that their professional honor was at stake, as they had failed to correctly identify these three bulls. We had not yet seen the three we were after. The great bull elephant of the Emboni Forest had two such tusks. He also had two askari elephants with him.

It was ten days later, after we had examined some thirty

other bull elephants in the vicinity of the water holes, that we found the tracks of three lone bulls. These, at last, were the ones we were after. The great bull of the three made very large oval tracks with his hind feet; he was the one that carried the tusks which reached the ground.

The meandering tracks of the three bulls carried us in an easterly direction along the fringe of the Emboni Forest. We found the spot where the elephants had fed the night before. There were marks in the crotch of a tree some twelve feet above our heads; there the big tusker had rested his ivory for a while, to ease the strain of his neck muscles.

From early dawn to the middle of the afternoon we trailed the erratic course of the feeding bulls. The tracks on the hard ground were almost invisible, but the devastation among the scattered trees was easy to follow. It was perhaps four o'clock in the afternoon when the leading Somali tracker pointed his spear and whispered in Swahili, "There they are!"

The trackers melted to the background. Andrew and I pressed forward cautiously. Ngoro was at our heels with the extra double rifle.

"Try for a brain shot if you can," Andrew cautioned me as we moved forward. "If you're in a hurry, shoot for the shoulder."

We had talked this over a hundred times as we sat around in front of the dining tent in the evening. The brain shot is immediately lethal. But if you miss by so much as an inch, the elephant only gets a bad headache.

The bodies of the three bulls loomed out of the brush like wrinkled gray mountains. We could see the movement of the great ears, and the occasional upward curve of a trunk, as the elephants fed slowly away from us. As it was still warm, they moved lethargically. Slowly, first one and then another of the bulls would break off the top of a tree with a splintering crash. We could hear the rumbling of their great bowels.

Andrew and I were within fifty or sixty feet of the nearest of the bulls. Still, we could not be sure which was the great monarch that carried the heavy tusks. The ivory of each of the elephants was hidden in the foliage through which they walked. We caught only an occasional glimpse of a yellow-based tusk as a bull hooked over a tree or scooped out a root from beneath.

Andrew and I were crouching, so that we might see beneath the bushes. Ngoro whispered something to Andrew and pointed. The nearest bull stiffened. His trunk went up like the spout on a teapot. The tip turned toward us. I could see the flaring pink inside of the trunk's tip. Two great ears, like giant sails, flapped out on either side. The elephant turned and charged.

"Shoot!" hissed Andrew in my ear. "Shoot—Shoulder!"

When an elephant charges, there is little to shoot at. A brain shot from the front is so difficult that even an expert with plenty of time seldom tries it. I am no expert, and there certainly was no time.

A moment ago there had been brush and trees between the bulls and ourselves. Now there was nothing. The charging elephant had flattened all this as though the wooden tree trunks had been dry straw.

The bull swerved toward Andrew at the side. I saw the great shoulder beneath the flapping ear. The double rifle came up like a shotgun. There was the spot. The rifle bellowed. I did not feel the recoil.

The elephant stopped. He staggered back a step. He turned even more to the side. There was the whole shoulder. I shot the second barrel. Again the bull staggered back.

Ngoro pressed the second gun into my hand from behind.

"Once again," Andrew said quietly. I fired once more into the bull's shoulder. He seemed to wilt. He fell backward and on his side, with a crash like a house dropping through a grove of trees.

The other two bulls had apparently not scented us. They shuffled off among the trees. Andrew and I ran forward with our guns ready. The two tusks of the fallen bull curved out seven or eight feet in front of his lips. They were perfectly formed and big at the base.

"Man alive, look at those tusks," I exclaimed excitedly. Andrew was standing beside me. There was a look of utter disgust on his face. "You got yourself a nice pair of knitting needles." Abruptly he turned away.

Ngoro cut off the bull's tail, which is the age-old African way of claiming ownership of a dead elephant.

Andrew would have nothing to do with the fallen elephant. "You got one of the askari bulls," was all that he would say. We found out later that the two tusks weighed eighty-four pounds apiece, which is very fair ivory. But Andrew was inconsolable. He would not even wait until the Somalis had gone to get some of the Embonis to cut up the dead elephant for meat. Instead, he walked toward where we had left the safari car several miles back. Even when we had gotten into the car, and Brownie asked us if we had found the great bull, Andrew would say nothing. Instead, he started the safari car and drove along the jungle track like a madman.

It was many miles farther on that Andrew explained to us that we were on our way back to the town of Garissa where we could telegraph to Nairobi for a second elephant license to be issued to us. In vain I explained to Andrew that I was tickled to death with the first elephant, even though he was an askari. Furthermore, I could hardly afford a second elephant license. Andrew scarcely listened to these protests. We drove most of the night and the next day.

At Garissa we found that the Commissioner at Nairobi was in his office. The clicking key under the hand of the native boy in the hot little room at Garissa gave us the message that a second elephant license had been issued in my name. We could start hunting.

Back we went along the dusty miles down the Tana, then off along the jungle track through the Emboni Forest. We had not had a real sleep for two nights. Andrew hadn't slept at all. He was a man possessed. He kept saying over and over, "Biggest bloody bull I ever saw."

After two days and two nights, we came to the point where we had left our safari car before. There was one of the Somali trackers, squatting on his hunkers with his tablecloth-like skirt stretched over his knees. He rose and greeted us by lowering the tip of his spear. Without a word he turned and walked into the forest behind. We loaded our double rifles and followed.

After a walk of about four miles, we came to a place where two elephant trails crossed, and there was another Somali tracker. Andrew talked to this man for a few moments in Swahili. The tracker pointed with his spear to the north. I gathered that while we had been gone to get the second elephant license, the Somali trackers had been following the two remaining bulls. How they had managed to do this and leave some of their number so that we could follow, I will never know.

We walked in single file for another three or four miles. Behind a screen of thick-growing thorn trees, we picked up another Somali tracker. This man pointed ahead. We moved off again. I heard a tree crash to the ground off to our right. Then another branch broke. The Somalis moved to the rear. Andrew and I walked forward on tiptoe.

There again were the two gray backs looming out of the brush. Andrew whispered in my ear, "Careful, old boy. If these bulls make up their minds to kill us this time, they'll probably get it done."

We edged forward again. Ngoro pointed to the bull on the right. "*Makuba*," (the big one), he whispered. Andrew shook his head. "Not sure," he whispered back.

The elephants were feeding diagonally away from us. We could catch only a glimpse of the white gleam of ivory between the spiny leaves of the plants as the bulls moved their great heads from side to side. One of them was kicking out roots from the hard soil with his foot, then scooping them all up with one tusk and the end of his trunk.

We crawled alongside of the bulls, perhaps forty or fifty feet away. Ngoro was ahead. He crouched behind the splintered limbs of a tree which one of the elephants had just pushed over. I knelt behind the trunk of the same tree. Andrew stood in the shadow of the upturned roots. Ngoro signaled us with his hand: it was the bull on the right. I raised the double rifle. The elephant in front of us stopped. The loose folds of gray skin seemed to tighten. The ears swung out. He straightened his trunk in front of him. There was a scream. He whirled like a cutting horse and came at us.

The head and the outflung ears seemed like a gray cloud over us. Ngoro was swinging his arms to attract the charge. Andrew yelled something. The bull swung toward Ngoro. There was the gray shoulder. The double rifle kicked back once—twice. Dust flew from the hide before me. The bull's brown eyes had a look of surprise. I dropped the empty gun. Ngoro pitched me the loaded one. I swung it up. There was the right barrel—then the left. The bull had stopped. He swung his head and looked down at me. Then slowly, a step at a time, he began to walk backwards.

"Reload," yelled Andrew frantically.

Fortunately, there was no need. The foreleg crumpled first. Then the bull rolled on his side. Two trees snapped off like matchsticks. The blood bubbled in his trunk, and then he was still.

Only then did I see the great bull. He stood there facing us, with his trunk outstretched. Two massive curved tusks reached clear to the ground. They were blunt and scarred and looked a foot through. We had shot the other askari elephant!

Slowly I kept repeating this over and over, as though I were drugged. "We shot the other askari."

The great bull walked forward a few steps. He turned, and with his massive tusks he attempted to lift the body of his dead friend. But the inert carcass slipped away as he prodded beneath it. With the end of his trunk, the big bull explored the hide of the dead elephant before him. He sniffed at the spots of blood on the shoulder. He straightened out his trunk toward us. The screaming trumpet was like the blast of a thousand brass horns in our faces. He flapped his ears again, then turned slowly and walked away.

All of us let out a long breath. "That was a very sticky business—a very sticky business," Andrew said quietly. "Anyway," he added slowly with a smile, "I know where there's a bloody big elephant for next year."

4 · Elephant Stampede

It started with elephants and it ended with elephants. We had gone to the Samburu country to look for elephants, but we didn't expect three hundred of them to run over us.

Like trophy game of any other kind, a really big elephant is hard to come by. A trophy class bull elephant, ever since the old ivory trading days, is usually considered a "hundred-pounder." Elephants carrying tusks weighing one hundred pounds or more apiece were scarce during the nineteenth century. They are a lot scarcer now, especially when one considers that a bull with that much ivory on a side is eighty years old or older. On previous trips I had found that the code of East African white hunters forbids the shooting of a bull with only one tusk, no matter how big that tusk might be. A hundred-pounder, then, means a bull with two tusks, at least one of which is the specified weight. Furthermore, only in a few spots of Africa does the forage contain sufficient minerals for elephants to develop heavy ivory. Usually, the biggest tusks come from beasts of semi-arid brush country, not from those feeding on lush, tropical forage. As a rule, forest or jungle elephants have slender ivory of no great weight.

I suppose I never would have gotten the elephant hunting fever if I hadn't seen the hundred-pounder on our safari in the Emboni country. I could not forget the majesty and size of the great Emboni bull. (We had seen him only after we shot his two askaris.) After this episode, the big Emboni bull disappeared from the region. The Somalis reported he had gone south across the Tana River.

Out of the hundreds of elephants shot by all of the safaris, in all parts of Africa each season, only one or two of the hundred-pounders are brought in each year. An elephant specialist, Don Hopkins of Spokane, Washington, has spent most of the last several years in East Africa trying to find a bull elephant carrying one hundred fifty pounds on each side. Don has spent most of his time in eastern Kenya and in northeastern Tanganyika. Any elephant hunter will tell you that the bush country near the coast, near the Tana and Galana rivers, is the best bet to find a bull with the biggest ivory.

When I determined to bag a hundred-pounder, I wrote to Don Hopkins, and to several other hunters lucky enough to have found hundred-pound tusks. Most of these advised me to get Andrew Holmberg, Eric Rundgren, or Stan Lawrence-Brown for a guide. Andrew Holmberg had been shot through the foot by an elephant rifle. I wrote to Stan Lawrence-Brown, one of the old-time elephant hunters of Kenya. It was Stan who shot the elephant pictured in the movie, *King Solomon's Mines*. During his lifetime, he had brought in several hundred-pounders, including one monster bull carrying 142 pounds in each tusk. Also, Stan knew the brush country south of the Tana. He said the natives there reported several big bulls in the hundred-pound class.

But Lawrence-Brown's luck ran out at last. Before our trip started, Stan, hunting with a European client, had been cornered by two bull elephants. Stan managed to down one bull with a brain shot, but the other one picked Stan up in his trunk and crushed his back.

When Brownie, my wife, and I arrived in Nairobi at the end of May, Stan met us on the porch of the Norfolk Hotel. As he limped up to us and extended his hand, he smiled wryly. "Bit of nonsense with an elephant," he apologized. "I can't go myself, but I know where to find your hundred-pounder."

As we sat on the shady veranda, sipping the very good East

African beer, Stan told us of his plans. He had contacted some native poachers in the Samburu country, near the Kenya coast, who had just been arrested and brought in to Mombasa. The men told of four large bull elephants in the Samburu country, along the Voi River. These bulls had been so large, their tusks so long, that the poachers had not dared to attack them.

"The Samburu country . . . the Voi River. . . ." That had a familiar ring, I thought. Then I remembered: Colonel Ray Harrison, my hunting friend at home, had told me of the Voi country. He had shot two bulls with hundred-pound ivory during his long hunting career, and he had got them both on the lower Voi River.

"There are some mighty big elephants in that Samburu country," Ray had said. "But watch out for those herds of cows and calves. The poachers torment the beasts with poisoned arrows. Those Samburu elephants will charge at the drop of a hat."

Stan Lawrence-Brown was still talking enthusiastically about the elephant hunt. "I'll have Nick Swan, my young assistant, take you down there," he said.

We had met Nick Swan, the son of a local farmer. Nick was a young, stocky lad, just starting his career as a white hunter. As Stan told us he was sending us elephant hunting with this young fellow, he must have seen the doubt in our eyes. "Nick is a good hunter," he assured us, "and he has a fine gun."

Later that day we saw the gun which Nick proposed to use. It was a .577 double rifle which he had just purchased from an old elephant hunter who had gone out of the business. The next category larger than a .577 is field artillery. If the size of Nick's double rifle was any indication, the elephant was going to be a cinch.

Our start to the Samburu country was delayed, as I had "a bit of nonsense with the fever," as Stan expressed it. I had picked up tick fever in French Equatorial Africa, and was still feeling pretty shaky the first week in June when we drove our safari car and one truck through the little railroad town of Samburu. We had a good piece of luck here, as we picked up one of the original poachers who had told Stan about the big elephants. This old fellow, Ndege by name, had been let off with a ninety shilling fine by the magistrate in Mombasa, and was starting right back to Samburu to kill elephants again.

The Samburu country is not beautiful. It lies along the edge of the East African plateau, just back from the coast. It is both dry and wet, and looks like a semi-desert. The scattered trees are stunted and small; cactus-like plants and spiny clubs grow in thickets so dense that only an elephant can force through them. Sanseveria, which reminds me of our western yucca, grows everywhere. And yet, at night, across this arid country, the sea fog rolls in from the Indian Ocean. In the chilly mornings, the spine-tipped bushes are dripping with dew.

In the vast bush country of Samburu, old bulls carrying heavy tusks can live out their days and never see a hunter. Perhaps, I thought, as we drove the safari car across the rolling ridges north of Samburu, I will find a hundred-fifty-pounder, and beat Don Hopkins at his own game.

Outside of a few scattered grass huts with small shambas of maize near them, there are no large villages north of Samburu for one hundred fifty miles. We camped near one of these small groups of houses, where the natives were using water which had collected in a crack in the bedrock during the rainy season now long past. Water is a problem both for humans and elephants in the Samburu area.

Both Brownie and I thought, as we sat in front of the tent that first evening, that this was not the most romantic part of Africa by any means. For one thing, there were none of the teeming herds of game which are commonplace on top of the grassland plateau farther to the west. Also, it was damp and cold as the sea air moved in from the southeast. A lion coughed in the distance. Brownie wondered how the lion would avoid freezing to death in that awful place.

But pleasant camping or not, Samburu is the land of the big elephants. The trick is to find them. We were looking for either the Emboni bull, which probably still traveled alone, or for the group of bulls which the poachers had reported. Throughout the next week, we moved through the area north and northeast, both on foot and in the safari car. Many of the Naswahilis burn the hardwood trees of the bush country into charcoal, and we followed the small trails and roads that wander everywhere through the bush, leading to these charcoal stations. (Charcoal burning is a good cover for poaching, and the illegal ivory is usually taken out in trucks under a load of charcoal bags.)

Whenever we found the huts of charcoal burners, we inquired about big bull elephants. Generally, we got very little information, as the natives thought that we were government scouts, searching for poachers. However, we did learn that there was one group of five bulls feeding together, and another group of three very large bulls. Either of these might be the one we were after. Any natives who would talk at all said that there were lots of elephants, and usually added that their shambas were being trampled and eaten by the "tembos," so that they ought to be killed.

At the end of a week we had seen much fresh elephant sign, but had not seen a single square inch of elephant hide. Unfortunately, Swan had never been in the Samburu before, and we had to depend entirely upon Ndege, our poacher guide. This fellow seemed quite friendly, once he had decided we were not government game scouts. He showed us how he stalked and shot animals with his poisoned arrows. "This makes the elephant very, very angry," the man assured us.

But even the master poacher could not find the Emboni bull, or the other large bulls that had been reported. Several groups of elephants were watering at a muddy pond, which lay about eighteen miles north of our camp. Several mornings, after driving half of this distance in the darkness over the rutted charcoal trails, we got an early start in tracking the bulls from the water. The wary elephants came in and drank at night, and then walked several miles back into the bush before feeding or resting during the heat of the day. We never caught up with any of these bulls, even though we tracked some of them ten hours or more. I began to wonder if we were ever going to get a close look at one of these animals. We had planned only to stay in the Samburu country for about three weeks at the most. Now it appeared that this was not going to be enough.

We had driven to the water hole just at daylight one morning, as we had done before. After several days of tracking on foot, Nick and I were getting tired of seeing some thousands of elephant tracks—but no elephants. We had picked up a charcoal burner, the evening before, who knew of another mud puddle, about five miles to the east, where elephants also drank. We decided to send Ndege and this native to the other watering place to look for signs of elephants.

While they were gone, we shot a very nice lesser kudu, which had stood on the edge of a clump of sanseveria for a few seconds before diving into the thicket. We had seen lesser kudu and oribi every day we had been elephant tracking.

About nine o'clock in the morning the two natives came back at a dead run.

"*Mingi, mingi!*" they shouted as soon as they were in sight. "*Tembo mingi!*" They had found a lot of elephants.

We left Brownie with the native driver at the safari car. Nick and I snatched up our rifles, and started after the two men. They had already run three or four miles, and yet they started back toward the elephants at top speed.

We did not get so far as the second water hole before we heard the elephants. A shrill trumpet came from far ahead. (An elephant trumpet sounds like a French horn with a broken reed.) Usually trumpeting indicates a herd of cows and calves. Harrison had said to stay away from cows and calves. Well, it would do no harm to take a look.

After another half hour of walking, we could hear elephants screaming and trumpeting to the south of us, but the thick scrub blocked the view. The elephants now sounded close. Ndege climbed up a small tree, and looked out over the bush, then beckoned to us to climb up beside him.

Nick and I shinnied up the scaly trunk of the thorn tree with considerable difficulty. Even at a height of twenty feet or so we could see out over the thickest mass of thorny bush. A couple of hundred yards away, a rounded gray boulder the size of a house stuck out of the scrub. An ear flapped. A puff of dust from the dirty back drifted off in the wind. The gray mass moved a little. A trunk snaked up at one end, curled around a branch, and jerked it off. There was a crack of splitting wood.

As we shifted in the tree, we could see another elephant, and then another. Three or four hundred yards away, a group of gray-brown backs appeared and disappeared among the stunted thorn trees. All of the elephants had recently dusted themselves. All were dirty and brown. After fifteen minutes of investigating from every angle in the tree, we could locate about thirty animals. All of them seemed to be full-grown, and some were obviously very large. From the trumpeting and squealing that came from that direction, we knew that some of the elephants were certainly cows. But off to the right were three big brown backs that could only belong to large bulls. It was impossible to see their tusks, although I did catch one glimpse of heavy ivory between the branches as an elephant moved. The thing looked as big around as my thigh.

"Those three are bulls," said Nick, swinging his binoculars as he clung to a branch of the tree. "Certainly one of them ought to carry big ivory. We'll have a look."

Nick and I dropped down from the tree and crawled forward together. As we inched through the bush, I remembered that sometimes big bulls stay around a herd of cows even though their breeding days are long past. The Samburu poachers had said that there were three very large bulls in the area. Perhaps the veterans with the big tusks were hanging on the outskirts of this bunch; or perhaps they had been attracted to the area by all the trumpeting and squealing, just as we had been.

It was fairly easy going toward the herd. From the tracks and droppings it was obvious that this group had been feeding in the area for several days. In the trails before us were large cuds of sanseveria, where the elephants had jerked off trunkloads of the plant and chewed it to get the moisture. We picked up several of these sanseveria cuds to see if they were wet and fresh. They were.

Nick tested the wind by shaking a little bag of wood ashes. It was steady from the southeast, as always. We had gone about two hundred yards, and figured we should be close to the first bull we had spotted from the tree. Suddenly there was a gurgling rumble, like water going down the drain of an old-fashioned bath tub. That was an elephant's intestines working. The noise was just ahead.

We could just make out a hind leg with loose folds of grayish skin. As Nick and I crawled forward on our hands and knees, the hind leg shifted back and forth in a monotonous rhythm. Apparently the bull was half asleep. He was rocking back and forth, and swatting flies with his long tail. If he would only stand there until we could crawl around to the side and have a look at his tusks!

We worked our way slowly through the brush. The bull was standing in the only available trail, so we had to crawl through the thick stuff. Nick and I were just negotiating a clump of cactus, when a branch splintered off almost over our heads. There was a thunderous belch. Wood and leaves crunched, like grain going into a sorghum mill. We saw the black ear of an elephant flap forward and back. The beast was almost above us. We had not seen this second bull.

Nick and I scrambled back past the cactus. We made a lot

of noise, but there was no help for it. Fortunately, the bull was breaking branches and crunching twigs so loudly that he didn't hear us.

When Nick and I got back to the tree where the natives waited, we were sweating in rivers, though it wasn't a particularly warm day.

"That was close," Nick commented. "My head was almost between that elephant's forelegs. I thought they were two trees."

We climbed our observation tree again, to reorient ourselves. We could not see the bull which had given us such a bad scare. Again we picked out the larger body of the biggest bull. He had not moved. If we circled even farther downwind, we could come up on his other side, and get a look at his ivory. If the tusks were a hundred pounds or better, we could polish him off then and there.

Again Nick and I made a wide circuit downwind. In the distance, we could still hear the trumpeting of the cows and calves. Apparently none of the animals were really moving.

We circled a hundred yards beyond the elephant trail where we had crawled before. Within a few minutes, we could again see the bulk of the largest bull through the stems of the bushes. He cleared his throat with a thunderous noise; his bowels rumbled and bubbled. The gurgling of his guts was so loud that Nick and I could not whisper to each other. The noise seemed all around us. I could see one tusk very thick at the base. I could not quite see how long the ivory was. Nick was punching my thigh from behind. I motioned him back irritably, looking over my shoulder. Nick was pointing to the other side.

About twenty feet to the right of us, a trunk coiled among the brush, like a headless serpent. Just behind, I saw elephant legs, several of them. No wonder the rumbling was so loud. I was already backing up like a startled crab. Nick had turned. Crouching low, we bolted from the brush.

Behind us, one of the elephants trumpeted. There was the

noise of splintering wood. I looked over my shoulder. I could see three domed heads above the bushes. The elephants were not following. The wind still blew steadily towards us.

Personally, I had lost my enthusiasm for trying to crawl up on those particular bull elephants. Apparently, instead of three bulls, there were a dozen or more. If we tried to get up to any one of them, we would surely get stepped on.

Nick was talking Swahili to Ndege, who kept shaking his head and spreading out his hands in a flat denial. Our own tracker, Nduyai, was showing no more enthusiasm than Ndege. Nick explained his plan to me. "If these fellows circle around on the other side of the elephants," Nick said with a sweep of his arm, "the bulls will catch their wind and drift this way. As the bulls go past, we can take our pick."

The bulls might not go past, I thought. Furthermore, from all the trumpeting in the distance, the main herd seemed in no mood to be chivied in any particular direction. However, as I couldn't think of any better plan, this one seemed worth a try. "One or two of those bulls over there certainly carry heavy ivory," Nick added as a clincher.

Nick ordered the two trackers to start circling the herd. The men were sullen and resentful. I didn't blame them especially, except that both of these fellows were elephant experts. They had spent their lives getting close to big elephants. The boy carrying the cameras we sent back a safe distance toward the safari car. We figured he might bolt in the wrong direction, and ruin the whole plan.

Nick and I sat down in the shade of a tree and waited. An hour passed. From the occasional trumpet of a cow elephant, it seemed that the herd had not shifted its location. It was, by this time, two or three o'clock in the afternoon, and the elephants were still quiet. Later on the animals would begin to move and feed.

Another hour went past. Nick began to fidget. He paced up and down an elephant trail in front of us. Twice we climbed up the tree to look at the elephants again. We could see about thirty of them. The big bulls were still almost in the same place, over to the right of the herd. Occasionally, one of these would jerk down a branch, and munch it slowly. Most of the elephants were still standing, but they seemed restless. Another half hour passed.

"Those bloody trackers have gone back to the village," Nick commented viciously. "When I get back—"

A shrill trumpet cut him short. A second elephant, and then a third, took up the cry. We could hear the shuffling of heavy feet. The noise increased to a rumble.

Over the brush, we could see the heads of elephants. They were coming straight at us. The dark shapes rose and fell. They were running. The crash of trees and brush was lost in the thunder of jostling feet. The elephant heads seemed a solid line; dark-colored bodies appeared out of the brush as far as we could see.

"Quick! Into the tree!" yelled Nick. He had already thrust his big double rifle into my hands. He turned, and leaped at the tree trunk. It was not a large tree. The first branch was perhaps twelve feet up, where the tree fanned out like an open hand. Nick shinnied up the trunk, and gained the main fork. Recklessly I tossed up the rifles to him. He caught the first one, and then the other. The noise of elephants was all around me. I scrambled up the trunk. I never knew how I got to the first branches. In a second, I was there.

Choking clouds of dust billowed everywhere. The first elephants passed by us in a solid wave of indistinct bodies.

Clutching my gun, I looked out over the brush. There were elephants everywhere. Through the dust, I could see cows with their trunks upraised. There were medium-size elephants, and baby elephants. All of them were trumpeting and screaming. Just ahead, a tree went down, but the crash of splintering wood could hardly be heard above the confusion of noise.

Nick was yelling something at me, although we were only three feet apart. "If they push this tree, we've had it," he shouted.

I could see what he meant. The jostling elephants were not moving along the trails. They crashed straight through the brush. Trees, thickets, and cactus were flattened before them.

As they ran, they crowded each other. Just below our tree, I saw a big cow with long, slender tusks. She reached out her trunk to protect her baby. The little fellow was no bigger than a sheep dog. The cow turned, and viciously gouged the flank of another cow who had come too close. The offending elephant didn't even flinch. At full speed, she rushed past. Her shoulder just grazed our refuge. The tree shook under the impact. Though I was holding on to a limb as big as my arm, I was jarred off balance, and almost dropped my rifle. As I held the gun in one hand, I could have touched the back of the cow elephant with the muzzle.

I swung back into the main fork. A half-grown elephant saw the movement. He stopped. He pointed his trunk straight at us. He screamed at us. I do not remember hearing the noise at all. The end of his trunk flared out like a trumpet, and his eyes looked as big as dinner plates. The African elephant isn't reputed to have good eyesight. This one did. He stood his ground, and stared straight at us. His trunk stretched out toward us like an accusing finger.

"If that elephant's mother comes up," I thought, "we're cooked. A big cow could pick us out of this tree as easily as if we were apples." A group of cows and young bulls surged from behind. Still, the young elephant stood under our tree, and pointed us out. "Here they are," he seemed to trumpet. The other elephants jostled against him. They paid no attention to the young elephant. None of the bigger bulls or cows looked up. Another cloud of yellow dust moved over us. The young elephant was gone, swept away in the stampede.

"Must be three hundred elephants!" Nick shouted again. His voice was lost in a new blast of trumpeting and squealing. What was Nick counting elephants for? It would just take one bull or one cow. At that moment, another mass of running forms rushed past. I noticed that they all seemed to be bulls.

There were big bulls and little bulls. Beyond, through the dust, the elephants were now scattered. Most of the herd had already swept by. "I believe we are going to make it," I yelled over my shoulder.

"Look at that bull!" I noticed for the first time that the noise of splintering brush and trumpeting was lessening. Nick's shout was over-loud. One of the bulls beneath us swung out his ears, and his trunk went up like the spout of a teapot. I could have touched the red tip of it with my hand. Certainly he would smell us. But he moved on. Just behind, I saw an enormous bull. He came straight at us out of the dust. His tusks were very thick.

"He's a hundred-pounder!" Nick said in my ear. "He'll go a hundred pounds."

I hitched the Weatherby rifle up on top of the branch. It was going to be awkward. The big bull swung slightly to one side. A knot of other bulls came just behind him. I threw off the safety of the .460 rifle, and lay at full length along a tree branch. As the big bull swept past, I could see his shoulder through the sight. There was the spot, just below the edge of his ragged ear, right on the point of his shoulder. There were branches in the way. Now! The recoil of the gun jerked my shoulder back. I saw the bull half turn, and go to his knees. I lost my balance. It was difficult to bolt another shell into the chamber. Six or eight bulls were coming straight at us. The rifle shot seemed to drive them berserk.

"Shoot!" Nick yelled. "Shoot—!"

I could see the muzzle of Nick's big .577 thrust out past me. I was having trouble getting my balance in the tree for a second shot. Nick's double rifle blasted out. The end of the limb which I held disappeared. I half turned. Nick's gun was sailing through the air. So was Nick. Both barrels had some-how gone off at once. Nick shot out of the tree like a rocket. Thrown against a branch, he clutched desperately at it. It broke. He grabbed at another, hanging by one hand. The elephants thundered beneath us. The feet of the bulls broke

Nick's double rifle into splinters. They could not miss the man hanging in the air before their faces.

I stuck my own gun between two branches, and leaped out along the limb. Nick was struggling up. I reached the back of his belt, and pulled him into the tree. An elephant ran by beneath us. Nick's feet dragged on its back.

Nick lay over a limb on his stomach. "That was a bit sticky," he said with a wry grin. He looked down at his gun. We could make out some of the pieces in the trampled earth. "Getting stepped on by an elephant would be awfully messy, wouldn't it?" he commented.

We might yet be down there with Nick's shattered double rifle. At the sound of the shot, the main herd of elephants had wheeled in panic. They were coming back at us again. For another ten minutes the earth shook under their running feet, and the air was filled with noise, dust, and confusion. Nick and I clung to our tree of refuge and waited. We did no talking, and we did not move around. If the elephants ever stopped running, they'd smell us or spot us in a second, and jerk us down.

But the elephants did not stop running, at least for a couple of hours. The main stampede had broken up into small groups of fifteen or twenty animals. These now rushed aimlessly back and forth. Some elephants stood. They raised their trunks in the air, and took the wind. Far off in the distance, we could hear broken fragments of the herd, still trumpeting and running. By sundown, some of the elephants had quieted down and begun to feed. Those downwind from us moved off, still screaming.

There was no sign of our native trackers. For all we knew, they might have been caught in the middle of the stampede. Our camera boy, too, had disappeared. If an elephant stepped on my cameras, I thought, they would look worse than Nick's double rifle.

It was almost dark when Nick and I slipped down from the tree. We could still see seven or eight elephants nearby. We took no time to go and look at the bull I had shot. We had to move quickly. There were a lot of elephants downwind of us.

At a half run, we moved cross wind. I still hoped to find the camera boy. Chances were that he had run when the stampede started. Nick and I rounded a clump of trampled brush at a dead run. There was a bull elephant not thirty feet from us. The bull shook his head and stuck out his ears. He turned and ran.

Brownie, at the car, had heard the trumpeting of the stampeding herd even at that distance. The two trackers had already come in, and the camera boy had showed up soon afterward. The natives had been smarter than we were.

The next day we worked our way cautiously back to our favorite tree. We had a bad moment when we saw twenty or thirty elephants not far away. Fortunately, the animals were already moving off. We waited a half hour, to make sure they were gone, and then worked our way back to the stampede grounds. The area looked as though the greatest of tornadoes had swept by. Trees, clumps of brush, and cactus were flattened like cobwebs. The earth itself was churned into powder. There was no square foot of that area that didn't have an elephant track on it.

My bull lay about thirty yards from our tree. He had apparently been carried part of the way by the stampede of his fellows before he dropped dead. His tusks weighed only eighty-one pounds, as they proved to be fairly short. He had looked awfully big coming straight at us out of the dust and confusion. Nick was picking up the parts of his double rifle, to see if anything could be salvaged. "I think," he said ruefully, "that this is the wrong way to get a big elephant."

5 · *Walk Around a Rhino*

A GRAY BODY heaved out of the brush before us. Two red-billed tick birds danced up and down on its folded skin. Their shrill *tchick, tchick, tchick,* had done the damage, warning of our approach. The rhino whirled, his little eyes glaring straight at us.

Andrew Holmberg was already pulling me backward by one shoulder. "Poor quality horn," he whispered in my ear. "Only fifteen inches."

While he was speculating on the horn's length, I was thinking that both of us were likely to be impaled on that horn in the next second. Sure enough, the rhino snorted, lowered his head, and came rumbling toward us. Apparently he was charging in the general direction of our sound and scent, however, without having a good visual fix on us. At any rate, he went pounding by to one side, and kept on going.

This was a typical blind rush by a rhino, and Holmberg was no more disturbed by it than a city dweller would be by a careening taxi. It seems you're usually fairly safe from a general-direction charge if you step behind a tree or bush. Only when a rhino gets you lined up in his short-sighted eyes do you have serious trouble to contend with.

Holmberg, who started shooting African rhinos as a boy on his father's Kenya coffee plantation, almost invited the brutes to come at him. "The best way to judge the length of the horn," he blandly assured me, "is to get the rhino to look straight at you."

This proved to be true, but there were difficulties—even for a man as experienced as Holmberg. Only a year before, Andrew was seriously injured while reviewing rhinos from his favorite head-on perspective. He had taken a client to within a few yards of a female feeding with her small calf. The cow charged, as usual, and Andrew stepped behind a bush. As he watched the cow gallop past, the calf crashed through Holmberg's screening bush and knocked him flat, breaking a couple of his ribs.

A grown African black rhinoceros will weigh two tons or more, but its brain is smaller than a human's. Yet low mentality is precisely what makes the rhino so dangerous. He'll charge an elephant, another rhino, a safari car, or even the sound of his own dung dropping. Rhinos have tipped over trucks, spilling the people out and trampling them to death. Charging rhinos have stalled trains on the Mombasa railroad, and crumpled cars on the highways.

Because of his witless willingness to charge, the African rhino has been purposely killed off as new roads and farms are established in his habitat. Kenya is practically the last area of all Africa where the black rhino can be hunted at all. Since the rhino is a slow breeder, as well as a menace to settlers, there seems little question that his days are numbered in most parts of Africa. In Kenya and northern Tanganyika, the normal range of the black rhino, it is already difficult to find one with a good head and a long front horn. The bush rhino, which lives in the low scrub country, generally has a short, stubby front horn. The long, graceful horns, so much sought after by hunters, are almost always found on animals living in mountain country, such as the slopes of Mount Kenya. One such animal met a military patrol in single file on a narrow game trail in the Mount Kenya jungles, and spitted the first two men on his horn before they could avoid him.

Mount Kenya was closed to our party, however, because bands of Mau Mau terrorists were again operating there, so we turned instead into the mountainous country to the south and west. Here, beyond the famous Rift Valley, Andrew had located a good rhino range while acting as military scout some years earlier. There were no native villages within miles. Our only difficulty was in getting a wheeled vehicle within striking distance of a particular isolated valley, in which Andrew had located several rhinos with trophy-sized lengths of horn on their snouts.

Our truck, the second vehicle in our entourage, never did make the grade across the rocky escarpment which blocked the entrance to "Holmberg Valley," as we called it in honor of our white hunter. But we finally got our safari car up an old elephant trail which crossed the Rift escarpment and into the valley beyond. This valley, surrounded by thorn-tree-covered mountains and broken by lava cliffs, is as wild as any in Africa today.

We spent three weeks there and saw about fifty rhinos. The first we sighted as our car topped the last rise of the trail beyond the Rift Valley. Andrew had stopped the car to look at some fresh buffalo tracks, and a pair of dik-diks suddenly skittered in front of us. These tiny antelope were frightened of something beyond a screen of bushes.

Sungura, our second gunbearer, pointed beyond the bush. There we saw a horn on top of an ugly snout. An ear with frayed edges tipped backward and forward, as though to catch sound. The head that showed above the brush looked like a prop from a Hollywood movie about dinosaurs.

The head swung toward us, and an explosive snort funneled through the two nostrils below the menacing horn. "If he charges the car, we've had it," Andrew whispered in my ear.

We had walked a few yards from the car, following the buffalo tracks. We bent low and sneaked back. Ngoro, our Masai gunbearer, silently handed down a pair of .470 double rifles. Then Andrew and I crawled toward the brush again, followed by our two gunbearers. We moved rapidly in a quarter circle, keeping perhaps fifty yards from the rhino.

The beast snorted from time to time, swinging his head back and forth. He'd heard us but hadn't spotted us—yet.

At a break in the bushes I saw another form, standing quite close to the flank of the first.

"Calf," breathed Andrew in my ear. "I thought that first one was a cow. She has a good horn, though. About twenty-five inches." Although it is legal to shoot female rhinos, most sportsmen won't do it, especially if the cow has a small calf.

Gunbearer Ngoro was now trickling dust between his fingers, watching a faint breeze drift the stuff in the direction of the animals. I heard the cow stamp her feet. Brush and branches crashed. Andrew and Ngoro stood up.

The rhino charged in our direction, but not straight at us. She pounded past us, the calf keeping pace at her flanks. A cloud of dust boiled up behind them. Then they were gone.

"Our first rhino, and a twenty-five inch horn," Andrew said enthusiastically. My own reactions were different. I was not only learning about rhinos, but also about white hunters.

On this safari we shot elephants, buffalo, lion, and a fine leopard. In all of these encounters we moved in close. Even when it was possible to shoot from one hundred yards or so, these professionals practiced the theory that one accurate shot at close range is worth several poorly placed ones at a greater distance.

I argued that I could place my shot as well at a fair range. Then, if something should go wrong, there'd be time to form a different plan, or at least to sprint for a tree. My words were lost on Andrew. I had to hunt his way—easing up within twenty or thirty yards in an effort to make the first shot count.

I also learned that a white hunter joins in the shooting only as a last resort, and Andrew's idea of a last resort was nothing like mine. It seemed to me that dangerous animals came within a hair's breadth of doing me in a dozen times in the course of our safari. At one point, I explained to Andrew that if something had me down and was chewing on me, he should feel free to shoot.

"You'll make out all right," he shrugged.

Andrew was no doubt trying to build up my confidence, but the rhinos kept tearing it down. If the brutes charged the car, as they often did, it took a wild ride through rocks and trees to get away. On one or two occasions we had a rhino huffing and puffing right at our rear wheel.

On foot the situation was even worse—especially in Holmberg Valley. Here the rhinos were concentrated along a small stream that was flanked on both sides by a solid mass of jungle-like vegetation. Rhino trails, worn deep, led down from the hills into the area. Apparently the rhinos spent a lot of time on the mountain slopes.

Some rhinos, especially cows with calves and younger bulls, stayed in the valley most of the time. We would often sneak up close to these to get a good look at their horns. Their usual response was to lower their heads, and snorting like donkey engines, come charging our way.

"You know," Andrew observed one morning, "there are a lot of rhinos here that we haven't seen. I think we'll try that heavy cover right over there."

We'd already seen a dozen rhinos that looked good to me, but Andrew was more particular. "Somewhere in these mountains there's a record-size rhino," he said, as we started out. "He may be in that heavy cover along the stream."

We drove the car to one of the open parks near the middle of the valley. Then we took the first game trail that led toward the creek in the center. Sungura and Ngoro followed us, each carrying an extra double rifle.

The open grassland was like a sunny park. Entering the jungle growth was like going into a darkened room. Every leaf, fern, and circling vine was struggling for light. When our eyes became accustomed to the gloom, I saw great woody vines hanging like serpents above our path.

I noticed that Ngoro and Andrew paused at almost every

step, looking intently into the shadows ahead and on both sides. At no time could we see farther than twenty or thirty feet.

We pushed along as silently as ghosts for perhaps an hour, encountering nothing larger than a flock of dark-colored partridges. Then, in a particularly dense place, Ngoro stopped— so suddenly that I bumped into him. He stared intently to the right. I'd noticed that Ngoro had seemed to be following the track of one particular rhino, turning from one trail to another as the distinctive track followed the stream's bank.

I stared in the direction Ngoro seemed to be looking, but I could see nothing. Ngoro turned and looked at Andrew. They both nodded knowingly. Andrew beckoned for me to move forward, and put his finger against his mouth.

We now redoubled our efforts at stealth. Ngoro carefully leaned over and moved small sticks from the path, so that we might make no unnecessary noise, and at every step he stopped to listen. I heard the piping of a faraway bird, but that was all.

We tiptoed forward a few yards more. Ngoro pointed. Two small birds were perched on a rounded boulder in the dense shadows. They were excited, and ran back and forth calling *tchick*, *tchick*.

The boulder beneath the two birds quivered. Then it was still again. Andrew made motions to Sungura. Slowly, with great caution, Sungura began climbing a tree at one side of the trail. He reached the first big limb and looked intently over the screen of bushes just before us. He stared for a moment, shook his head ever so slightly, and started to ease himself down the trunk. As he dropped lithely to the ground, a twig snapped.

The gray bulk heaved up before us. As part of the same movement, it whirled to face us, and I clearly saw the snout and the curved horn. It wasn't thirty feet away. Automatically, I brought up the .470 double.

"Poor horn," muttered Andrew behind me. In that second the rhino charged, and we plunged into the brush.

The brute passed us like a truck out of control, flattening small trees and brush in its path. We could hear the thud of its feet far up the trail; then all was silent.

"The wind from that thing almost took my hat off," I said.

"Poor horn," Andrew said again. "We didn't want him."

A few minutes later and a few yards farther along the trail, Ngoro again spotted a huddled form beneath a tangle of low-growing vines. Once more we tiptoed forward. There were no tick birds here, but we saw a flick of motion.

Ngoro peered ahead, then got to his feet. There was a look of disgust on his face. Andrew stood up. "It's no rhino," Andrew said to me. "It's a bushbuck—but a good one."

Sungura silently handed me the .300 Weatherby, and I gave him the .470 double rifle. My hands were sweaty and none too steady. I stood up and saw that the bushbuck was lying flat with his back toward us. Occasionally he flicked his white-fringed tail, and that was the movement we'd seen. I shot him through the shoulder.

"Well, that shot ends the rhino hunting in here for some time," Andrew said. "It's hard to pick out a good horn in this thick stuff anyway." I readily agreed to return to open country.

For the next week we tried to catch the rhinos as they came down from the hills to water. We saw perhaps ten in that time, one of them a bull with a horn about twenty-five inches long.

"That one would look awfully big where I come from," I said as we studied the bull.

Andrew wouldn't compromise. "Ngoro has seen the tracks of one particularly large bull that comes down to water at night. That's the one we want to get."

We started out before dawn to inspect the baits we had hung to attract the lion we had heard roaring every night, over on the other side of the valley. As we drove up to the first, Sungura, who was perched on top of the car as a look-out, pounded on the roof. Andrew stopped the car.

We looked ahead, expecting a lion, but Sungura was pointing behind us. There we saw the head and shoulders of a rhino looming above the brush fringing the river. Even at a distance—the rhino was about three hundred yards away—we could see that the horn was long and pointed. Andrew didn't even raise his binoculars. He just handed me the Weatherby .300.

"You're so eager to shoot something big with this," he commented. "You can try it out."

I slipped some cartridges with solid bullets into the .300 and we walked forward. Ngoro tested the wind with a piece of grass. The rhino apparently had watered at the stream, and was now on his way back to the hills. After a moment, he moved out of sight among the scattered bushes.

We trotted in a wide half-circle, so that we might come up in front of the rhino on the downwind side. At the place where we hoped to meet the animal, there were several rhino trails with patches of brush in between. It was certainly no place to try out my long-range theories. There was enough brush to permit the rhino either to pass us unseen, or to charge from a few feet away.

We stood there wondering if we'd gone too far or not far enough. Something moved in the brush to one side of us. We whirled around. The horn looked enormous, and it was pointed straight at us.

"Shoot him under the chin," Andrew said.

I raised the .300, centered the crosshairs of the scope below the chin, and squeezed the trigger.

At the shot the rhino seemed to shrink backward. Then he turned sideways. Frantically I centered on a point on his shoulder, and jerked the trigger. The rhino went down.

"Flattened him," said Andrew behind me. But when I started forward he pulled me back. "Never head straight for a rhino," he cautioned.

Ngoro thrust the .470 double into my hands, and impatiently I let Andrew guide me in a half-circle.

Suddenly the brush shook. The brute was on his feet, the great horn aimed at us.

"Shoot!" Andrew snapped.

As in a dream, I raised the rifle and fired at the base of the neck. The rhino swerved under the impact of the heavy bullet. I fired the left barrel into the shoulder as he swept by not six feet from the gun barrel.

The rhino lurched to a stop and stood still. Then he turned his great head toward me. I fumbled for the extra shells in the loops at my waist. Ngoro pressed another rifle on me from behind. Dropping the empty one, I snatched the loaded one, and whirled around. The rhino sank forward on his face.

"That was sticky," Andrew commented. "I didn't even see this second rhino till he was right on us."

"Second rhino?" I asked, still in a daze. Andrew pointed, and I saw the great carcass of the rhino I'd shot with the .300 in the brush ahead of us. The second rhino had charged out of the same patch of brush, giving me the impression that I was still dealing with the first animal.

Our original rhino had a front horn measuring thirty inches. The pioneer African hunters took rhinos with much longer horns, but a thirty-incher is a remarkable trophy these days.

Andrew was both elated and dejected. Pleased about the trophy, he was nonetheless upset because it had been necessary to shoot two animals. The second one weighed about as much as the first, but its horn was only eighteen inches long.

Later, when we explained the double kill to the game warden, he agreed that it had been necessary. "Had an experience like that myself last month," he said.

Tangling with two rhinos is exciting, I'll admit, but I confess that I would never do it on purpose. I'm more loyal than ever to my notion that rhino hunters would live longer if they picked out lone bulls, and used scoped rifles to shoot from much longer ranges.

6 · Rhino Versus Bulldozer

THE RHINO hurtled out of the bamboo like the battering ram that he was. He struck the half-raised blade of the dozer at one side. The machine, laboring up the steep grade, stopped dead. Ndege, the driver, frantically worked at the controls to start the engine. The rhino whirled on stubby legs, and charged again. Ndege saw a trickle of blood from the flaring nostrils. The rhino came from the side. Just before he struck the bulldozer again, he lowered his head, then jerked his snout upward as he struck. The sharp-pointed horn caught the dozer under the top plates of the track. There was a sound like a bullet hitting hard steel. The whole bulldozer tipped precariously under the impact, and Ndege and his helper were thrown out of the far side of the driver's seat. One of the plates of the track ripped away.

"A rhino charge a bulldozer and stop it dead?" I asked incredulously. "An automobile, yes; maybe even a truck if the rhino hit it on the side; but a bulldozer. . . ."

David Ommanney, the white hunter, shook his head, and stuck his pipe in his mouth at a belligerent angle. "Couldn't believe it myself till I went to look. They're repairing the bulldozer now. That driver, Ndege, is still the color of wood ashes."

David Ommanney, my wife Brownie, and I were at that moment in a wet camp well up on the slopes of Mount Kenya in East Africa. We had been there for two weeks, hunting bongo, that elusive, forest-dwelling antelope considered by many sportsmen to be Africa's top trophy. As secondary prizes, I hoped to get a forest leopard and a wide-horned, forest-dwelling buffalo. During our bongo hunt, we had been charged by forest elephants and snorted at by buffalo. I had shot one buffalo bull just above our camp on a forest road. The buffalo turned out to have a very disappointing head of horns. We used the carcass for leopard baits, up and down the same road. After three nights of vigil, we finally surprised a mongoose eating the buffalo meat. While looking at the mongoose, I bagged a giant forest hog, which looks like a cross between a bacon pig and a black bear. We wanted bongo, forest leopard, or at least a good Mount Kenya buffalo. We had everything else but. All of this is to say that our hunt was not the most successful African safari in the records.

Not that Mount Kenya isn't about the most interesting country in all of East Africa. Camped as we were well up on the slope of the 17,040 foot mountain, we found ourselves in another world as far as Africa was concerned. Even in our camp the weather was wet, cold, and dark. We had pitched our tent in a small clearing, formerly occupied by a sawmill. From the sawmill radiated forest roads along which the foresters had hauled in the saw logs before World War II. Farther up on the mountain, the forest roads enter the bamboo zone. Here, most of the roads stop. Some of the Mount Kenya tracks up the main ridges were extended by Army bulldozers during the Mau Mau emergency, so that truckloads of scouts could more easily get at the terrorists. Our white hunter, David Ommanney, was one of the scouts. He showed us where he and his men had surprised a camp of Mau Mau, killing sixteen in a hot fire fight. We could still see the ashes of the old fires, and the remnants of the brush shelters where the terrorists lived.

We had spent most of our time in the bamboo, as that is where the bongo lives. We had found the bamboo forest wet and nasty, and bongoless as far as we were concerned. Finding one of the rare forest antelope in that monotonous stuff was like trying to find a flea on a hound's back when you are the size of the flea. So when David heard that the men at Keith's sawmill, some thirty miles north around the base of the mountain, had sighted a big bull mountain rhino, he took the safari car and drove around to find out.

"See a mountain rhino!" the foreman of the sawmill exploded. "We've done nothing else but see the bloody beast. He's disabled my only dozer, kept two of my men up a tree all night, and charges every time we go up there. The bloody thing lives there."

Next morning, David and I went to see for ourselves. Native mechanics were fitting a new plate on the broken bulldozer track. Even when the machine was repaired, however, Ndege claimed that he would not again go up on the ridge where the rhino lived.

"We'll go up there and shoot him for you this afternoon," Ommanney said confidently.

Confidence is a good thing in a white hunter. As a matter of fact, I was very confident myself. Shooting a three-ton rhino was going to be a cinch, compared to the elusive bongo. But four days and a hundred miles of mountain trails later, we still had not eliminated the bulldozer rhino.

He was there all right. The foreman had said that he lived there, and we found tracks to prove it. He was a bull, too. The print of his hind foot was as wide across as my hand from outstretched thumb to extended little finger. This is a big track, even for a mountain rhino. We followed some thousand of these distinctive tracks every day, but the bulldozer rhino seemed to be as retiring as one of the rare Mount Kenya orchids that Brownie was always looking for. With a guide from the sawmill, Ommanney's gunbearer, Longolo, and a second gunbearer, Kwakai, to carry lunch and ammunition, we tracked, rested, and tracked again. As we rested, David told me about mountain rhinos.

"The mountain rhino is a lot different from his lowland cousin, the bush rhino, although they both belong to the same species. The mountain variety of the black rhino, like this one here,"—David indicated one of the deep three-lobed footprints in front of us—"has a bigger body, a lighter color, and a long, slender horn compared to the short, blunt snout of the bush rhino. These mountain beasts are usually shyer than bongo," David added with a wry smile.

Apparently our mountain rhino bull had reverted to type. We hadn't even gotten a good look at him, much less a fair shot. I did have one glimpse the second morning of the hunt. I saw the rhino's eye and his front horn, about five feet from my face.

David and I had found tracks on our first reconnaissance, which showed that the bull usually bedded down very close to the spot where he had effectively stopped the bulldozer from scraping a road up his home ridge. A hundred yards above the gouges in the earth where the bulldozer had been working, a thick stand of bamboo began, extending upward into the sodden clouds that always hung on the flank of the mountain. On the second morning, we went directly to this bamboo thicket, after driving our safari car as far as we could along the unfinished road. At the edge of the bamboo, where the tunnel of a game trail showed like a black doorway, was a dollop of dung, fresh and wet. Longolo stuck his bare toe into the dung, and grunted in a whisper. David translated the Swahili: "Dung's warm. We'll find your rhino in there." He gestured with the barrel of his .470 double rifle.

We followed the fresh tracks and droppings into the dark-ness of the bamboo. I was third in line. We went a few yards, then stopped where three game trails came together. Just to my left I thought I saw a dark form. It certainly wasn't the matted stalks of several fallen bamboo. At a crouch, I moved off several yards to the left, and stuck my head around a corner of the game trail. I could see a bright eye with wrinkles around it. Above was the base of a horn, brown and shredded like a coconut husk.

"Come back, you fool," Ommanney hissed behind me. The

bamboos crackled as the rhino heaved to his feet and lunged. I threw up my Weatherby. The barrel caught on a bamboo. I could see nothing. The noise of breaking bamboo was deafening. Just to my left, the stalks jerked and splintered. The crashing died away.

"That was sticky," David commented as we got to our feet. "If he had charged straight at you, he would have stepped on your head." I gathered from his tone that at the moment David wished that the rhino had done just that. Longolo was taking the wind by shaking a little bag of wood ashes. He muttered something in Swahili. "That bull circled on his own trail and had our wind," David commented, shaking his head. "Can't fathom why he charged a bulldozer but didn't take on four men on foot."

Just when the bulldozer rhino lost his nerve, I do not know. The natives at the sawmill told us that, as far as they could remember, the bull had lived on that ridge for the last three or four years. He had systematically charged and driven off every native who came that way, and ultimately even the bulldozer which had invaded his domain. For some reason, he figured we were different. That night he left his bamboo ridge, crossed a deep canyon to the south, and disappeared. It took us a whole day of tracking to find where he went. When we did follow the sliding tracks in the mud, I could not comprehend how a three ton beast could go down that muddy track, across the volcanic rocks in the canyon bottom, and up the other side. The terrain would have tried the ability of a mountain goat. Late on the third day, we jumped the rhino in a thick clump of bamboo, and he ran again.

During the fourth day of tracking, we were tired, wet, and discouraged. The belligerent bulldozer rhino had turned into a running coward. We had jumped him twice on the bamboo-covered ridges, high up on the flank of Kenya. Each time he had smelled us or heard us, and galloped off through the bamboo like a frightened rabbit. Each time he ran, he circled wide, and headed back to the north. Late in the afternoon, we figured he was going back to his home range, and we would all be just where we had started, which was nowhere.

We stopped in a little opening where the spreading limbs of a giant cedar had stunted the bamboo. In the sodden mess at the base of the tree, we built a fire with great difficulty (and a lot of Boy Scout lore), and ate a late lunch. The cold mountain mists were already beginning to roll down Kenya. The tree hyraxes were tuning up, as though night had already fallen. The tree hyrax, an animal about the size of an American groundhog, makes love to his mate in the next tree by screeching, a noise that sounds like a woman having her throat cut. A group of louries, with their brilliant red underwings, fluttered and settled for the night in the tree above us. Longolo and Kawkai stretched out on the wet ground with their feet to the fire. Even Ommanney seemed discouraged. "We're either going to have to get cracking and head for the car, or spend the night under this damn tree," he remarked sourly, as he sucked at his dead pipe.

I nodded glumly, but added, "Let's track old bulldozer a little farther. It's almost in the direction we have to go anyway."

David shook his head, prodded the two gunbearers into life with his foot, and motioned Kwakai to carry his double rifle. While David was stamping out our sputtering fire and knocking out his pipe, I stepped along the game trail on the tracks of the bull. The tracks had never been hard to follow. In the mud of the bongo trail, the rhino had sunk two inches at every stride. I saw by the splayed-out imprints that old bulldozer was still running. "Probably be clear on the other side of the mountain," I thought glumly.

A couple of hundred feet beyond our fire, the bongo trail ended abruptly in a tangle of half-broken bamboos. This was to be expected. We had passed a hundred places like it on that day. Bushbuck, bongo, buffalo, and other animals using the forest track had made a detour around the windfall. As I stepped into the side trail, David was at my shoulder. I crouched down to crawl beneath a couple of bamboos, and then stopped on one knee. Just ahead, in the open trail, were four tree trunks. They didn't look natural. The closest one moved a little. A leg! A gray head moved from behind the bamboo. There was a rasping snort. A bamboo cracked. Old bulldozer charged straight through the bamboo.

Apparently the old bull had decided to run no more. Why he had taken his stand just there can be explained only by another brainless rhino. Behind that windfall in the trail, it was easily possible to hear our voices as we had stood by the fire and talked for over an hour. Certainly the old rhino could smell the smoke. But when he made up his mind, he made up his mind. He didn't take the detour around the mass of fallen bamboo, but came straight through. Bamboo stalks as big as my arm snapped like straws. David yelled something, and grabbed for his rifle. Kwakai, at the sudden appearance of the rhino's horn through the bamboos, turned and ran, carrying the double rifle with him. David matched him, stride for stride, screaming like a madman. Meanwhile, it was up to me.

I was still on my knees in the mud. The rhino had apparently seen me. He came straight at me. I saw him lift his ugly head in a vicious uppercut, to toss away the bamboo stalks. Automatically I raised the Weatherby. There was no time to sight. There was no need. The rhino was twenty or thirty feet away. The solid bullet struck the rhino on the shoulder. He squealed and whirled, and he ran in a complete circle. Bamboos splintered and cracked as the great body cut through them like a scythe. Here he came again. Ommanney was running up the trail. He had snatched the double rifle from Kwakai.

The rhino saw the movement, and charged again. The bull was in the open trail now. I cranked in another shell, and fired at his shoulder as he passed me. David, crouching and running, fired the first barrel, then the second. He and the rhino were running at each other, and only a few feet apart.

David would never have a chance to reload. At the impact of the 500 grain bullets, the rhino fell to his knees, and slid in the mud. I bolted in another shell and fired blindly. My gun barrel was not ten feet from the flank of the rhino as he heaved again to his feet.

Ommanney was frantically trying to reload. Usually, a hunter with a double rifle carries two extra shells between the fingers of his left hand, but David had not been carrying his own gun and was not ready. None of us were ready. Now he was trying to dig two shells out of his belt loops, and stuff them into the breech of his gun. I was trying to reload, too. I could not remember whether I had fired two or three times.

But old bulldozer was through. He got to his feet shakily, turned, and ran back through the swath of destruction in the bamboo which he had made seconds before. David and I reloaded, and followed him with our rifles thrust forward, the safeties off. Just ahead, we heard the bamboo crash again. A heavy body rolled down a little slope. There was a gasping snort—and then silence. As we came up to the bull, he raised his head and glared at us with his little pig eyes. I shot again at the base of his neck. He quivered, and then was still. We left him there in the wet bamboo, and started the long walk back to the road and the safari car.

The next morning, with cameras and extra bearers, we walked back to the spot where old bulldozer had made his last stand. In the soft ground, just beyond the bamboo windfall, we found where he had fallen, gotten up, and fallen again. He had waited for us at that particular place. It was no accident. "More like a buffalo than a rhino," was David's comment. The rhino had been fifty feet from us when I had seen his four stubby legs and he had started his charge. My first bullet from the .378 Weatherby had entered at the base of his neck. We found the bullet beneath the skin of his hip on the opposite side. David's shots had struck the rhino in his chest. Any of these would have been fatal, but perhaps not

quickly enough. Outside of a skinned place on one side of
his flank, and the broken tip of his horn, the bulldozer rhino
had come off better than the bulldozer which gave him his
name.

7 · Three Bad Buffs

A RUMBLING SNORT exploded in our faces. I saw the polished tips of black horns, and dark, evil eyes beneath. A glob of frothy saliva whipped away from the open mouth. As the vague gray body behind surged toward us, the widespread horns dropped suddenly and came forward.

"Shoot!" yelled Andrew Holmberg in my ear. "Shoot low!"

I held the .470 double rifle at an awkward angle. Those awful horns, only a few feet away, seemed paralyzing. My muscles would not move. The muzzle of the gun would not come up. "Don't shoot at the horn!" Andrew had told me before. "The bullet won't go through."

When we had first started this safari, I had wondered if I would stand up under the charge of one of the Big Five. A man never knows until he has actually tried it. To shoot a deer, or even a bear, across a canyon is one thing. To face a charging African Cape buffalo a few feet away is another.

When Andrew first met my wife Brownie and me in our room at the Norfolk Hotel in Nairobi, I could sense that he was sizing me up. He had had many clients in the past. He told me afterwards that he had taken out some hunters who had nerves of steel, and others who threw their guns away and ran when a dangerous animal attacked. Professional hunters do not like to take an unreliable client close to dangerous game. This is the way white hunters get killed.

"Any one of the Big Five can kill a hunter—and often does," Andrew said in his slow, meticulous manner. "Of all these animals, the Cape buffalo is probably the worst. We'll go after buffs first."

"What do you mean 'the worst'?" Brownie wanted to know.

"The cemetery on the edge of Nairobi here," said Andrew as he waved his hand vaguely, "has more customers put there by buffs than by all the rest of the Big Five altogether." With that comforting thought, Andrew got up rather abruptly and left.

As we drove out of town at sun-up the next morning at the start of our sixty-day safari, I was thrilled, but somewhat apprehensive, too. Andrew's logic of starting with the Cape buffalo first had not been lost upon me. Undoubtedly, he figured that if I stood up well to the buffs, the elephant, rhino and the rest would be a cinch. I had found out, too, in talking with some of Andrew's friends, that there was probably no man in all of East Africa who knew more about Cape buffalo than Andrew. He holds the world's record buffalo head, a magnificent bull with a horn spread of fifty-eight inches. When Andrew said these animals were dangerous, I was sure he knew what he was talking about.

During the trip to southwestern Kenya, where we were to begin our safari, Andrew did not elaborate on his opinion of the Big Five. I plied him with questions about the habits and characteristics of Cape buffalo in general. He summed it up by saying, "Buffs are not only big and hard to knock down, they are dangerously intelligent. If a buff makes up his mind to kill you, chances are that he'll get it done."

Our safari was a comparatively small one. Our Willys safari car was followed by a single truck, which carried our tents, extra gasoline, and food, and perched on top, our twelve safari boys, representing six separate native tribes. With this light equipment, we moved by a circuitous route into an area of Kenya west of the Rift Valley, which had been hunted little since the Mau Mau uprising. As we camped that evening on the bank of a little stream that flowed out of the Nguti-

gushe hills to the west, Andrew pointed out the first buffalo
tracks on a well-trampled trail that led down to the water.
"Just across those hills there," he remarked, "is where I shot
the world's record buffalo, two years ago. I think there are
some bigger heads than that one in this country."

During our first two days of hunting, we found evidence
of Cape buffalo on both sides of our camp. In the immediate
vicinity were two herds of perhaps fifty animals each. These
moved along trails far out into the open country at night to
graze. Generally by early morning, however, they returned
to the thick cover of jungle-like scrub, which grew in a solid
band of vegetation on both sides of the little stream. The trick
was to catch the buffalo in the open long enough to judge
their horns, and to shoot a big bull.

On our third morning, we had a chance. We drove out of
our camp before dawn, to make a reconnaissance of a pride
of lion that we had heard roaring during the night. We passed
close to the strip of jungle along the river. Our first tracker,
Mohammed, who was riding on top of the safari car as a
lookout, pounded frantically on the metal roof.

"*Mbogo, bwana* Andrew, *mbogo!*" he said, as he pointed
his arm toward the fringe of forest on our left.

How the devil could the man see a thing in that blackness?
It was not yet dawn! Andrew seemed to read my thoughts,
for he said, "Mohammed hears buffalo bawling." He stopped
the car, and motioned me to silence. Quietly also, Ngoro, the
first gun bearer, unshackled the .470 double rifles from the
rack in the safari car, and handed one to me. I had borrowed
this gun for the trip, and had tried it out on the first day of
the safari. With its open sights it shot very well indeed. There
was one difficulty, however. I found out that this particular
gun had an interesting habit of firing both barrels at once, if
you pulled the front trigger too enthusiastically. The result-
ing kick had laid me flat on my back. Anyway, I thought, if
those 500 grain bullets have that much punch backward, they
will knock down anything in front of them. It was comforting

to feel the cold barrels of the .470 in my hand as we stepped off into the heavy cover.

In the semi-darkness of dawn, we could hear and smell the buffalo herd much easier than see them. A calf bawled from time to time. Occasionally there would be a heavier-voiced grunt, as some cow hooked another with her horn. The smell was like that of a freshly-used cow corral, and the droppings were those of domestic cattle. We could hear the buffalo feeding just ahead of us. As the light grew stronger, we could see trees bending down, and trailing vines being jerked from beneath, as the buffalo stripped the leaves away.

Andrew motioned us backward. "We'll circle them to find the herd bulls," he whispered. Ngoro led the way off to the left, through a tunnel-like path which skirted the center of the heaviest foliage. The path had been worn by generations of Cape buffalo and other animals. There were fresh buffalo tracks in the black earth beneath our feet, and the smell of buffalo was everywhere. We gripped our guns and swung around, as a startled bushbuck jumped beside us and disappeared around the corner of the path. Then we heard a branch break to our right. Andrew pointed, and motioned me ahead. We bent over, and, at a crouch, silently moved forward, turning into a cross trail. Ngoro pointed through the stems of the close-growing bushes. I could see a dark patch of hide move. I could make out cakes of mud and dirt on the side of the thing. Another branch broke with a splintering crack. I saw one split-edged ear, and an ugly head. I raised the double rifle. This was my first look at a Cape buffalo, and he wasn't thirty feet away. There was his ugly snout with a dark gray horn upon it. Another horn was just behind.

"Rhino," breathed Andrew in my ear. He was already pulling me backward. Ngoro and Sungura, our gun bearers, were backing up too. The rhino swiveled his frayed ears backward, and raised his head. He had caught some sound. If the ugly beast whirled and charged in that narrow trail, he would flatten us all. We backed up slowly. Then, when we were

out of sight behind a tree, we swiftly retreated to the main
buffalo trail.

"Boy, what a beauty! Did you see that horn?" I whispered
to Andrew.

"Only about eighteen inches," Andrew answered, in a non-
committal way. "Very mediocre head. An old bull, but probably with a nasty temper," he added with a smile.

We traveled for several hundred yards along the buffalo
trail which paralleled the stream. From time to time, we could
hear the grunts and bawling of the main herd off to our right.
If the wind held, I saw that we could get ahead of the feeding
animals, and then look them over as they slowly moved past
us. Just ahead of us, on one side of the stream, was a little
clearing of perhaps an acre or so. The tall dead grass which
covered the place was partially burned away—by the natives,
no doubt, as they always fired the grass when it dried suf-
ficiently after the wet season of April and May. We crouched
by the edge of this clearing, as the noise of the herd was now
quite close. We could hear some of the animals splashing in
the water and walking up the bed of the stream beyond.

Suddenly, a black head appeared from behind a bush, almost beside us. Slender black horns with shiny tips stood out
on either side. The eyes were dark-colored and malevolent.
The animal was not much more than a short stone's throw
away.

"Cow! Don't move!" whispered Andrew out of the corner
of his mouth. "If she charges us, we're dead."

Ahead I could see other black forms moving through the
bushes. Another head appeared on the edge of the clearing.
The horns on this were massive, swinging low on both sides of
the head, and then up in a graceful sweep. I knew that this was
a bull, and he looked tremendous. Ngoro prodded Andrew
quietly in his side, and pointed with his eyes. Off to our left
was another bull. He was standing stock still, looking straight
at us. Still farther to the left was another dark form. I heard
a shuffling noise on the trail behind us. I looked back out of

the corner of my eye, and saw another evil head with wide-sweeping horns. There were buffalo all around us.

"Shoot the one on the left," Andrew said quietly. "Aim for the lower third of the shoulder, and *don't miss.*"

I slowly raised the .470 double rifle. Fortunately, the gun was so heavy that it seemed comparatively steady. The open sights seemed just like those of the .22 I used when I was a kid. Perhaps when I touched off that shot, we would have African buffalo all over us. I squeezed the trigger gently. The heavy gun recoiled like the kick of a steer, but I didn't notice. As the bull turned, I shot the left barrel at his flank, and heard the solid "thunk" of the bullet in hard flesh.

There was a trampling and bellowing all around us. Andrew stood up. Ngoro thrust the extra .470 into my hands, and snatched the other from me. The buffalo in the trail behind us turned and ran. The others circled past. One old cow galloped by within fifteen feet, but she did not see us. Within a minute, the trampling of hoofs and the breaking of brush had receded down the valley.

I started forward toward the bull I had shot. Andrew pulled me by the shoulder. "Never straight for them, old boy," he said softly. "Not for a buff."

We circled widely, keeping to the middle of the little clearing before us. The place where the bull had disappeared was the mouth of one of the game trails which criss-crossed through this strip of jungle. We could see the black opening of the tunnel now. There was something bright protruding at one side. The thing shook, then moved out. It was one horn of the buffalo bull. The animal was on his feet, standing quite motionless, with only his head sticking out of the leaves. He seemed to sense that we saw him, and a bellow rumbled in his throat. He lurched forward. I saw that he came on three legs, and slowly, but his eyes were fixed upon us. I shot him once in the chest. The impact of the heavy bullet turned him half around. I fired the left barrel into his shoulder. Still he stood shaking his massive head.

"If you had followed him close around that bush, he'd have had that horn through your belly," Andrew said. Then the bull collapsed all at once. We walked forward.

"It's not a big head, but it's stylish," said Andrew, as he tilted the horns this way and that. "It will do for our first buff."

A week later, in another valley, we tried again. As no natives lived in the valley, and no safari party had ever penetrated this far, the buffs semed unafraid, and had been grazing in the open the afternoon before we first spotted them. This time we would have a chance to look them all over, and pick out the mightiest head of horns in the bunch.

Andrew, Ngoro, and I started out late in the morning, to stalk the big herd. We left Brownie and the safari car in the middle of a grove of thorn trees near the stream. Mohammed and Sungura were enjoined to stay with her, as the place was full of rhinos. We saw thirteen on that one day alone. After carefully testing the wind, so as to keep the morning breeze in our faces, we circled perhaps a half a mile to come up on the flank of the buffalo herd. They had moved during the night, but not very far. We soon located them by the bawling of the cows and calves. They were moving toward us, apparently coming down to the little stream in the middle of the valley to water.

Just before the first scattered groups of animals came into view, we hid ourselves in a thick clump of sanseveria. Instead of passing by us a hundred yards away, as we had anticipated, the lead animals of the herd turned down a game trail which led within forty or fifty feet of the sanseveria where we crouched.

Fortunately, the light breeze down the mountain slope held. The first group of animals stalked past at a walk. In the lead were some dry cows. Then there was a group of bulls, youngish and with long, gracefully-upcurved horns. As group after group of the animals passed by—so close that we could see the lashes on their eyes—I began to understand why Andrew claimed that there were no two buffalo heads just alike. Some had long sweeping horns, with comparatively narrow shafts. Other horns were massive, with a solid boss of bone which covered the whole tops of the animals' heads. Still others had a wide gap between the two horns. There were straight horns and back-sweeping curved horns, some with perfect tips, and others broken and worn.

Half a dozen times I whispered out of the corner of my mouth into Andrew's ear, "That one?" Each time he shook his head slightly. Then he whispered back, "These are the herd bulls. The big busters will be at the very end of the herd. The very last bull will be the one."

Even at these words softly spoken, a huge bull on our side of the moving line stopped dead in his tracks, and swung his head toward us. His horns were caked with mud, and a bit of one tip was broken off a little. But the whole top of his head was covered with a spreading cap of scaly horn. His dark eyes looked directly into our own. If we so much as batted an eye, the whole herd would be upon us. He stood there for a long minute, looking at us steadily. Then he rumbled in his throat, and swung away. I heard Andrew let out a long breath beside me.

I had counted roughly two hundred animals that had already passed us. The last straggling bunches were coming into sight further up the slope. There were some tremendous bulls among them. One old fellow with enormous handle-bar horns looked like a sure bet. Again, Andrew shook his head, ever so slightly. "The last one," he whispered.

There, at last, was the gray-black back of the last buffalo, between the trees. He did look big in body. In a moment he would be before us. There he was! He held his head low, and he was looking behind. It was a cow! Behind her, still wet from birth, was a forlorn little humped-back calf. The calf tottered along behind her with faltering steps. I glanced at Andrew with withering scorn. "The last one will be the big bull," I reminded him.

When the cow buffalo and her new-born calf had finally
walked slowly out of sight, we stood up and moved away
down the valley.

We made a wide circle of perhaps half a mile to avoid a
rhino that we had seen sleeping in the shade under a fever tree.
Beyond was a park-like place of evenly-spaced flat-topped
thorn and fever trees. There Ngoro spotted three lone bulls.
He stopped and pointed. Down below us, in the big grassy
flat, the animals looked like three black boulders.

"They have very heavy heads," Andrew said after a moment. "One—the one on the right—has a good spread."

"The distance between a buff's ears is about thirty-six
inches. You can tell how wide the spread is by how far the
horn sticks out on either side beyond the ear tips," Andrew
commented, again reading my thoughts.

Although it was late in the morning, the buffalo here had
not gone into heavy cover. As we walked through the waist-
high grass, yellow-necked spurfowl and quail kept flushing
before us. I noticed each time the birds went up that Andrew
looked worried. I was thrilled. Africa certainly provides the
world's best bird shooting. We had a 16 gauge shotgun back
in the safari car. I determined to try some of this fabulous
bird hunting as soon as we had finished with the buffalo
business.

When we approached closer, we crouched to take advantage of the cover of the long, straw-colored grass. From time
to time, Ngoro would cautiously thrust his head up, and then
whisper something to Andrew in Swahili. We moved forward
until we were well within a hundred yards of the nearest of
the three slate-colored forms. Still we moved in closer. We
were within fifty yards now, creeping on our hands and knees.
I heard one of the buffalo belch, like an old man after a heavy
dinner. Ngoro, after cautiously raising his head, signaled us
to the left with his hand, and again we moved forward. Then
Andrew removed his terai hat, and slowly looked over the top
of the grass. Behind his shoulder I also took a look. One of

the three buffalo had disappeared. The nearest one was still grazing. He wasn't fifty feet away. The third bull had turned away from us. Two tick birds skittered along his backbone. The tick birds had spotted us.

"One is lying down," Andrew whispered, as he pressed his mouth against my ear. "They all have big heads, but I can't get a real good look. Keep ready." He touched the .470 in my hand.

We moved forward again, although this seemed foolhardy. I hunched along on both knees and one arm, so as to keep the double rifle ready. Suddenly there was a blur of motion before us. Two spurfowl spurted out of the grass, almost under my hand. A black form moved out of nowhere. It was the bull which had been lying down. I could hear the two tick birds with their frantic "tchick, tchick!" I raised to my knees. The three buffalo were moving toward us. They broke into a run.

"Shoot!" said Andrew tersely. The middle bull was just before me. I covered the corner of his shoulder with the sights, and jerked the trigger. Both barrels went off with the deafening blast. I was knocked backward against Ngoro, who was already pushing the spare double rifle into my hands. The first bull had gone down, Ngoro and Andrew were on their feet now, yelling wildly. The two other bulls passed close beside us. One swerved away, stopped, and then turned.

"Get ready!" said Andrew. Ngoro took two or three steps toward the bull, and sailed his hard felt hat along the top of the grass, into the buffalo's face. The bull snorted, pivoted on four legs, and ran off after his companion.

Andrew was looking down at the fallen buffalo. My two shots had entered the animal's shoulder a finger's breadth apart. I had shot too high, but the bullets had broken the beast's neck. The bull was not yet dead.

"A whole valley full of trophy buffs, and we had to pick this one!" commented Andrew sourly.

I saw immediately what he meant. The horns were massive,

perhaps the heaviest and widest spread we had yet seen, but one of the tips was a freak. Instead of curving up, it stood out straight.

"Anyway," Andrew commented as we finished our photographs, we'll get another chance at buffs south of here in Tanganyika. I know a particular herd in the Loliondo country which produces some very exceptional heads."

Unfortunately, we could not get at that herd; we were turned back from Loliondo by a military patrol, which had a group of Mau Mau terrorists surrounded just north of us. We swerved west, to hunt along the Grummetti and Mara rivers. We carried permits to take two buffalo in Tanganyika, but there was little point in taking another mediocre or freak head. We wanted only one, and Andrew knew a place on the Grummetti which had produced some of East Africa's biggest buffalo heads.

The country along the Grummetti and Mara rivers is difficult to hunt. Although it is relatively open, with an abundance of game, here the buffalo have been shot at for years, and have become extremely wary. The buffs spend all of the daylight hours securely hidden in the dense cover of brush along the water courses. Buffalo are very plentiful in the Grummetti country, but a casual hunter would seldom see one.

In all of our buffalo hunting, I had found that the major difficulty was Andrew himself. I am sure that by this time we had looked over five hundred buffalo bulls, but on each occasion Andrew had shaken his head, and if I too eagerly raised the muzzle of the gun, he would slowly push the barrel down with a disapproving look.

"You'd be ashamed to take *that* one back to Nairobi," he had said a hundred times. I had pointed out, on an equal number of occasions, that some dozens of buffalo bulls that we had passed up—and a lot of other game, too, for that matter—would look awfully big back home. Actually, I saw Andrew approve of only a very few animals during our whole trip. Most of these turned out to be world records, and he had been able to identify them as such a quarter of a mile away.

It was almost the last day of our stay on the Grummetti when Andrew suddenly became enthusiastic. We had stopped the safari car alongside a small tributary, which was overgrown with the usual tangle of vines and jungle trees. We were looking at a bushbuck, standing motionless at the edge of this scrub. The animal was orange-colored. Even I could see that the horns were of mediocre length and development.

"There's the one we want," Andrew said quietly. "That head will go forty-five, and maybe forty-eight inches."

I looked at him in surprise. He was looking through the side of the windshield, across a little flat toward another tangle of jungle growth. Two buffalo bulls stood motionless staring at us. The right-hand animal had a set of horns like a gendarme's hat—all boss and no points. The left one had everything.

As silently as we could, we got the double rifles out of the rack, and crawled out the far side of the safari car on our hands and knees. Even this movement, however, alarmed the animals. Before we could slip down into the sheltering cover of the scrub along the river, they whirled and ran. In a single jump, they had disappeared into the close-growing brush behind them.

We broke into a jogging run up the sandy course of the donga (or arroyo) into which we had dropped. The place was a natural pathway, screened on both sides by the belt of vegetation which arched in a solid growth of branches and leaves overhead. I saw rhino tracks, and the cat imprints of lion which used this same tunnel-like path. We rounded a sharp corner, and turned into the side wash where the buffalo had disappeared. In a few minutes, we saw where the damp sand had spurted from their massive tracks as the heavy-bodied animals had jumped down into the wash and run along it. In a few yards, the tracks turned up the bank on the far side, and along a game trail. Ngoro pulled a pinch of down from a feathery-looking plant, and dropped it between his fingers to test the wind. There was practically no current of air at all.

We crawled out of the donga, and up along the game trail. Andrew cautioned me to silence as Ngoro moved ahead. I gathered that Ngoro and Andrew did not think that the two bulls had gotten our wind and were not badly frightened. We moved on a few yards, to where the vegetation was thinning on the far side. Ngoro pointed ahead. I could just see a dark form with the light making a vague outline from behind. Andrew motioned me to crawl past him. "It's the big one," he whispered. "Shoot him in the chest." Ngoro sank down, so that I could shoot over him. I raised the gun quickly, centered the sights in the middle of the massive chest, and fired. The buffalo turned and ran. Only then could I see the great up-sweep of his wide-spreading horns. He was a monster. I had no chance for a second shot.

I reloaded the empty right barrel, and we moved forward slowly and cautiously. The game trail opened out into a tiny clearing. I could see the tracks of the buffalo in the dark-colored dirt. There was a splash of blood close by them. Ngoro knelt, and examined the tracks carefully. He and Andrew held a whispered consultation in Swahili. Ngoro was pointing to several places on his own body as he talked. I could tell that he thought the shot had gone too high to be immediately fatal. Andrew looked questioningly at me. I shook my head.

We trailed the buffalo a couple of hundred yards farther. Here, the second animal had split off on another game trail, but the drops of blood continued straight on.

"We've got a wounded buffalo on our hands," Andrew said quite unnecessarily. "Ngoro will go first. We will look ahead while he does the tracking. Do not look down. If you see anything black-colored, shoot! Don't try to pick a spot—just shoot."

Ngoro went to follow the wounded buffalo. In a short distance, the blood disappeared almost entirely, another indication that the wound was not lethal. Occasionally I had an

opportunity to watch Ngoro cast around like a trailing hound.
The game trails over which we moved were pock-marked
with tracks. There were buffalo, rhino, eland, and a dozen of
the lesser antelope. All had used these paths recently. Unerringly, Ngoro led the way. From time to time, he showed
Andrew a drop of blood on a stick or a blade of grass, as an
indication that we had not switched trails or were following
some other bull. Andrew and I moved behind with our rifles
ready. We had the attitude of those who expect a cock pheasant to flush at any second—only this wasn't going to be a
pheasant. It was going to be an African Cape buffalo, weighing close to a ton, and in a very nasty frame of mind as far as
humans were concerned.

The worst places we passed were the spots where the game
trail dipped into patches of high-growing cane and thick trees,
forming complete tunnels shutting out almost all of the light.
We talked in whispers, and made no other sound as we crept
through these ambuscades on our hands and knees. I gathered
from Ngoro's and Andrew's actions that they expected the
wounded buffalo to stop and hide in just such a spot, to try
to kill us. It was just a question of where he would do it. We
must see him first.

A dozen times I had raised my .470, and covered some dark
shadow in the jungle beside us. Once it turned out to be a wart
hog. I noticed that even Andrew was edgy. Only Ngoro
moved ahead methodically from track to track.

After about two hours of steady tracking, we found a place
where the bull had laid down. It was a dark pocket, beneath
an overhanging tree, surrounded entirely by tall grass and
brush. The ground beneath the tree had been raked and fur-
rowed. There was a great deal of blood and phlegm. Ngoro
looked the tracks over for a few seconds, then pointed to his
throat. I had shot too high, hitting the bull at the base of the
throat.

Hours dragged on, and the day became hotter. The tension
was beginning to tell. We sweated profusely, and were taking

more chances as we moved through narrow trails with blind corners ahead and behind. I noticed, also, that the buffalo had traveled in a giant half circle, always keeping to the heaviest cover. We were now along the main Grummetti, skirting the edge of the heaviest jungle along the stream itself. Actually, we had covered no more than three or four miles at the most. In the middle of a small clearing, Ngoro and Andrew held another conference.

"Ngoro thinks he's headed for water at a pool down below here," Andrew whispered to me. "There's one place there with an open buffalo trail leading to it. He'll wait by the water. We'll get him there."

We turned to go. Ngoro strode along more confidently now, passing through a series of tiny glades separated by clumps of bushes and trees. Andrew and I stepped faster, to keep up with Ngoro. We were still on the track of the wounded bull, but we now knew where he was going.

Ngoro paused by a bush. He turned a single leaf toward us; a ruby red spot of blood glittered in the sun. There was a bellowing roar. The whole bush flattened out. Ngoro rolled to the side. His rifle was knocked out of his hand. The bull came out of the bush like a jack rabbit leaving cover. His first bound carried him clear over Ngoro, still rolling on the ground. Andrew and I scattered like quail. My gun came up. I fired it like a shotgun. There was no time to aim. As in a dream, I saw the bull charge Andrew first, then turn toward me. Vaguely I heard the thud-thud of Andrew's double rifle as he fired both barrels at point blank range. Before I could shoot again, the bull had hurtled between us.

The momentum of his charge carried the buffalo beyond us. Still he bounded, bellowing and grunting as he lurched. He spread his great feet, and slid to a stop. As agile as a cutting horse, he whirled, and faced us again. At one side, Ngoro was frantically trying to get to his rifle. Andrew was reloading. I had one barrel left.

The bull lowered his head. In a single jump, he would be

upon us. He semed unwounded. I tried to center the sights on the shoulder, just past his head. As he swung his horns low, I pressed the trigger. At the blast of the shot, he went to his knees. His hind legs jerked, and pushed him end over end. I jumped to the side to avoid the flailing feet. Just then, Ngoro pressed the freshly-loaded rifle on me from behind. I waited there on my knees, but it was unnecessary. The bull bellowed once again, and then lay still.

Andrew was also sitting down, wiping his forehead with his sleeve. "That was sticky," he said weakly, and I knew he wasn't talking about the weather. Only Ngoro seemed unmoved. He was already measuring the width of the bull's horns with the barrel of his rifle.

Andrew and I looked at our tracks in the earth where we had separated and fired at the charging buffalo. There were the gouged imprints where the bull had jumped between us. Andrew and I had been only six paces apart when we had fired. Our three shots had all gone too far back, and through the flanks of the bull. These shots might just as well have been paper wadding for the effect they produced. My first shot, the one which had caused all of the trouble, had hit the animal low in the neck, and passed clear through without breaking the vertebrae.

"This was a bad buff," said Andrew as we admired the animal. "But a very good one after he is dead. A very good one indeed."

8 · King of the Cats

THE FACE was feline and evil, the wide-set green eyes fixed intently upon us. The beast's mouth opened and closed as he panted, the canine teeth appearing and disappearing like white daggers in a sheath. A coughing grunt rumbled from the animal's throat.

Ngoro squeezed my leg from behind. *"Simba moja,"* he whispered.

I looked where he pointed with his eyes. A second lion also had risen to his feet. He, too, turned toward us. Their manes stood out around the two lion faces. Two tails moved rhythmically from side to side. They were both going to charge at once. There was no cover. Ngoro and I were as exposed as a couple of sheep on a golf green. Why had we crawled into this mess?

The whole safari had been a series of tense situations, especially as far as the cats were concerned. Andrew Holmberg wanted desperately to get an outstanding lion to enter in the annual East African Big Game Competition. East African white hunters covet the prize in this competition more than Hollywood stars want Oscars. I was as anxious as Andrew to get outstanding trophies, but I found, during the course of the safari, that bagging record trophies of the Big Five is a dangerous business—especially if you go with Holmberg.

Andrew Holmberg knows thoroughly all types of game, but he specializes in the cats. Lion are becoming very scarce in Kenya and Tanganyika. Leopard have never been easy to get.

Most of the safari companies append a paragraph of fine print to their booklets, which reads, "We cannot guarantee our clients a lion or a leopard." This situation has become even worse during the last few years. Lion have been shot out of some areas completely, very often, surprisingly enough, by control officers, who kill them because they prey on native cattle, and, for the same reason, by the natives themselves. And really big lion—the ones with heavy, dark-colored manes —have always been scarce.

For this reason it is practically impossible to bag an outstanding lion with a long and heavy body and an outstandingly good mane. I was well familiar with this general situation, as my wife Brownie and I had planned the hunt with Andrew in Nairobi before the start of the safari.

"I know a place—" Andrew had said, after I had explained to him that I wasn't going to leave Africa without a trophy specimen of the one animal symbolic of the Dark Continent. I further explained that, as I had successfully hunted the American mountain lion, had received a college degree because of my study of lion, and had written a book on American lionine types, my interest in lion was more than transitory.

I found out later that Andrew *always* "knew a place"— especially for each of the Big Five: elephant, rhino, Cape buffalo, lion, and leopard. Not only did Andrew always know a place, but these particular spots were usually impossible to get to. But, when we did finally arrive, we didn't find the tracks of other safari cars before us, and the game was there.

The particular place which Andrew knew in Kenya turned out to be a wild spot which he had found when hunting Mau Mau terrorists during what East Africans call the "Emergency." I discovered, also, that Andrew had located, and laid by for future reference, several such places while he acted as military scout for the Kenya Rifles. As white hunters of East Africa jealously guard the secrecy of their hunting places, I will not divulge the specific location of this one. Suffice it to say that it was in southern Kenya, and a pride of eighteen lion lived there.

The process of hunting African lion is more than just knowing where they are. A hunter might be in the very middle of a nest of lion, hear them roar every night, and yet never catch a glimpse of one. In the game parks, the lion lie around in the shade of trees and stare stupidly at tourists with cameras. Wild lion, however, usually don't. Lion may sometimes ignore a safari car, apparently thinking it a peculiar kind of rhino or other animal. They never ignore a hunter on foot.

One of these natives, our first gun bearer, was Ngoro, a Masai who had hunted with Andrew for fifteen years. Masai and lion are practically the same word. What Andrew and Ngoro don't know about lion isn't worth bothering about.

When a pride of lion is located, a white hunter who knows his business carefully places some lion baits to attract the cats, so that he may get a look at them. This, in itself, is a specialized task. A zebra or a wildebeest is usually selected, as they are a lion's natural food. The bait must be shot in the middle of the day, and a considerable distance away from where the lion are lying up, so that the cats will not be disturbed. The bait is then dragged behind the safari car—usually across the path which the lion take to water. The time of the drag must be one or two days after the lion have made a kill of their own and finished it up, to insure the cats' being hungry. Most important, the drag must be made in a natural way, with no human scent accompanying it. The usual method is to toss the stomach contents of the bait animal from the rear of the safari car at intervals, to blot out any human smell. The zebra or wildebeest is then hoisted into a tree—which must be just the right kind of tree, in just the right position. (The tree chosen must enable the hunter to approach unseen from behind, and on a side which is usually down wind.)

The bait animal must be suspended in the tree at precisely the right height; if hung too low, the hyenas—always the first to follow a drag trail—polish it off within ten minutes after the humans have left, and if suspended too high, where vultures can sit on an adjoining limb, the carrion birds will leave the bait animal a clean-picked remnant of bones before the lion ever get there. Even if all of this is done correctly, some lion, especially the wary and big ones, will not follow a drag mark, but prefer to kill their own meat. There is many a professional hunter in East Africa who does not have the skill or know-how to bait a lion successfully.

On our first night in the lion country, we heard the roaring of the carnivores in the distance. As Andrew had told us, the noise sounded more like an owl with stomach cramps than the hunting cry of the king of beasts. But this was, indeed, noise of Africa. I had heard it on the sound tracks of Hollywood movies, and sure enough, it was the real thing.

"The pride is on the move," Andrew remarked, as we turned in beneath our mosquito netting that evening. "If they don't make a kill tonight, we'll see lion soon."

Just at daylight the next morning, I shot the first zebra. Andrew chided me for shooting the animal behind the shoulder. In vain I explained to him that behind the shoulder was the way we did it back in North America. "Here you shoot them *in* the shoulder," he said with emphasis. "And remember that when you shoot a lion. He uses his front paws to gather you into his mouth. See that you place the first shot through the shoulder, so that he can't reach for you." Andrew then showed me his own .470 double rifle. The hard steel of the barrel was deeply dented by two freshly-scarred depressions above and below. "Ngoro held this gun in a lion's mouth after a client had shot the beast through the middle. It gave me time to reload. If you look at Ngoro's shoulder, you'll see where the lion's claws dug in." Andrew would say no more about the incident.

That first morning, we set up a zebra bait, and another of a big wildebeest bull. I saved the wildbeest's head, as he had an exceptionally heavy set of horns. I hoped that the lion wouldn't mind the head's absence.

During the night, the lion roared again, especially just before daylight. Brownie and I were disappointed that we didn't hear them, but the day's hunt had so exhausted us we slept soundly, not only through the coughing of the lion and the throaty yipping of the hyena, but also a baboon fight that had broken out in the fig tree just over our tent. Andrew remarked that if the baboon stayed there and continued throwing wild figs and other ammunition down on us, we would have to move camp.

It was daylight when we drove our safari car within three or four hundred yards of the place where we had hung the wildebeest. With binoculars we could see the carcass was only half its former size. The lion had taken the bait! We checked our rifles. I was using the Weatherby .300 magnum, with some special soft-pointed and hard core bullets which I hoped to try out. Andrew and Ngoro carried two .470 double rifles, which are standard artillery of the white hunters of Africa. Sungura, our second gun-bearer, carried an extra .470 just in case.

When I asked Andrew about so many rifles, he just smiled. "It isn't the lion you're shooting at that makes the trouble," he remarked. "The others with him sometimes charge. It's the females, especially, that are cheeky. I remember a very sticky situation when we shot a big male out of a pride of 25 lion. Three lioness charged us. . . ."

Ngoro interrupted and pulled quickly at his sleeve. We looked with our glasses where he pointed. A lioness had risen out of the grass. She looked at us intently. The skin on the back of my neck prickled with excitement. We crawled to a little knoll and lay on our bellies. We looked carefully over. There were two other lion close by. Their ears and the tops of their heads were showing above the grass tops.

"A lioness and two big kittens," said Andrew shortly. "A bad dish of tea." We squirmed backward and retreated behind the knoll.

After taking some pictures from the car, we moved on to

the next bait. This one also had been eaten. As we walked forward at a crouch, we saw that some twenty or thirty vultures were sitting in the top of the fever tree above the frayed carcass. No birds were on the ground. Four lion were stretched out in the shade beneath the tree itself. As we came up, one dashed out to strike at a vulture which had flapped down from the tree to pick up a scrap of meat on the ground. We crawled up to look at the lion from behind a line of high grass. One lion was a male, big, heavy-shouldered, and gray in color. Ninety per cent of all African male lion are as maneless as the females. And hardly ever do they have the big bushy collars that the farm-raised Hollywood lion have. But this male looked enormous.

"Too young," said Andrew tersely. "We'll leave him to grow up for a few years." We photographed the lion from a distance and moved cautiously away.

Farther up the little valley we set out an additional bait of a hartebeest which had been fighting and had broken one horn. He seemed a straggly specimen, fit for lion bait. We also shot an ostrich which had magnificent long black and white plumes. After the four Mohammedans of our safari crew had appropriated the fat of the ostrich, which they highly prize as a medicine, we used the ostrich also to add to our string of baits.

The next morning, we saw four more lion. Another young male was among them, and the rest were females. We saw the tracks of a very large male lion in a little sandy wash. Apparently he was living apart from the main pride and was making his own kills.

On the fifth morning we got a look at the big male lion of the pride. We bumped into him quite accidentally as we stopped to admire a group of impala along the riverbank. There were two magnificent impala bulls. As we looked them over, we saw that they were staring with all of their attention at something off to the right. We focused our binoculars on the spot. There he was! He stalked along like the king of beasts that he undoubtedly considered himself. Even Andrew became enthusiastic.

"A very, very big-bodied lion," he commented.

In a few seconds the lion had walked majestically into a thick tangle of head-high grass and low brush beyond the impala. It would have been foolhardy to follow him.

The next morning we caught another glimpse of the big male, but at a great distance. Apparently he had heard the noise of our safari car and already had begun to walk down a small donga into heavy cover. Two other males lay on top of a small hillock near our zebra bait. One of them would dash out from time to time, whenever a foolhardy vulture dropped down toward the meat. The two lion seemed comparatively unconcerned but watched us steadily as we crawled toward them. One of the pair, a heavy-shouldered lion of a noticeably dark gray color almost tempted us. After a long look we decided that neither of these two was as large as the one we had seen near the impala. Somehow, in our discussing the merits of the various male lion in the pride, the big male we had seen near the impala came to be called "George."

Before dawn on the following morning we laid elaborate plans to set an ambush for George, the king of the pride. We had, by this time, seen all eighteen of the cats, and could speak with some authority. We had photographs of most of them. With this knowledge of the lion tribe, we were certain we could get a shot at George if we played our cards right. As it turned out, it wasn't so easy.

On approaching the string of baits just at daylight, we had a disagreement with a big bull rhino, which loomed out of the dawn darkness right beside us. We circled him, but he charged anyway. The snorts of the rhino, and the pounding of his heavy feet along the game trail, alerted the lion. We could see eleven big cats standing by the carcass baits. Just beyond the farthest carcass, we could make out two big male lion, still lying down on a little bluff overlooking the stream. George was nowhere in sight.

With Ngoro in the lead, we crouched behind the high grass and made a wide circle behind the baits. We finally crawled out on a low headland beyond the farthest lion. Down below was the little valley and the belt of jungle along it. If George tried his usual tactics of slipping away into the heavy cover, we could see him before he got there. On the point across from us, we could clearly see the other two males, about two hundred yards away. Both of them stood up and advanced a few steps toward us. In the early sunlight they looked like two statues of bronze. George was gone. We crawled a few yards farther on to look over the edge of the bluff itself. At a crouching run, I moved forward. There was George, thirty or forty yards away. He was moving at a swift trot down a gully toward the cover along the stream. I fell forward. The rifle came up. The crosshairs of the scope settled on his shoulder as he moved diagonally away. The powerful leg muscles moved beneath the gray skin. I squeezed off the shot. There was no time to get excited or to wonder what the other male lion would do.

I could see the impact of the bullet. It was a little high. George jerked around and snarled. I think he meant to bite the thing that stung his shoulder, but in that instant he saw us. He gave a coughing grunt. He turned toward us. His ears were laid back. He crouched low to charge. I shot him again through the same shoulder as before. The bullet knocked him down. He fought to get on his feet, his great eyes still glaring straight at me. The roar in his throat became a gurgle, and he fell back.

"About the biggest-bodied lion I ever saw," Andrew said, as we stood over George. "If he had a thick mane, we'd have a good show."

George was indeed a monster of a cat, but his mane was a farce. He had only a scruff which ran down the back of his neck like the clipped crest on a blooded horse. George was big-headed and big-footed. As a matter of fact, George was big all over. But his size alone would not win the game competition at Nairobi.

"We'll just have to try again," said Andrew, as we turned George over to Matingy, our skinner. "We have a lion permit for Tanganyika. I know a place there. . . ."

It was several weeks, and many shots, later that we arrived at the spot in northern Tanganyika where Andrew knew of a pride of lion of a particular strain which usually sported big manes. As it turned out, there were two prides in this area, one of eleven lion and another of eight.

As the country was more thickly grown with vegetation, and laced with small dongas fringed with heavy jungle growth, it was more difficult to get a look at these Tanganyika cats and pick a really good one. Also, this area was teeming with game. As it was then late in August, the country had become green with new grass. Scattered herds of wildebeest, hartebeest, zebra, eland, Tommy gazelle, and impala were everywhere. We found that baiting lion was extremely difficult. Several of our carefully-placed baits of zebra and wildebeest were not touched at all. These lion would rather kill their own meat.

Actually, we saw most of our lion in the Tanganyika hunt by following the vultures. These keen-eyed birds hovered over the lion as they moved out to make their kills. A group of vultures circling and diving down was a sure sign that fresh meat was there. If the birds kept off the ground, perched in the trees nearby, we knew that the king of beasts also was there.

In a week of intense activity, we never once saw a really good maned lion, although we got at least a glimpse of most of the cats in the area. We collected an impala which will place among the world records; a very fine wart hog; and several of the lesser antelope during this time; but our lion hunting had been a bust.

Two days before we were to return to Kenya to finish our hunt there, we put out one more zebra bait along a small wash about four miles from camp, where the lion had been roaring every night that we had been there. It was a forlorn hope, as the flat on both sides of this wash was teeming with zebra. The movement of the herds was so great that they trampled out most of our drag marks. If the lion were to find our bait, they would have to do it by scenting the carcass itself.

On a sultry morning we crossed the several dongas which lay between our camp and this grassy flat. As our safari car labored up out of the last wash, a big maned lion stood before us. Sungura, who, as usual, was on the car roof as lookout, pounded frantically on the metal top for us to stop. The two safari boys sitting in the back seat whispered together in an awed voice, "*Simba!*" This was the one word which, to us, meant Africa.

The lion before us looked like a painting. His mane was a great reddish ruff around his face. Before we could get out of the safari car to begin the stalk, however, the lion whirled and ran. Andrew followed him with his binoculars.

"That will be one of the two big males that the natives told us were running by themselves," Andrew said, as we watched the lion trot into a thick mass of low-growing scrub across the flat. Ngoro pointed to the right. Under an isolated acacia tree, in full sight, were two more lion, both males. Again Andrew focused his glasses. I could see in my own binoculars that both lion had big manes that extended well down on their chests.

We did not stop to wonder where the first lion had come from. A glance at our zebra bait over across the flat told us it was untouched. The circling vultures just beyond the two lion beneath the thorn tree indicated that the lion had made their own kill, and in sight of the bait which we had hung up for their benefit. Andrew quickly issued a string of orders. Ngoro and I were to advance on foot and keep the lion in view. Andrew would take the safari car back into the wash from which we had just come.

We were on the edge of the grassy flat and in plain sight. Ngoro carried the extra .470. I carefully loaded the

Weatherby .300 with soft-nosed ammunition. Ngoro and I moved forward.

We began to crawl to the left, where the grass was higher, and where a scattering of small thorn trees offered a little cover. We had gone a few steps when Ngoro pulled my arm and pointed to the ground before us. A brown snake moved off swiftly. It must have been six or eight feet long. I had seen my first cobra.

But even the king of snakes could not hold my attention when the king of beasts was so close. We looked once and saw that the two lion were still staring at the spot from which the safari car had disappeared. Ngoro and I hitched ourselves forward on knees and elbows. It was evident that Ngoro had no intention of waiting until Andrew caught up with us. Perhaps the two maned monarchs would whirl and disappear into the heavy cover, as the first one had.

We had moved forward perhaps two or three hundred yards under fairly good cover. Beyond this, the only screen was a very tiny tree, with a trunk no bigger around than my arm. Ngoro was flat on his belly now, squirming forward. I moved along behind him. I could see the two lion clearly. They were both lying down in the patch of shade beneath the acacia tree. Both of them stared fixedly at us. I noticed also, rather incongruously, that a Tommy gazelle buck was grazing within a few yards of the two carnivores. Apparently their distended bellies after a full meal was reassurance that they did not mean to kill again. I noticed, too, that the lion differed as to their color. One had a very blond mane, the other a distinct reddish cast. A blond and a red-head, what a vicious combination!

Ngoro looked back along his shoulder, and motioned me on with a turn of his head. He signaled me to pass him. That little tree just before us was our goal.

Behind the spindly stem of the tiny tree, I cautiously gathered my knees beneath me and raised up. Undoubtedly the two lion had thought that we were skulking hyena. Now they

knew we weren't. I saw their interest quicken. A stiffness
came over the two bodies. Ngoro signaled me to shoot the
right hand one. That was the blond. So be it!

I crouched behind the little tree. The palms of my hands
were already sweating. The two lion were only thirty or
forty yards away. With a low growl, the red-maned lion got
to his feet. He turned toward us. Should I shoot? We should
have waited for Andrew. Ngoro had the extra .470. If both
lion charged, we wouldn't have a chance.

The second lion reared up. He walked menacingly forward
a few steps. I centered the crosshairs on the point of his shoulder. In another moment he would be turned straight toward
me, and I would not be able to see his shoulder at all. The
crosshairs of the telescopic sight danced crazily up and down.
I couldn't hold the thing still. There it was! I squeezed the
trigger.

Viciously I bolted another shell in. I took all the skin off
the side of my thumb, but didn't even notice. I saw, as in a
dream, that the first lion was down. I had shot too high and
broken his back. The range was too close. The second male
wrinkled back his lips. A guttural, coughing grunt came from
between his teeth. He stood there, his mouth half open. This
was it. He swung his head. He turned toward us. "To fight
or run?" seemed to be in his eyes. Then he turned and
bounded away. A few yards farther on, he stopped and looked
back at us. I followed his shoulder with the crosshairs of the
scope. Then he turned again, and ran off into the brush along
the donga, with the thick fold of skin beneath his belly swinging from side to side.

"*Mazuri, bwana, mazuri sana,*" Ngoro said, wringing my
hand. I had to stop him a moment to fire another shot at the
lion on the ground before us. He was still moving a little, but
now his body stiffened. He stretched to full length like an
athlete. Then he was still.

Ngoro and I walked forward together. Andrew came puffing up with Sungura at his side. Andrew cursed Ngoro in a

stream of Swahili. We should have waited. What about the second lion? But even Andrew could not wait to see the maned lion at close range.

Eventually Andrew showed his pleasure. Our lion had a full, well-developed fourteen-inch mane. When we had finished measuring the beast, and had hung him up for photographing, we found that in bodily proportions he was not the equal of maneless George, our first trophy. George had the size, this one had the mane. Andrew held his chin in his hand.

"We'll have to change heads to get it to come out right and win that competition," he commented with a wry smile.

The competition, as it turned out, was won that year by a very fine greater kudu.

9 · Let Sleeping Lion Lie

WITH A coughing grunt, the lion launched himself at us. All I could see was the huge head, ears laid back. The open mouth was coming straight for my face. Frantically I tried to bolt another shell into my rifle. Those teeth would be at my throat before I could raise the gun.

I hadn't set out to hunt this lion. As a matter of record, I wasn't even interested in desert lion, as they are usually maneless and make a poor trophy. The lion of Somalia on the east coast of Africa are about as maneless as they come. Furthermore, Guliano Belli, an Italian hunter, and I were busy trying to find an elephant carrying one hundred pounds of ivory in each tusk. In the Somalia desert country, it is the elephants that are big; the lion are scrawny.

Somalia became a new African country on July 1st, 1960. Her transition to independence had been a peaceful one, and her new government was functioning fairly smoothly when I arrived in Somalia about six weeks later. Unlike most of the new African countries, the Somalis realize the value of their game, as they have a hunting tradition which goes back hundreds of years. With independence, they established a new game department, and declared that a hunting season should begin August 15th, 1960.

Guliano Belli del Isca remains from Benito Mussolini's day, when the Italians had hoped to form a vast African empire. When Guliano had been district commissioner under the Italians, he had found that his district in southern Somalia was teeming with big desert elephants. After independence, Belli decided to start a new safari company. He wanted to advertise to all who might be interested that Somalia was first class game country, and contained some very intriguing specimens of a good many varieties. That's why I was there. I had come to Somalia to see just how good Guliano and his hunting area might be.

To anyone who has hunted in East Africa, especially in the Northern Frontier of Kenya, Somalia seems familiar. The country is semi-arid, but far from a complete desert. Two very large rivers flow down from the highlands of Ethiopia and through Somalia to the sea. These are the Giuba and the Uebishabelli. Guliano's best elephant country is around the Giuba, and southward toward the Kenya border.

Guliano had bought a fairly creditable Land Rover from a Kenya dealer, and had commandeered an Italian truck which was already a relic when Mussolini was a young man. Guliano met me at the airport in Mogadiscio, the picturesque capital of Somalia, and we moved southward toward the Giuba, with the truck following behind like a wounded animal. I looked under the hood of the thing once to see what made it go. Beneath the hood the engine looked even less prepossessing than the battered body outside.

With this equipment, we traveled some four hundred kilometers south over a road which the Italians had built. We crossed the Giuba River on a modern bridge. Around the Giuba is a belt of plantations, where several Italian farmers raise bananas to ship to Europe. Beyond the banana plantations, the country quickly becomes primitive, and the road virtually disappears.

We set up our elephant camp near the small border town of Beles Cogani. It is well to camp near a town, as some Somali tribes are still a little high-spirited at times, and have been known to kill travelers for their guns or other knickknacks which the Somalis covet. There is also a good deal of raiding back and forth from the Ethiopian border. When I asked what

Beles Cogani might mean, I was told that it was the name of a sheik of the Galla tribe who had been eaten on the spot by a lion. I was very fascinated by all of this local color, and thought that it added considerable zest to the elephant hunting.

The metropolis of Beles Cogani itself is not inspiring, in spite of the fact that it serves as the port of entry for camel caravans, and for the occasional lost and wandering automobiles which might find their way in from Kenya. The Somalis, distinctive from other Africans in physical appearance, culture, and religion, are tall and clean featured, and dress in turbans and the loose garments which they have adopted from the Arabs. The Somalis are Mohammedans, and adhere rigidly to the Mohammedan principle of not eating meat unless the knife of a true believer cuts the throat of the animal in the ceremony known as "hallel." A considerable amount of our hunting time was taken up in shooting lesser kudu and gerenuk, so that our Mohammedans could cut the throats of the animals and have meat.

Just beyond Beles Cogani, toward the Kenya border, is a large depression in the desert floor filled with water from the spring rains. This place, called Tabda by the Somalis, is a favorite spot to water camels, fat-tailed sheep, goats, and cattle. Actually, the watering at Tabda takes place in a certain rhythm. At night, about three hundred elephants come in from the surrounding bush country to drop their trunks in the green, slimy water of Tabda and drink their fill. By day, hundreds of Somali herdsmen, with thousands of head of assorted stock, converge on Tabda from a dozen desert trails. Between the elephants and the humans, other animals of the region try to squeeze in a little drinking time. Among these were a dozen or so lion.

We had seen the lion tracks at Tabda on several mornings, as we went there to find out what bull elephants had used the drinking hole the night before. We had heard lion roaring in the distance not far from Tabda, and I had idly wondered how the elephants, camels, cattle, sheep, goats, humans, antelope, and lion all managed to avoid each other when coming and going from water. The answer to my speculation is that they don't avoid each other. Embarrassing meetings of domesticated and wild animals are frequent.

The third day of our hunt at Beles Cogani, a Somali herdsman, driving a small bunch of his humpbacked cattle to the Tabda pool, met a lion in the middle of the trail. The man, Gedo by name, raised his spear when the lion did not move out of the way. The bull of Gedo's small herd was in front of the line of cattle. The lion knocked Gedo's bull down with a sideways blow of his paw, and then bit the animal through the back of the neck, killing it instantly. Gedo threw his spear and missed. The lion ran off into the thickets at the side of the trail.

We did not hear about the death of Gedo's bull until the next day. We would have had no occasion to hear about it even then, except that Gedo pastured his cattle and a few camels some twenty miles north of Tabda. In that same area, he had reported seeing three gigantic bull elephants. We maneuvered our safari car along the camel trail to Gedo's grass hut in the north. When we reached his modest home, his wife and daughter talked to us shyly. Gedo himself was away. The thrifty Somali had cut up the bull which the lion had killed, and packed the meat back to his wife. He had then taken his bow and quiver of poisoned arrows and set out to track the lion down and kill him. "A very sporty business," I thought as I looked at the thick desert brush of the area. Then Belli and I got on with our elephant hunt, and forgot about Gedo and his problem.

Two days later, the police sergeant in charge of the small border contingent of Beles Cogani visited our camp in the evening. He talked a little Italian, as he had been part of a military garrison under the former regime. The police sergeant told us that Gedo had not returned from tracking the lion. This was very strange, as Gedo was *Arganti*. (Belli explained to me that the Somalis recognize a succession of hunters. When a Somali kills his first animal, he becomes a first grade hunter, called *Irin*. An Irin would probably shoot a Hunter's hartebeest, or one of the smaller antelope, with a poisoned arrow. The Somalis use poison made from a kind of grass called "uabahayo," which they trade from the tribes in Kenya. If an animal is struck with this potent poison, he dies in an hour or so. The trick is to get close enough to an antelope to get an arrow into him. When a Somali hunter gets good enough to kill an elephant, rhino, buffalo, giraffe, or a lion, he becomes *Alghen*, or the highest grade of hunter. Anybody with audacity enough to punch a poisoned arrow into one of these animals certainly deserves the first prize, I thought. I would hate to see what a lion would do after he was hit and before he died. The giraffe is included in the list of hard-to-kill animals because it is virtually impossible for a bowman to approach a giraffe unseen. A very few Somali hunters have killed all of the dangerous animals including giraffe. Such a man is a superhunter, called an *Arganti*. If any Somali survived all of these dangerous encounters and became Arganti, he set himself up as a patron of the area in which he lived. Any hunter of lower rank who killed an animal in the Arganti's territory had to give the local Arganti part of the kill —usually a brisket.)

Gedo, the Arganti, had been a mighty hunter, but his luck had run out at last. I was sorry that I hadn't known the fellow. Belli told me that the Somali often killed lion which were attacking their camels or cattle. Gedo had killed several lion, and more than ten elephants. However, he certainly had followed one lion too many. If he had not returned from his private lion hunt in three days, chances were that his wife shouldn't expect him at all.

The next evening, the police sergeant came to see us again. We were rather sorry to see him, as Belli and I had trailed five bull elephants over twenty miles that day, and we were dog tired. But the sergeant sat at our little camp table under the thorn tree and sipped tea for twenty minutes before he came to the point of his visit. A large male lion had killed a woman and her twelve-year-old daughter just north of Tabda. Apparently the lion had killed the girl first, as she herded a little flock of sheep toward the water. The Somali woman had rushed to drive the lion away from her daughter, and the lion had killed her also. The lion had dragged the girl beneath the brush at the side of the trail and had almost completely devoured her. Her chewed and bloody clothes had been found there by other herdsmen. The woman had been killed by a blow of the lion's paw and a bite through the base of the neck, but had not been eaten. The fat-tailed sheep still grazed around the spot where the bodies lay.

"This lion is the same male lion which killed Gedo's bull, and which killed Gedo," the sergeant continued gravely.

"How can you be sure it was the same lion?" I broke in. "The track of any male lion looks the same."

"Not to a Somali," said Belli. And I took his word.

The sergeant wanted to know if we would help to kill the lion. "There is no other hunter around Beles Cogani except the one whom you have," he added as a clincher.

When Guliano translated this, I thought that the sergeant was paying a compliment to the great American hunter (myself) who was visiting their troubled village. If my fame had reached all the way to Beles Cogani, I could do nothing else but abandon my elephant hunting for a couple of days and help them out. It turned out that the police sergeant was not thinking of me as even a first grade hunter. He was referring to a man named Kula in our camp, who had been tracking elephants for us. We had picked Kula up near the town of Afmadu, on our way south to Beles Cogani. It developed that he was the finest lion tracker in all southern Somalia, and furthermore, that he was an Alghen grade hunter in his own right. Kula certainly was the finest elephant tracker I had ever followed, and I didn't want to lose him. We called him to the conference under the thorn tree. Kula readily agreed to track down the man-eating lion of Beles Cogani. I gathered from his enthusiastic expression that he had been planning to do just this anyway, ever since he had heard about poor Gedo.

The next morning, before daybreak, we moved past the still sleeping town of Beles Cogani. Our headlights picked out a herd of wart hogs in the very middle of the town. Being Mohammedans, the villagers never bother the pigs, which are considered religiously unclean. We swung north on a camel trail toward the spot where the two women had been killed the morning before. The place was perhaps five miles from Beles Cogani, and a little more than that distance from the water hole at Tabda. We found no lion tracks until we reached the spot itself. Here the Somalis had made one of their typical graves. The mother and daughter had been buried in an area between three thorn trees. Around the grave had been built a solid wall of heavy limbs and split pieces of wood. Outside of this was a thick *boma*, or fence, of thorn branches, to keep off any hyenas or other predators.

Outside of the trampled area where the grave had been made, Kula circled like a beagle. He soon found the track of the lion. It was, of course, twenty-four hours old. Kula started along the old track with the same assurance he displayed when on the trail of an elephant bull. I can track most elephants myself, but Somalia lion tracking is another matter. A lion, being soft-footed, does not make much impression on hard ground, and this was stony desert terrain. In the sandy spots, the tracking was easy; but over the hundreds of yards of hard surface, it seemed impossible. But Kula did it anyway. Without reservation, Kula is the finest tracker I have ever seen. Even at that, he was constantly losing the track and having to cast ahead. The track of the single lion had been blotted out completely where herds of camels and cattle had been driven along the trails toward Tabda. The lion had gone in a generally southeasterly direction toward Beles Cogani. By two o'clock in the afternoon, we had tracked the beast about five miles, and were not far from the town.

This whole lion hunt now began to seem bizarre and incongruous. In every other place in Africa, lion are hunted by hanging a bait and then shooting the beasts when they come in to chew on the meat. I had never heard of hunting lion by tracking them through thick brush. I couldn't believe it was possible.

But the question was academic, as late in the afternoon even Kula lost the trail. In the welter of tracks on the outskirts of Beles Cogani, the faint imprint of the paws had been blotted out. We could only tell the police sergeant that the man-eating lion had circled the outskirts of his town the evening before. We sent the truck driver back to retrieve our safari car, and we walked back to camp. The lion hunt had been a bust.

That night I slept badly. For some reason, the hyenas were especially annoying. Hyenas were always bold in the vicinity of Beles Cogani. But they had never come into our camp before. I was awakened by some of the men throwing sticks at them. Some time after this uproar, I heard a heavy panting in my tent. Belli's going to have to do something about that asthma of his, I thought to myself, forgetting for the moment that Belli's tent was fifty feet away. I went back to sleep.

In the morning, the cook reported that the hyenas had jerked down a gerenuk carcass which had been hanging in the tree over his bed. The contemptible beasts had devoured the thing on the spot. Kula came up to where I was brushing my teeth with my eyes half open. He touched my elbow and pointed to the ground in front of my tent. There were the clear imprints of two big lion paws, where the cat had stood and looked in. The lion had walked straight through the middle of camp, past the dining tent, and within twenty feet of a dozen sleeping men. It was the lion that had pulled down the gerenuk. He had walked off a few yards when the cook threw a piece of firewood at him. Then he had lain on his belly and had calmly eaten the gerenuk, crunching the bones within thirty feet of the entire camp.

"The same lion—?" I asked.

Kula nodded. The same lion which we had trailed all the

day before had calmly spent most of the night in our camp. Belli was greatly perturbed. The cook was so upset that he couldn't make breakfast. Most of the camp boys got into the parked truck and stayed there, even though it was now daylight. Kula, Belli, and I started out on the track. We made a good early start. There was no breakfast, and we were anxious to track the lion before the Somalis began to move their herds and obliterate the trail.

Belli clutched a .375 Winchester and I carried a .375 Weatherby. Usually I shoot a lighter gun, but after the lion looked in my tent, the heavier artillery seemed to be appropriate. Belli and I crouched behind Kula with our guns ready. Several yards in the rear, Sherif, the manager of the camp, carried an extra gun and a bottle of water.

The lion had moved from our camp along the edge of the road toward Beles Cogani. Within the town are several large cisterns, or catch basins, where the inhabitants trap water in the rainy season. The Coganians put hedges of thorn brush around these to keep out the wart hogs. The lion had raked away the thorns at the edge of one of these cisterns, gone through the gap, and drunk his fill. Just as the good citizens of Beles Cogani were coming out of their houses to fill their own water jars, four grim figures stalked past, crouched and ready. No one spoke to us as Kula followed the track past the customs house station, past the corrals on the edge of town, and southward.

Somehow I expected to see the lion still lurking on the outskirts of town. Certainly a cat of that temperament would be standing somewhere out of sight, watching the people, and planning his next meal. But the tracks led on.

The morning sun rose hot and high in the African sky. We followed the track of the lion in a circle almost around the town, then at a sharp angle south again. Surely the lion, with his belly full of meat and water, would lie up somewhere.

About eleven o'clock, Belli and I sat down in the shade of a wait-a-bit thorn and drank the last of the water. The lion had outwalked us. He was obviously leaving the country. In the heat of midday, Belli and I soon slumped against the bole of the tree in a half doze. Sherif also nodded. Kula slipped away, and followed the track.

About one o'clock we decided to head for camp, to get something to eat. As we started off, Kula slipped up behind us. He tapped me on the shoulder and grinned broadly. Sherif translated Kula's Somali. "He has found the lion asleep."

If the Somali hunters can slip up to a sleeping lion, and stick a poisoned arrow in him, I thought to myself, I guess I can do the same with a rifle. But it certainly is an interesting way to hunt lion.

Kula led us on tiptoe through the thickest brush I had seen in Somalia. The packed thorn bushes and stunted trees were interlaced with clumps of the thick cactus they called "galole." As we came into the dense growing stuff, I noticed that Belli was panting hard, and Sherif had fallen well to the rear. Kula kept cautioning us with his finger on his lips. In his bare feet, Kula was absolutely soundless. He grinned continuously. Obviously he was enjoying himself. I was not sure that I was.

We tiptoed to a little opening in the cactus. Kula crouched and pointed. I took one more step behind him. There was the lion.

Whatever I had expected, this was not it. All I could see was a fat stomach about fifteen feet from me. The thing rose and fell with regular breathing. The lion had made a nest underneath the cactus. I could see neither head, tail, nor feet.

Which end is the head, I wondered. I had the Weatherby to my shoulder and the safety off. Maybe it was the click of the safety. Maybe man-eating lion have guilty consciences. The lion did not wake up and look at us. He came out of his bed in one movement—with a roar like an exploding boiler. There was no doubt now which end was the head. It came straight at us. I fired as I saw the lion's chest. At that range, I couldn't miss. The lion jumped past us, tore a hole in the solid brush, and was gone. Belli and I stood dazed.

Kula beckoned us forward. He pointed to where the lion had crashed through the cactus and brush. It looked like a slaughter house. The soft-nosed bullet of the Weatherby had apparently ripped away the lion's chest. I stepped forward confidently behind Kula. There was blood everywhere. The lion had torn a hole through the thick cactus like a bulldozer. We walked perhaps fifty feet. Here was an opening in the brush as big as a small room. As we stepped into the opening, the lion roared. I have heard of sounds being blood-curdling, but this roar was congealing. It certainly was not the roar of a lion in his death agony. The roar came again, and again, from across the little clearing. Both Belli and I had our guns up. We couldn't see a thing.

Then suddenly, there he was! I could see the curve of yellow hide through the green brush across the clearing. A tiny termite hill stood just to our left. I got up on the low mound. At the movement, the lion roared again. The sound shook the leaves around us. I pushed Kula to one side. He had been standing there grinning. I could see the outline of the lion fairly clearly now. He was crouched on his belly, facing us. His head and shoulders were behind a solid tangle of limbs and stems. He gathered his hind feet beneath him. I shot.

At the sound, the lion grunted and jumped. In one bound he cleared the brush. In the next, he was in the air before us. I heard Belli's gun go off. Frantically, I clawed at the bolt to get another shell into the chamber. I half raised the gun and fired. In the same instant, the lion hit us. I scarcely realized that the impact of the bullet had jerked his body sideways. Instead of his mouth and claws, he struck me with the back of his shoulder. Belli and I went down, with the lion on top of us. We were mashed flat by the crushing weight. The lion was still struggling. His three good paws thrashed and his mouth opened and closed. I rolled from underneath the flailing claws in considerably less than one second. Kula was standing there laughing.

My first shot had struck to one side and broken the lion's

shoulder. My second, when the lion was crouching ready to spring, had hit the same shoulder. The lion was still in good working order when he made the final leap. My last shot hit the lion in mid-air at the base of the neck. His momentum carried him on top of us. I found out later that I had two broken vertebrae in my back as a result.

Baiting African lion is thrilling sport. And if you crave real excitement, you should get a Somali tracker to lead you into heavy brush after a sleeping lion. But if you take my advice, you'll let a sleeping lion lie.

10 · Leopard Bwana

THE OPEN JAWS were at his throat. The rifle barrel was knocked aside. Stumbling backward, he raised his hands to fend off the cat's face. The leopard seized the hunter's pith helmet instead of his throat, and with teeth and claws the animal tore it into fragments.

In those few seconds, Andrew Holmberg was able to raise his rifle and fire at point blank range.

This story, and many others of his own experiences with leopards, Andrew had told us. He showed the scar on his forearm, which had been made by the teeth of a charging leopard. "A wounded leopard will always charge," Andrew had said. "Pound for pound, the leopard is the most dangerous of the Big Five of African game."

On that particular safari we had not yet bagged a leopard, though we had seen almost every other kind of game that Kenya and Tanganyika could produce. We had taken two excellent lion—one maned and one maneless—and had seen a family of cheetahs make a kill. As this was in Kenya, where cheetahs are considered royal game, we did not bag a cheetah. We did, however, locate and collect a serval cat, which looks like a small leopard. But we very much wanted a leopard of trophy size.

We had also learned something of the ways of white hunters. The white hunter operates by a strict code. Even with very dangerous game, the hunter does not shoot unless the situation is extremely critical. Andrew's idea of "critical" dif-

128

fered radically from mine. We were charged repeatedly by
rhino. Two elephants tried their best to kill us. We had a very
intimate experience with a nasty Cape buffalo. During all of
these "sticky situations," as Andrew described them, he stood
impassively behind me with his .470 double ready. But he
did not shoot. It was nice to know he was there, but just the
same. . . .

"Andrew," I remember saying somewhat bitterly on one occasion when we were hunting lion, "if one of these friends of
yours has me by the throat, please shoot."

Andrew just smiled, and pointed his gun barrel at the lion
which was trotting away. I had just shot one large male out of
the pair. The remaining male advanced threateningly from
the body of his dead friend.

"Lion will hardly ever charge," Andrew said quietly. "It's
different with leopard."

As far as leopard were concerned, it looked as though we
were going to be skunked anyway. Leopard were indeed
scarce, but we had seen two of these elusive cats. Early in our
safari in southwestern Kenya, we had put out some leopard
baits. Our safari boys, under Andrew's direction, had tied
Grant's gazelle carcasses in the trees in just the right manner.
We also placed a string of four baits along a small stream
which flows into the Mara River. After three days, we had
two leopard on two of these baits.

We saw the first leopard just at daylight, as we came to
look at the string of baits. The cat was in the tree next to the
gazelle, and had already fed on the rotting flesh. I could see the
leopard clearly against the gray morning sky. He was draped
in a relaxed attitude over a couple of limbs. His tail twitched
back and forth nervously. He looked straight at us.

Andrew pressed my gun barrel down. "Too small," he
whispered. "Much too small. We don't want him."

The leopard looked immense to me. It certainly was far
bigger than any of the mountain lion that we had bagged in
our Southwestern country back home.

It was the same with the second leopard. We found this one actually feeding on the carcass, again early in the morning. Again Andrew had said, "Too small," and he added, "It's a female."

The major difficulty on our whole safari had been getting Andrew to let me shoot anything. If the animal did not seem to set a record of some kind, we didn't fire. Now, toward the end of the trip, it looked as though Andrew's particular attitude was gaing to cost me a leopard altogether. Many safaris do not bring back a leopard in their bag. I didn't want to be one of those.

It was while we were after an especially large buffalo along the bank of the Mara, farther north, that we found a leopard track. Immediately, Ngoro and Andrew were on their knees in the dirt, talking in Swahili about the imprint. They gesticulated excitedly, and measured the outline of the track with their hands.

"Biggest leopard track we've ever seen," Andrew said, as he rose to his feet and dusted his knees. "He came to water here last night."

The buffalo hunt was abandoned for the time being, and all our energies were turned to the baiting of the leopard. We shot a zebra and a Grant's gazelle. As a leopard will seldom follow a drag mark, we had to place these two baits in a position where the cat would actually smell the carcass after we had placed it in a tree. We carefully cached the gazelle and the zebra about a mile apart, each bait placed so that the evening breeze would carry the smell of the fast-decaying flesh along the bank of the stream where the leopard would come to water. Still farther down, along a small side stream, we shot a big male baboon, and placed this in the fork of a thorn tree well back from the creek, near the mouth of a side canyon, where the leopard had evidently come down the night before. With these preparations completed, we carefully withdrew. We did not shoot any other game close to or between any of these baits, as such a disturbance might drive the leopard off.

The next morning, we approached the Grant's gazelle cautiously. It had not been touched. As we drove our safari car toward the zebra bait, along a game trail which paralleled the river, we saw the leopard's track again. There was no mistaking that big cat's imprint. It was as big as a good sized lion. Farther on, we saw another track in the dust of the trail. The leopard was heading straight for our biggest bait.

As we approached the zebra, Andrew stopped the car, so that we might investigate with our binoculars. One hind leg of the bait animal had been eaten. The heavy carcass had been hoisted higher in the tree, and pulled into a different position. We crawled out of the safari car and moved forward at a low crouch to get a closer look. (We had earlier constructed a sketchy blind some fifty yards from the base of the tree which held the bait.) It was now our intention to work our way up behind this screen. The leopard should be there, guarding the meat.

Before we had crawled half way to the tangle of vines which served as our blind, Andrew, who was hunching along in front, stiffened. He motioned me up beside him. "There he is," he whispered in my ear. "It's the biggest leopard I've ever seen."

As slowly as I could, I crawled forward a few feet to the bole of a big thorn tree. Behind this, I slowly pulled myself to my knees, and looked out through the crotch where a heavy limb left the trunk. I could see nothing.

"To the right on the ground," Andrew whispered hoarsely.

There he was! I could just make out the top of the head and the erect ears in the long grass. The leopard was standing beneath the bait tree. There was no doubt that he had seen us. In a second he would whirl and go. If only I could stand erect, and rest my rifle over the limb of the thorn tree just above my eyes. . . . Such a movement, though, would certainly frighten the leopard. The largest leopard Andrew had ever seen! I must not miss.

Clumsily, I placed the gun alongside the thorn tree trunk.

I flipped off the safety and rose as high on my knees as I could. Still I could make out only the upper half of the leopard's head. "I'll never hit him in the head at this distance," I thought. "I'll try for the chest."

I centered the crosshairs of the sight at the point where the chest of the leopard certainly would be, hoping that the thin screen of grass stems would not deflect the shot. I squeezed the trigger.

At the blast of noise, the leopard's head disappeared abruptly. Andrew scrambled to his feet, and the safari boys came running. In English or Swahili, everyone was asking the same eager question: "Did you get him?"

"I don't know," I answered tersely. "I just don't know." When I explained to Andrew that I had shot for the leopard's chest, his face took on a pained look.

"But he was standing with his tail toward us," he explained, as he might have to an imbecile child. "He was looking back over his shoulder. You shot under his chin."

That evening, Ngoro and the other safari boys would not speak to me. Andrew was more than usually courteous and cold. We had all wanted an outstanding cat trophy, but I had muffed the greatest chance on the whole safari. Andrew assured me (in a rather distant manner) that there was no chance that the leopard would come back to the bait.

"Once he's wounded, the African leopard is the fiercest thing on four legs. But otherwise the leopard is as shy as a school girl. We've seen the last of the biggest leopard in all Africa."

In spite of this, I told Andrew that I would wait by the bait tree that evening. Ngoro, who apparently felt that his own honor had been dimmed as much as mine, volunteered to wait with me. Andrew shrugged his shoulders eloquently, to indicate that if we wanted to lie there and be bitten by tsetse flies to no purpose, we richly deserved whatever awful thing might happen to us.

About four o'clock that afternoon, Ngoro and I crawled

into the blind near the leopard bait tree. Andrew's prediction
of tsetse flies was fulfilled. We were bitten unmercifully.
There was also a species of black ant to torment us: these
large insects, red underneath, had pincers on their mouths
which felt like pairs of tin snips.

But the panorama of African life that moved before us was
worth even this discomfort. Four hyenas circled within a few
yards of us, as they sniffed upward toward the delicious rotting zebra in the tree. Flights of brilliant, orange-headed para-
keets flew past on their way to the water at the stream behind
us. A herd of lesser kudu grazed by. There were two beautiful
bulls in the bunch, which snorted and ran when they got the
smell of the dead zebra. But no leopard came.

The next morning, at dawn, I persuaded Andrew to pass by
the place. The bait had not been touched and no leopard was
in sight. Another leopard had appropriated the Grant's gazelle,
however, and a third leopard had taken over the dead baboon.
This one had jerked out great mouthfuls of baboon hair and
eaten about half the carcass. Ngoro and Andrew examined
the tracks. These were all lesser leopards, none of them worth
a real try. The whole safari company seemed dispirited. What
was the use of trying for a scrawny, half-sized leopard, when
the big bwana had missed the king leopard of them all?

I didn't know what I could do to regain everybody's esteem.
Here I was, a "two simba" man; and I had blown my whole
reputation by miscalculating where a leopard's chest ought to
be. That next afternoon, I persuaded Ngoro to go back with
me to the leopard bait, just to get away from the critical
glances of all of my companions. Brownie wanted to photograph a rhino we had seen, and Andrew said he would be glad
to take her, with the inference that this, at least, was a worth-
while trip.

Ngoro and I slipped up to the leopard bait as before, and
lay on our stomachs behind the sketchy blind of vines. The
tsetse flies were happy to see us back, and the big ants must
have told all their friends about us. Even the hyenas seemed

to be in greater force. We watched eight of them circle the tree and sniff in a pathetic manner at the meat which they could not reach.

Just before dark, the hyenas drifted away. We heard a baboon chitter off in the thorn trees behind us. Ngoro, beside me, seemed half asleep. In a few minutes, we would have to walk back and report another failure.

Two or three baboons barked. Ngoro tensed and raised his head slowly. He squeezed my arm and pointed with his eyes. I looked through the vine stems. There, a pair of ears were moving along above the grass tops beyond the bait tree. The leopard was returning.

Slowly, I hunched forward to my knees. I steadied the rifle against one of the vine stems. The great cat's ears moved forward, then turned from side to side. The leopard was cautious. Whatever was the thunder which had driven him away before, he was taking no chances this time.

After perhaps five minutes, he moved cautiously to the edge of the grass beneath the trees. Only then did he look up at the bait. I could see his chest now, and his two forepaws. I could also make out the tail. I moved the crosshairs of the telescopic sight to the very center of the leopard's chest. Slowly and deliberately I squeezed off the shot. This was it!

The leopard went down. Ngoro jumped up with a Masai warwhoop. He thumped me on the back, and pounded on my hat. "*Mazuri, mazuri sana*," he shouted at the top of his lungs.

The leopard was flopping on the ground like a beheaded chicken. Suddenly he seemed to regain his faculties. He pulled himself to his feet. He whirled, and in an arching bound, ran off into the high grass behind.

Ngoro and I stared numbly at each other. Another Masai shout died in Ngoro's throat. We could hear the safari car coming. Brownie and Andrew had heard the shot. The car wove crazily among the thorn trees and slid to a stop.

"Did you get him?" Andrew asked excitedly.

"I killed him. But he ran off," I said weakly.

Fortunately, Ngoro came to my assistance with a flood of Swahili. "Indeed, the big bwana, the slayer of simbas, had killed the monster leopard. Then the leopard, possessed of many lives, got to his feet and galloped off!"

It was almost dark. Quickly, Andrew organized us. "We've got a wounded leopard on our hands," he said tersely. "Even if he should die tonight, the hyenas will eat him before morning."

Ngoro held one .470 double rifle as a spare. Andrew carried another, and I stuck by the Weatherby .300 magnum. As we stepped into the yellow grass, Andrew said tersely, "Shoot him as he jumps for your gun barrel."

As the three of us moved forward in a line, I thought of Andrew's description of a charging leopard. "Of all the Big Five," he had said, "the charging leopard at close quarters is the worst."

I remembered how Carl Akeley, years before, had told me of his experience with a wounded leopard. The cat had sprung at him so viciously, and from such close quarters, that he had had no time to get in a shot. The leopard seized his arm with its teeth. With one hand in the leopard's throat, Carl had wrestled the cat. The leopard's claws raked up red furrows of flesh on his thigh and stomach. Carl fell forward with the cat beneath him. With one knee, Carl had cracked the leopard's ribs one after the other. With brute strength he crushed the chest of the leopard. Carl Akeley was a extremely powerful man, but wrestling with that leopard had put him in the hospital for six months, and nearly cost him his life.

The hair on the back of my neck prickled. My hands were sweaty. Could I hit a charging leopard head on? I wasn't sure. And yet, I was the one who had set up this awful situation. What could have happened? Why wasn't the leopard dead?

A growl ripped from the grass just ahead. The rasping sound was like tearing cloth. I stiffened. Andrew had said, "When a leopard growls, he's on his way."

We stood there, the three of us, in the gathering dusk. Our rifles were pointed. Our fingers rested firmly on the triggers. The line of grass was a dark shadow. No leopard appeared.

Andrew jerked his head to motion us backward. We retreated slowly, still watching every clump of grass and fallen leaf that might suddenly become the open mouth and awful face of a charging leopard.

With Ngoro and I standing guard, Andrew maneuvered the safari car so that the lights would shine in the direction from which the growl had come. We then climbed on the metal top of the safari car. Still we could see nothing. There was no gleam of green eyes in the grass. We moved forward with the light at our backs. Suddenly Mohammed, the first tracker, darted ahead and into the brush in the full gleam of the lights.

"Come back, you fool," Andrew yelled. Mohammed plunged into the brush like a terrier. He grasped a long black and yellow tail and pulled it out. The leopard was stone dead.

It was a safari car full of wildly celebrating hunters that drove into camp that night. The safari boys wanted to carry me on their shoulders. They made up impromptu songs about the great leopard bwana. Frankly, I didn't feel so great myself. A stroke of blinding luck had pulled me out of what Andrew would have described as a "very sticky situation."

The leopard was a male, seven feet ten inches long. The bullet I had fired had entered his chest exactly in the middle and had come out behind the right foreleg, smashing straight through the lungs. And yet the leopard, with this lethal shot through him, had lived ten or twelve awful minutes before he died. This leopard is not only one of the largest ever shot in Africa, but certainly one with the most stamina. For my money, at least, it is the leopard that is the king of the cats.

11 · The Killer Leopard
of Manyara

THE MOUTH was open, the lips were wrinkled back. Two eyes were streaks of green-yellow light.

The cat head lunged forward. The open teeth were a blur of motion. The impact knocked the gun from David's hands. There was a paralyzing blow on his throat. He was thrown and pinned like a wrestler in a match for death.

It was no accident that the leopard stood over the body of David Ommanney. David himself could have foretold that this would happen. For one thing, there were the bad omens; and, for another, there were the leopard themselves. Only that morning he had told his client, Baron von Boeselager, that the African leopard is the most dangerous animal in existence. "For its size and weight," David had pronounced solemnly, "the leopard is the most ferocious game on four legs. When a leopard is wounded, he *always* charges. And when he charges, he usually gets there with his teeth."

It was not that Baron von Boeselager did not believe David. Actually, the Baron had hunted twice in Africa before, and had shot all of the African Big Five, the animals that bite back. Even though the leopard is usually mentioned last in the list of the dangerous five, he is considered by many white hunters to be the most deadly of the whole quintet. Both the Baron and David Ommanney had heard, just before they started on this trip, that Eric Rundgren of the safari firm of Ker and

Downey had been mauled by a leopard in the Narok district in southwestern Kenya. Dave Lunan, another white hunter, had also been badly chewed by a leopard near Lake Manyara, in northern Tanganyika, only a short time before.

And yet at the close of January, 1959, Baron von Boeselager and his white hunter, David Ommanney, had set up camp in the very country where Lunan had almost met his death. The reason was simple. The Baron wanted a male leopard at least two and a half meters in length. Dangerous or not, some of the best leopard in all of East Africa are to be found in the Lake Manyara district. So David directed the safari boys to set up the camp on the flat plain two or three miles back from the edge of Lake Manyara itself. The country is level with scattered palm trees. Game is fairly abundant. There are many Grant's gazelle, impala, and wart hogs. Around the salt pans of Lake Manyara a herd of some five hundred buffalo habitually feed. Perhaps because the smaller varieties of game are abundant, the plain around the lake is crawling with leopard. For some reason, the Manyara leopard are more aggressive than leopard elsewhere. In the last ten years, two fatal leopard attacks and a dozen maulings have occurred in the Manyara district.

David Ommanney is one of the youngest full-fledged white hunters in East Africa. Nonetheless, he felt supremely confident as he directed the safari boys to set up camp and sent the trackers out to look for leopard sign. David was born in India in 1928, and lived most of his life at Nanyuki, on the slopes of Mount Kenya in Africa. He had been hunting leopard, and every other kind of game for that matter, since he was old enough to lift the butt of a rifle. David had dealt with the forest leopard on his native Mount Kenya, and had collected on safari dozens of the beautiful spotted cats in the brush country and grasslands of both Kenya and Tanganyika. By the time he was twenty, David had personally accounted for over twenty-five leopard.

It was an old story to David as he directed the Baron to

shoot some small game for leopard bait. The first evening, on January 20, the trackers brought in the information that at least four leopard were working within a mile of camp, and were watering some distance back from the edge of the lake. The next morning, the Baron shot two wart hogs, a Grant's gazelle, and an impala. With the cunning born of long experience, Ommanney directed his first gun bearer Salim, and his second gun bearer, Mutia, to drag these baits, one at a time, through the grass and palmettos where the leopard would pass. Then, as each leopard moved down to drink after dark, he would smell the drag and go straight to the bait. Each carcass was placed high in a tree.

That very first day, the stage was set for tragedy. Baron von Boeselager shot a hyena. Perhaps the Baron did not know that hyenas are considered very bad luck. Most of the Masai tribe (and there were several Masai among David's safari boys) regard the hyena as bad because the animal is full of evil human spirits. When a Masai dies, his relatives never bury the body. They simply place the dead on the ground outside the village. In the evening, the ever-present hyenas eat every scrap of the human body, then crack the bones and eat those too. Hyenas often do not wait for native villagers to expose bodies, but will attack a sleeping man and bite off his arm or his face in a single snap. To the Masai, the hyena is a powerful animal, full of the evil of death.

The safari boys murmured among themselves, and rolled their eyes at the ground, when the Baron shot the hyena. None of them would touch the dead animal. When the Baron wanted the animal skinned, and its head fixed for his trophy collection, not one of the skinners drew out his knife or made a move to save the carcass.

In the several days that followed, the incident of the hyena was almost forgotten, except by the most superstitious. During that time, the party found several leopard. Each of the leopard came to a bait which had been hung in one of the thorn trees on the plain. In two instances, the trackers could tell by the small size of the spoor that the leopard were but half-grown cats, not worthy of further attention. Three of the leopard, however, which had been to feed on the baits provided for them, were apparently large animals.

On each of three evenings, David and the Baron squatted in the high grass near one of these trees. At the first bait, they ascertained, by looking with binoculars at the carcass in the tree, that a leopard had appropriated the meat and was feeding upon it. From the amount of flesh eaten, they judged that the leopard was a large one, probably a male. They did not try to go near the tree from which the bait hung to get a closer look at the tracks. Such a rash action would either drive the leopard away, or, worse, provoke him into charging.

When leopard appropriate a kill, they feed upon it, and then lie up nearby, so as to keep an eye on the remains. If they kill the animal themselves, they usually haul the carcass into a tree for safe keeping. If the wily human places a Grant's gazelle or an impala in a tree, therefore, it seems very natural to a leopard. The leopard feeds by night on his kill. He usually comes in the evening, jumps into the tree, and fills his belly. After that, he will lie in some place of concealment near the tree, to guard the remains of the meat against would-be predators in the form of other leopard, hyenas, or birds of prey.

When David and the Baron slipped up to examine a leopard bait, they did so downwind, stealthily. They squatted in the high grass among the palmettos with only the tops of their heads showing. They made no unnecessary movement. The eyesight of a leopard is extremely keen. In whispered tones, Ommanney directed the Baron as to what to do. As the Baron had shot leopard before, he was steady, and the hunting went well.

But Baron von Boeselager was particular. The first leopard which they saw was a large male, better then seven feet in length. The animal appeared suddenly out of the grass. As the leopard jumped up into the thorn tree, the last slanting rays of the sun lighted up the orange-yellow body marked with beautiful black rosettes. This was a trophy of which any sportsman would have been proud.

The leopard was hungry. He looked around only once, and then lay at full length on a large limb and began to feed. David had laid his hand upon the Baron's elbow, so that there would be no movement which the leopard might see. When the cat began to eat, gulping down the rotten meat in great chunks, David signaled the Baron to raise his gun and fire. The Baron shook his head. "Two and a half meters," the Baron said firmly. Just behind Ommanney and the Baron, Salim, the gun bearer, swore a Moslem oath. The curse of Allah be upon this European. The misfortune of the hyena would overcome them all. Here was a fair shot in good light—and the leopard was a beauty.

But the Baron was a man of principle. He was determined to have a big leopard or none at all. On three successive evenings, the Baron shook his head firmly at three successive leopard. David himself was becoming irritated. For one thing, it was no small feat to attract five leopard in as many days. Not only had the leopard been induced to take the baits of gazelle and wart hog, but each bait had been placed just right.

Each leopard had fed for two or three nights so that the hunters had had a chance to look him over. Ommanney had led the Baron through the high grass in just the right way, so that the leopards would not be alarmed. Any one of the first five leopard they could have shot with ease; but still the Baron shook his head.

Perhaps it was the Baron's stubbornness; perhaps it was the evil human spirit of the hyena, as Salim said. The sixth leopard was the one.

David, with some show of justifiable irritation, had directed the Baron rather curtly to get another wart hog, which they would hang near a dry wash or donga some two miles from camp. There were leopard tracks in the sand of this wash. Two or three cats apparently used the donga as a highway going to and from water. The wart hog was appropriately placed in a thorn tree.

The next morning, as David swung the safari car within two or three hundred yards of the thorn tree, he could see that a leopard had taken the bait. The wart hog had been a big boar, yet almost all the carcass of the hog was gone. Only the head and one shoulder remained. These pathetic fragments, hanging by remnants of skin, had been hoisted higher in the tree, and now hung in the fork of a branch. The rope by which Salim had tied the wart hog carcass had been broken or bitten through, as if it had been string. Only a very large leopard could do this. Perhaps this one would be big enough to satisfy the Baron.

It was uncertain whether the leopard would come back at all. He had fed heavily that first night. Also, there was little left for another meal—even for a hungry leopard. But it was a chance. So David and the Baron squatted behind a group of palmettos some fifty yards from the thorn tree on the edge of the wash. Salim lay on his elbow behind them. As usual, Salim shook his head and muttered under his breath. The omens were bad. As the sun sank lower, a flight of pink flamingos flew into the lake from behind: a very bad sign. A hornbill stalked up and down a branch at the top of the thorn tree. The hornbill squawked through his ridiculous overgrown beak, and to Salim the cries sounded like "*mbaya, mbaya.*" This means, in Swahili, "bad, bad."

It was bad, too, when the sun lowered and the leopard did not appear. The last rays slanted over the escarpment beyond Lake Manyara. As though this were a signal, there was a rasping growl from the grass.

They saw the leopard at the edge of the donga. The end of his tail twitched back and forth in little jerks. The leopard was looking straight at them.

"He'll go eight feet, maybe more," David hissed into the Baron's ear.

The Baron was already raising his gun. He carried a European-made over-and-under effect, with an 8.64 rifle barrel mounted above a 16 gauge shotgun. This was not an easy shot. The leopard they had seen before were broadside, and in plain sight in a tree. This leopard was facing the hunters and looking straight at them. Any second the cat would whirl and go. The leopard's chest was a target the size of two human hands.

The Baron sighted quickly and fired. The solid ball struck too far to the right. Ommanney could see the spurt of fur as the bullet raked along the leopard's ribs. The leopard jerked sideways, and leaped into the air. The squawling scream that came from between the wet teeth was a mixture of pain and rage. In an arching bound, the leopard jumped sideways into the waist-high grass. Frantically, Ommanney raised his .470 double rifle and fired. The bullet was too late. It nicked the hind paw of the leopard as he sailed into the grass.

Just as the leopard leaped, he turned in mid-air. He turned toward the three men. He had been looking at the humans before the shots. Now he was coming at them through the grass.

Ommanney grabbed the Baron by one arm. They ran sideways a few yards to where a termite hill rose out of the grass. Around the termite hill, the busy little insects had cut down the vegetation for several yards. As Ommanney and the Baron scrambled up the rough knobs of the termite mound, a cobra uncoiled and slid into one of the passageways. The Baron flinched to one side. Ommanney jerked him higher on the bare dirt. Cobras usually run from humans; wounded leopard never do.

From the elevation of the termite hill, the hunters could look down into the grass. There was no sight or sound. Over across the plain of Manyara, the three rocky hills known as the pyramids were lighted by the evening sun. A lion roared in the distance down by the lake. The grass around the termite hill was empty of life.

Salim offered David the double-barreled 12 gauge shotgun

which he carried as an extra. A shotgun is standard armament
on a leopard hunt. At close range the shotgun is more lethal
than a rifle. Ommanney snapped open the weapon, and
checked the two shells of buckshot in the breach. He directed
the Baron to stay on top of the termite hill and have his rifle
ready. Ommanney stepped down and into the fringe of thick
grass to meet the leopard. With Salim at his heels, he moved
slowly toward the edge of the donga and the tree where the
remnants of the wart hog still hung. There was no noise or
movement to show that any animal was within a mile of this
quiet spot.

Perhaps ten yards from the place where the leopard had
stood, David hesitated. Here there were low-growing palmettos mixed in the high grass. The leopard might attack from
only a few feet away. He would need a second's warning to
catch the charging animal on the end of his gun barrel.

David raised the shotgun and fired one barrel at the palmettos. He could still see nothing, but he listened carefully, expecting the leopard to growl at the shot and reveal his position.
There was no sound. David reloaded and walked slowly forward. Again he raised the shotgun and fired, aiming at the
exact spot where the leopard had disappeared. He waited
tensely. Nothing. Even the birds had stopped their evening
chirping.

He reloaded the empty barrel of the shotgun. Perhaps the
Baron's shot had done its work after all. Ommanney stepped
forward. He stood in the very grass where the leopard had
jumped. With Salim peering over his shoulder, David swung
slowly around. The leopard had gone.

A palmetto rustled. There was no wind. Fifteen feet away
a yellow blur appeared. The thing was six feet in the air.
Blindly David fired both barrels. He saw white teeth in front
of his face. A paralyzing blow struck his throat. His gun flew
end over end. He fell backward. Salim behind him was
knocked down.

The leopard stood over him. When David looked up, he

saw a white throat from beneath. Bloody saliva dripped down over the open jaws. The leopard turned to growl at Salim. The cat's face bent downwards. David saw the open mouth lunge at his throat. Instinctively, he threw up his left arm. He tried to twist sideways. The weight of the leopard lay upon him. "Must keep those teeth from my throat," he thought. The fangs closed on his shoulder as he twisted. At the first bite, his leather jacket was shredded. Muscle and bone crunched between the teeth. The leopard growled deep in his chest. The teeth shifted their grip lower, to try again for the throat. Again David twisted frantically. The teeth sank in near his elbow. David could hear tendons and muscles breaking away.

Salim sprawled on the ground. The double rifle had been knocked from his hands. The leopard lay over bwana David. As the leopard lunged forward for the kill, Salim drew his knife—the curved knife that all Mohammedans wear. With it, Salim cut the throats of animals so that orthodox Mohammedans could eat the meat.

With the knife held high, Salim took one running step. He launched himself into the air in a flying tackle. As he struck the leopard on the back, he lunged downward with his knife. He felt the blade go through skin and meat.

The leopard squawled in pain. He turned. Raking talons curved from the side. Salim rolled clear over the leopard. He still held the knife. The leopard stood there. He swung his head, first at the unconscious Ommanney, then at Salim. Which of the two men would he kill first? With a low growl, the leopard turned and jumped into the grass.

Salim stooped over bwana David. Ommanney's eyes flickered. He raised his head weakly. Salim helped him to his knees. Blood was pumping in spurts from the severed arteries in his upper arm. Weakly, he tried to hold the blood back with his right hand. The muscles and tendons of his left arm were hanging in shreds. If he had not worn a leather jacket, his arm would have been gone entirely.

Baron von Boeselager and Salim supported David on either side. Ommanney's strength was failing rapidly, as blood poured down his left hand in a flood. By the time they reached the safari car, the pyramid mountains and the thorn trees were swimming before him. At camp, the Baron snatched rolls of bandage from the first aid kit, and with them he staunched the flow of blood. The native driver was already in the seat of the safari car. Arusha and the hospital were seventy-five miles away.

When David was on his way to help in the safari car, the faithful Salim began to wonder. Had his knife found its way between the leopard's ribs? Was the leopard dead, back there in the grass? It is the code of the hunters that a wounded and dangerous animal may not be left alone; otherwise, the next person to pass that way will surely be killed.

Salim went to the edge of the camp, where the safari boys were huddled together. They talked in low voices about the leopard which had nearly killed bwana David. Salim called to Mutia, the second gun-bearer. He thrust a .30-06 rifle into Mutia's unwilling hands. Then, having loaded Ommanney's .470 double rifle, he motioned Mutia to follow.

Twilight was beginning to darken the Manyara Valley when Salim and Mutia again approached the bait tree and the edge of the donga. There was the place in the matted grass where bwana Ommanney had fallen. There, too, was the pool of blood, already growing dark and sticky. Just beyond was the place where Salim himself had rolled, after he had knifed the leopard. And just there, in the high grass, was where the leopard had gone.

Salim took a step. The grass rustled. The leopard was already in the air. Salim half raised the gun. One barrel went off. The bullet plowed into the ground. The leopard caught him full in the face. One tooth ripped through his eye. As Salim fell over backward, raking claws tore at his belly and his thigh.

Mutia threw up his rifle and fired blindly. The leopard's tail was cut by the bullet. The leopard screeched wildly. The cat turned. Darting his head downward, he bit Salim through the shoulder. Salim could feel the teeth crunch through the bone. Then he lost consciousness.

Mutia managed to get another shell into the chamber of the .30-06. Again he shot. The leopard, writhing on top of Salim, was only feet away. The shot went wild. At the noise, the leopard stood up. He growled. Then he turned and leaped into the high grass. Half of the leopard's tail lay across Salim's knees.

Just after dark, Baron von Boeselager used the rest of the bandages from the first-aid kit to tie up Salim's thigh and shoulder. The teeth of the leopard had missed the jugular vein by a fraction of an inch. Salim's eye was gouged away. The Baron had the safari boys put the unconscious Salim on a mattress in the back of the truck. He drove the truck himself into Arusha. The hospital there received the second victim of the Manyara leopard a scant two hours after the first. From Mutia's story, they learned that the leopard still was not dead.

That night, over the telephone wires, went the story from Arusha to Nairobi: "A killer leopard is in the Manyara country. A safari is leaderless. We need help."

Theo Potgieter, a white hunter for the firm of Selby and Holmberg, was the only qualified hunter in Nairobi, as most white hunters were on safari. Potgieter, just in from his last hunting trip, answered the emergency.

It was Friday when the Manyara leopard had attacked David Ommanney and almost killed the brave Salim. It was Sunday before Potgieter could find his own gun bearer and drive the 150 odd miles from Nairobi to Arusha. It was Sunday afternoon, January 26, when Theo Potgieter reached the disorganized camp on the Manyara plain. That same afternoon, with Mutia and Baron von Boeselager, Theo went after the leopard.

Mutia still carried Ommanney's .30-06, but Mutia stayed well behind. From a safe distance, he pointed out the trampled

grass where the leopard had attacked Salim. Potgieter found
the spot. The matted ground was rusty with dried blood.
Jackals had carried off the leopard's tail. Of the tailless leopard
himself, there was no sign.

Theo directed the Baron to take his station on the termite
hill. With the double-barreled shotgun at eye level, and
the safety off, Potgieter walked slowly through the high grass.
David had described to him, from his hospital bed, the charge
of the leopard. "It was fast as light," David had said. "He was
in the air before my face when I saw him."

Theo moved slowly, the shotgun ever before him. He
kicked at the palmettos around the place where Ommanney
and Salim had met the leopard. There was no sound. The
leopard had gone. But just to make sure, Theo made a wider
circle. He beat up and down the high grass on the edge of the
donga for a hundred yards. He circled beyond the bait tree,
back and forth. The grass was undisturbed. The wounded
leopard had gone off and died.

Potgieter moved back towards the termite mound where
the Baron waited tensely. Again the sun was lowering beyond
the escarpment. A palmetto leaf rustled to Potgieter's left. He
jerked around. The leopard was already in the air. Potgieter
swung the gun. The first barrel burned fur on the leopard's
neck. Frantically he pulled the second barrel. The buckshot
tore into the leopard's shoulder. The momentum of the leopard's leap struck against Potgieter's chest. The gun flew from
his hands. He rolled away. The leopard stood there. His left
paw hung limp. The leopard was far from dead. His ears were
laid back. He wrinkled his lips. On three legs he lunged forward.

Theo threw up his arm before his face. In a second, the
leopard would be at his throat.

A shot blasted out. Potgieter did not feel the tearing teeth.
He raised his head. Three feet from him, the leopard twitched
on the matted grass. The bloody stump of a tail thrashed back

and forth in death. The Baron's shot had caught the killer leopard in the neck.

"Yes," said David Ommanney when he left the hospital with his left arm in a cast, "there are a lot of dangerous animals in Africa, but for my money, the leopard is the fastest and the worst. And," he added slowly, "I'm never going to allow a client to kill another hyena."

12 · Hippo Trouble

THE FACE before us looked like a dragon. The muzzle was shiny black, with round nose holes and loose lips. Bare rings of pinkish flesh marked the eyes. They were small eyes, too small for that wide and evil face. But it was the mouth that seemed the worst. It looked like a red cave as it opened wide. Curved teeth jutted out from above and below, as big as marlin spikes. It would have been a frightening face a hundred yards away. At twenty-five feet, it was paralyzing.

Something cold pressed against my shoulder from behind. It couldn't be Andrew. He was on the other side, and pulling back on my arm.

"*Bunduki, bwana*," came a voice from behind. It was Ngoro. Good old Ngoro. None of the rest of us had thought to bring a rifle. We weren't hunting. We were looking for a place to camp.

I snatched the Weatherby .300 from Ngoro, and bolted a shell into the chamber. There was no time to see if this was the soft-nosed or solid ammunition. Any ammunition would have to do. Ngoro should have handed me the .470 double rifle. But the size of the animal close before us made any rifle a matter of small importance. How could a gun stop that great thing? Where would I shoot? The open mouth seemed to cover the whole area. The body behind was almost hidden. A great red throat and the yellow tusks were all I could see.

The mouth snapped shut. The loose lips flapped together.

The two round nostrils dilated. There was a snorting roar like a bursting gasket. This was it.

Andrew Holmberg, Brownie, and I had not come to southern Tanganyika in British East Africa to hunt hippos. We hadn't even thought about hippos, although we had seen a few in the Athi River just outside of Nairobi. They had looked harmless enough. "River pigs," they had been called. It seemed a good name. Usually we saw only their eyes and ears sticking up above the muddy water. Even our photographs of the Athi hippos were not particularly remarkable. I remember thinking that of all of the animals we had seen, these were the most docile looking, and the hardest to approach and photograph.

I remember saying, when Andrew asked me if I wanted to shoot a hippo, "Don't think so. It would be like killing a pig in a puddle."

"There's a hippo on your game license in case you change your mind," he remarked. "Sometimes hippos can be exciting."

But we had forgotten about such minor matters as we entered enthusiastically into the bagging of the Big Five. In addition, we wanted to round out our safari repertoire with the two coveted and beautiful trophies—the greater kudu and sable antelope. Both sable and kudu are found in the south. The best greater kudu live in southern Tanganyika and northern Mozambique. Southern sable also carry the trophy horns. We would have to move south.

"I know a place," Andrew had said in his slow manner, "where only one other safari has ever hunted. I found it last year."

We had already had some experience with Andrew's aversion to places that showed "too many safari car ruts," or areas where, as Andrew described them, "the good game heads had been picked over." We had already taken one trip into a hidden valley which he had found when he was on patrol after Mau Mau terrorists. It was a fabulous spot for game, but an impossible place to take a four-wheeled vehicle. It is

no wonder that only one other safari had ever been there before us.

The long trip south to Arusha, and then west to Ngorongoro, the great volcanic crater which is teeming with tens
of thousands of head of game, was a wonderful trip in itself.
But by the time we had bumped over the rough roads south
to Tabora to pick up extra gasoline and supplies there, and had
then moved south again to the Ugalla River, we were saddle-
sore and weary. We crossed the Ugalla on a built-up dike of
mud and sticks, as the river in the dry season (this was in
July) had degenerated into a series of pools, with only
swampy ground in between. Andrew had told us that the
Ugalla country was where most safari parties went to get
the greater kudu and sable antelope. I could see their point,
because by that time they would be too exhausted to go any
farther in any event.

But the next day we pushed on still farther south. The road
became sketchier, and finally disappeared almost altogether.
Soon we turned off at an angle from even this dim track. The
turn-off place was a spot just like a thousand others that we
had passed in the last two days of steady driving. I could
only make out a very dim trail with the marks of elephant
feet upon it. We had become accustomed to seeing these
round, corrugated imprints along the elephant trails that criss-
crossed this country in every direction. But southern Tanganyika itself is almost flat, with few landmarks. It consists
for the most part of forested country, with only here and there
small glades overgrown with ten-foot-high grass. Along the
Ugalla these glades are larger, and when burned over by the
natives in the dry season, are relatively open. I suppose this
is another reason why most safaris hunt the Ugalla country.
South of the Ugalla the trees became thicker and the glades
fewer. As we turned off through the woods, I couldn't help
thinking it was like trying to drive through the Pennsylvania
woods without any road.

In addition to our Willys safari car with its special body,

we had a truck which carried our extra gasoline and drinking water, as well as the majority of our eleven safari boys, who perched on top of the tents and other equipment. By following the old elephant trail, the safari car could usually work its way between the trees. But the truck invariably got stuck. Twice we had to cut down good-sized trees with an axe. On many occasions, we made detours around close-growing groups of trees, to find a path wide enough for the truck to move through. As it was, our equipment was torn and raked by the branches. Everyone was exhausted with the work of moving logs and rocks out of the way. By the end of the first day, we had made barely fifteen miles.

Not the least of the hazards of overland travel through southern Tanganyika were the elephants. During the wet season, these animals had stalked all over the landscape, pockmarking the soft muddy soil with their huge feet. What had once been mud was now dried to flint-like consistency, but the elephant tracks in it were preserved intact. An elephant footprint is just about the size of the holes which the electric light company digs to set up their wooden poles. An elephant print also exactly fits the wheel of a car. It is the most effective automobile trap ever devised. In those places where we weren't stuck in elephant tracks, we were blocked by the trees which the elephants had pulled down or pushed over. In the areas where a herd of elephants had fed for several days, the country looked as though a tornado had passed over it.

I am not at liberty to say where we finally ended this long overland junket. (I probably wouldn't be able to describe it accurately anyway.) The white hunters of East Africa jealously guard their secret hunting places. Andrew had told us that the biggest greater kudu in all of Africa were to be found in this area. I hoped that they'd be big ones, after all this trouble.

On the second day, we found a small encampment of natives in the middle of the forest. (The place was wisely sur-

rounded by a heavy pole *boma,* or lion fence. We had heard
lion roaring on the last three nights of our trip.) These natives
made their living by gathering wild honey, packing it out on
their backs over the many miles to the settlements along the
Ugalla, where they would sell it to Indian traders. One of the
honey hunters volunteered to accompany us, and show us
the best elephant trails down to the water. If the elephant trails
along which this wizened little native led us were the best ones,
I would hate to see the others. The country was awful. As we
drew closer to the stream of water, the vegetation became
thicker, and there were gullies with naked rocks as well as
elephant-shattered trees to block our path. It was late in the
day when the little native pointed ahead, and we saw the glint
of water between the trees.

"I'll scout ahead and find a place to pitch camp," Andrew
said.

"And I'll go with you," I answered quickly. I was glad to
get out of the awful jolting seat of the safari car.

We had just rounded a thick clump of glossy-leaved bushes
when it happened. There were two hippos. The one closest
to us was a bull. The one behind I saw only dimly. (I thought
afterwards that the hippos must have been as startled as we
were. They had been lying down in a small cleared area on
the bank of the stream. By the dust and dried dung there it
would seem that they had been taking a dust bath.) But I had
few seconds to notice details, as the bull opened his mouth and
came toward us. I thought we were done for.

Andrew dragged me back by one shoulder and we stood
there, rigid, facing the bull hippo. Ngoro thrust the gun at
me from behind, but it seemed useless to shoot. We stood
there waiting. I held the gun ready. The bull hippo closed his
mouth with the noise of a wet mattress being hit with a base-
ball bat. He whirled and ran. I was amazed at the agility of
the animal on those short stocky legs. I was amazed, also, at
the size of his body as he launched himself over the river

bank in a running dive. The yellow spray spurted up to the tree tops as the two hippos hit the water together.

"That was a sticky spot," Andrew said mildly. "I thought that bull was going to take us in." And then, as an after-thought, he added, "As the hippos have mashed down all the brush here, this will be a good place for the tents."

Though I thought he was joking, Andrew proved as good as his word. He pitched our camp on the river bank, directly above the hippo pool in the place where the animals had been wallowing in the dry dirt. Fortunately, most of the hippos left that night and did not return. Only one old male remained in the morning. He was immediately dubbed "Harold, the Hippo." Harold, for reasons best known to himself, refused to vacate. During the ten days that we camped there, Harold blew and bellowed just below the canvas outhouse which our safari boys had thoughtfully pitched on the very brink of the river bank. Harold acted nasty, but was apparently just bluffing, with a lot of booming and snuffling to back it up.

The case was different with another bull hippo, who lived in a pool by himself a mile down the river. One of the honey hunters had pointed out this place to us as the only spot where we could get our safari car across the river. At this one spot, a gravel bar made a solid road for our car to cross. Hippopotamus trails, worn by generations of these heavy ani-mals as they had used this spot to climb up and down, had eroded the banks so that they formed an easy grade.

The first time we crossed the gravel bar, we were moving slowly. Andrew suddenly stopped the safari car. "Look," he said, pointing to his right and down stream. Close beside the gravel bar was a pool about the size of a city block. Beyond this was a tumble of rocks, and still farther down stream, an-other very large pool that seemed to extend for half a mile. In the middle of the far stretch of water was a great pile of rounded stones. A hippo bellowed in the distance, but cer-tainly there was nothing particularly remarkable about the scene, except perhaps for a small crocodile floating on top of the muddy water not far from our car. Suddenly one of the rounded stones moved. There was a squealing snort. Another one of the distant objects heaved up, and then another. The whole mass began moving. The pile in the distance was a solid mass of hippos! There must have been twenty-five animals, some of them lying on top of each other, three or four deep. The constant disturbance was caused by the lowermost ones, who were being squashed by the ten or fifteen tons lying on top. As we watched with the glasses, a fight broke out, apparently between two bulls. They opened their mouths wide and rushed at each other, sparring from side to side, as each tried to get a grip on the muzzle of the other.

"We ought to circle around with the telephoto lens and take some movies of that mountain of hippos," Brownie said.

"Better not," Andrew answered tersely. "I think we have company." Andrew was looking, not at the squirming mass of hippos in the far pool, but close beside us, at the edge of the gravel bar. A hippo's head had appeared above the yellow water. He snorted and wiggled his ears. This was standard procedure, and we had seen it a hundred times in the last day or two. The hippos would come up out of the depths, blow out their nostrils like a split steam pipe, look at us a moment, and then submerge again. The hippo now close before us, however, wasn't submerging. He wasn't even moving away as most of the others had done. He was coming straight toward us, the great black head and the red-rimmed eyes moving steadily. The hippo must be walking on the bottom, I thought, but why would he come so close?

"Must think our car's another hippo come to share his pool with him," Andrew remarked. "Some of these old outcast bulls are pretty frosty."

Andrew started the car and we climbed the far bank. When I looked back, the bull hippo was half out of the water at the edge of the gravel bar, and still moving toward us.

That evening when we returned, the bull hippo was still

in his pool. As we crossed the gravel bar, he again came menacingly toward us. Ngoro and Sungura, our two gun bearers, jumped out of the car for a minute, to examine the tracks of some greater kudu which had watered at this same pool some time during the day. At the sight of the two men, the bull turned toward them and opened his mouth. Ngoro and Sungura sprinted for the safari car, which was already in motion.

"Those cheeky hippos can be pretty dangerous," Andrew remarked, as we drove back along the river bank to camp.

That evening, Andrew regaled us with stories of hippos he had known. "The hippo is not one of the Big Five in Africa," Andrew said, as we sat around the table after dinner. "And some people think he's just a water-going clown. But I've known some nasty hippos in my time. Many of the river natives regard the hippos as the most dangerous animals in Africa. Some of my professional hunter friends have underestimated the hippo. There is the grave of one of these men in the cemetery in Nairobi. Only on my last safari, over toward Lake Tanganyika, we camped near a village where a native boatman had been killed the day before. He got between a hippo, feeding on the bank, and the water, which is the hippo's natural place of safety. The hippo bit the man in two with a single bite. The crocodiles had eaten the part of the fellow that fell into the water by the next morning when one of his wives came to look for him."

As Andrew talked, Harold the Hippo, not fifty feet from us, punctuated these bloody tales with bubbling roars and bellows that sounded like a water-logged French horn. Finally, well after dark, Harold climbed out on the far side of the river and went off to feed.

During the next several days, we saw the big bull by the river-crossing on every occasion that we passed his pool. The honey hunter who was acting as our guide had argued each time with Andrew that we should shoot this hippo. We hadn't paid too much attention, because the natives were always anxious for us to shoot more meat. However, we had killed a couple of impala, a Lichtenstein's hartebeest, and a very large roan antelope, and still our guide argued for the shooting of the bull hippo by the river crossing.

"This man says that sooner or later that bad hippo's going to kill one of his people," Andrew said one evening, as we came back from a hunt for sable antelope.

"Maybe we'd better make this river highway safe for legitimate travel," I answered light-heartedly, as I viewed the wilderness around us.

"So you've changed your mind about shooting a hippo," Andrew replied, looking at me. "Get three or four of those solid patch bullets for that Weatherby of yours, and we'll see what you can do."

We stopped the safari car several hundred yards from the edge of the river, so that the sound would not alarm our friend in the pool. Andrew and I walked forward together. We moved quietly, so as not to alert the bull. I don't think either of us thrilled at the possibility of shooting a bull hippo as he charged straight at us. We tiptoed along the bank, past the place where our car tracks led down to the gravel bar. At the very edge of the hippo pool was a gigantic sausage tree, with half its roots sticking out over the water where some flood had washed them clear. Using the tree as cover, we slipped up behind it and lay flat along the tangle of roots.

Over across from us, a large V of ripples moved across the surface of the muddy water. I could see the snout and head of a very large crocodile.

"A big one," Andrew whispered in my ear. "Must be fifteen feet long." He pointed across the pool.

There was the bull hippo. His eyes were already fixed upon us. Perhaps he had seen the motion of Andrew's hand as he pointed. I had no time to speculate upon the strange companions which the bull hippo had in his private pool. The crocodile simply sank from sight. The hippo turned in a wide arc, and came toward us.

"The only place is the brain," said Andrew quietly. "From this angle, it's between the eye and the ear. Don't miss," he added tersely.

I steadied the Weatherby .300 over the water-worn roots of the sausage tree. Through the cross hairs of the telescopic sight, I picked out the wicked little eye of the bull. It was fixed upon us with terrible intensity. As I swung the cross hairs with his movement, his feet must have touched the shallowing bottom. The great black head began to rise. Now!

I squeezed the trigger. The blast of noise seemed to blot out the great head. A plume of yellow water spurted upward. The pool boiled with motion from beneath. In the churning eddy, leaves and sticks from the bottom rolled up. Suddenly the dirty water was stained by a spot of red. Then a great three-toed foot rolled from the surface, stood rigid for a moment, straight up, and finally disappeared. Andrew clapped me on the shoulder. "*Mazuri!*" he said shortly. This was high praise indeed—the Swahili word for "well done." Andrew usually just grunted when I made a shot.

It was late in the evening. In any case, it would be necessary to wait until the carcass floated in the pool before we could drag it onto the gravel bar.

At sunrise the next morning, we drove the safari car out to the very edge of the pool. There was the bloated carcass, with a large crocodile sitting on top of it. The croc plopped into the water as soon as we appeared.

Volunteers to attach a rope to one of the stiff legs of the hippo bull were hard to find in our group. I didn't blame the safari boys, particularly as the crocodiles in that muddy water made the very thought of stepping into it seem like sure death. We finally rigged a crude raft of two or three empty water cans and a couple of spare tires. With this, one of the boys poled out and attached a heavy rope to the hippo. So heavy was the carcass, however, that even with the combined pull of the safari car on the hard gravel, with everybody else pushing, we could not drag the carcass out onto the bar. We managed it at last by rolling the great body over and over in the shallow water. Finally, we had to skin the bull at the very edge of the water, crocodiles notwithstanding. We saved the head, as the hippo proved to be an exceptionally large bull, with very fine and heavy ivory. The honey hunters were glad to have the meat. In skinning the head, we found a large iron ball, hand-wrought, and of about fifty caliber size. The thing was embedded in the cartilage against the hippo's skull between his protruding eyes.

I had seen a few of the natives of Tanganyika with muzzle-loading cap and ball muskets. In answer to my question Andrew told me that there are over twenty-five thousand cap and ball muskets in use in Tanganyika today. "They usually don't attempt anything as big and dangerous as a hippo with those antiquated guns." Then Andrew added, "Some one tried it, though, and a long time ago. It's no wonder this bull hippo didn't like people."

13 · Hunting the Sahara of Beau Geste

"OF ALL the dad-blamed double-breasted difficulties!" Tom Bolack was rolling around on the sand, flapping his arms like a trained seal. He licked his fingers where the hot metal of the wrench had branded him.

Tom crawled again underneath the stalled car and lay on his belly. We had both been working there for three hours, trying to fix the shattered fuel pump. The sun which burned down out of the African sky had heated the sand around us well above the hundred degree mark. We tried to keep the metal tools which we were using in the shade under the car. Tom had picked up a wrench which had been in the sun for only a few minutes.

At any other time, and in any other place, two full grown men lying under a stalled car in the middle of the desert would make a funny cartoon. Under the circumstances, however, it wasn't funny and it wasn't a cartoon. Tom Bolack, lieutenant governor of New Mexico and the man who had killed the world's record polar bear, had started out into the Sahara Desert with me to look for desert game. We did find desert game—and we also found other things. Most of these other things were several forms of death.

There is no dangerous game in the Sahara Desert. For this reason, Tom and I had thought that our desert hunt in the northern part of French Equatorial Africa would be a country stroll. We even had brought our wives. As my wife Brownie and I had been hunting the Sudan for some time, we had arranged with Tom and Alice to meet us at the small border town of Abéché, on the eastern edge of the Sahara Desert. The guidebook said that there was a local French airline into Abéché. It hadn't worked out that way. We had also arranged through Jacky Maeder and Company of Zurich, Switzerland, for a local French guide, one Jean Bepoix, to meet us at the Sudanese border, bringing with him a couple of vehicles and some natives as camp boys. That hadn't worked out either.

As a matter of record, Bepoix, who has spent most of his life in that country, has become almost as Arabic as the Arabs themselves. Outside of a penchant for French red wine, a copious supply of which he always had on hand, he was, in speech and manner of thinking, an Arab. We soon found that the Arabs have no words in their glossary for "close connection." There is an old Arabic saying, "Allah has given us the rest of the day, and all of tomorrow." Putting things off till the morrow makes sense in the Beau Geste country.

Abéché itself looks more like a stage set than a real town. The hotel, where legionnaires drop in for cognac, and the Abéché fort look as though Hollywood directors had built them. At the camel market near the fort swarm the picturesque desert tribesmen. In the eastern Sahara, the natives are mostly Gorans. They have been covered with an overlay of Arabic culture, too; they ride swift racing camels, and carry eighteen-foot-long spears. At the markets, Gorans barter for camels, rugs, and wives. Goran crones haggle over fly-encrusted chunks of goat meat, while Goran artisans pound out wrought iron spear points in the manner taught them by the Arab traders. It was these same spear points which were almost to cost us the hunt.

By breeding very fast racing camels, the Gorans have developed remarkable animals, with speed and endurance surpassing almost anything else that moves on the desert. Given anything close to an even break, a Goran cameleer can ride down a gazelle, and hamstring the fleeing animal with the razor-sharp edge of his spear. A French officer at Abéché told us that all of the desert game for a hundred miles around had been killed off by the Gorans.

Our caravan consisted of a fairly creditable truck, loaded mostly with Jean's wine, and a fossilized version of a United States Army command car. Apparently this down-at-the-wheel vehicle was left over from the campaigns against Rommel along the North African coast. The French had tied together the major parts of the weary old machine with wire, and had added a coat of paint to cover the original olive drab. From a hundred yards away, as a matter of fact, our safari car didn't look so bad. If you tried to ride in it, though, you had an experience worth missing. The wind shield had collapsed on top of the hood long ago. There was no other vestige of a top or sides. You had the feeling you were riding on top of a disintegrating gravel crusher. I considered it a mechancial miracle that it got as far as the frontier town of Oum Chalouba.

We were amazed and dismayed when the Bolacks showed up at Oum Chalouba in an exact duplicate of "Old Decrepit." Apparently two of these vehicles of World War II had been rescued by the French. The Bolacks had been delayed by a series of airplane adventures. Plane trouble had developed over the Atlantic, and they had missed connections from Paris. The ride out into the desert from Fort Lamy, with a maniacal Arab camel driver at the wheel of their vibrating vehicle, had just about finished them. If Tom and Alice had known the Arabic for "Turn around and go back home," they would have done so.

Certainly around Oum Chalouba there was game. This far north of the general range of the Gorans, desert gazelles of several kinds were fairly common. The population of Oum Chalouba didn't bother the wild life—mainly because there was no population. At the fort, there was a body of native troops, led by a French sergeant. Outside the fort, the one well in the bottom of the wadi had gone dry, and most of the people had moved away. We found that this was not at all unusual in the Sahara. Water is life; where there is no water, there are no people.

As for the desert animals, most of them do not drink at all. Some of the desert gazelles get moisture from the wild melons which grow just after the infrequent rains. Other desert animals do not even seek out green grass or melons. Their bodies are so remarkably adapted to conserving moisture that the scant water contained in the dry herbage is enough.

Within sight of the fort at Oum Chalouba, Tom and I bagged Dorcas gazelles, and their larger cousins, the Dama gazelles. The Dorcas is very much like the East African Tommy, and about the same size; the dama is a handsome animal, somewhat larger than our pronghorn antelope in North America, but of a similar appearance. Just south of Oum Chalouba, we ran into small herds of red-fronted gazelles, another of the small desert-dwelling members of the gazelle family. This was well and good, but we had not come to this far country to polish off pretty little gazelles for table meat. Our real objectives were the desert oryx and the desert addax.

The white oryx, or scimitar-horned oryx, is one of the handsomest members of the oryx family. Formerly common from the desert area of the Sudan westward through Libya and the French Sahara, the white oryx is now limited to a fraction of this range, and is mighty scarce even there. The oryx does not flourish when harassed by camel-riding natives with long spears or by men with guns. If humans move in, the oryx moves out. In addition to this shyness, the scimitar-horned oryx migrates at various times of the year, depending on the seasons and the occasional desert rains. At times, the oryx seems to migrate for no apparent reason at all. These migrations are not mass movements of hundreds of animals together, like some of the game treks in other parts of Africa; instead, the white oryx seems to drift in small groups of a dozen or so, or even singly. Generally, this fascinating animal lingers on the edge of the true desert. The oryx country which we saw north of Oum Chalouba as far as the Libyan border was desert enough, but not quite completely bare.

The addax, even more of a desert dweller than the white oryx, lives in the wildest solitudes of the Sahara, where there is practically no vegetation at all. We knew that we would have to go far out to the north and west to get addax, but we hoped to get oryx close to our base camp. By taking both of the disintegrating command cars, we made a sweep north and west of the fort at Oum Chalouba, as far as we could go in one day. We saw Dama gazelles, desert ostrich, and thousands of Dorcas gazelles, but no sign at all of an oryx or an addax.

Bepoix told us, on the third evening of our stay at Oum Chalouba, that he thought we should move north to the Camel Corps headquarters at Fada, and hunt from there. That same evening, a camel caravan moved through Oum Chalouba on its way south. The cameleers had just come from Fada, having made the journey in fourteen days, with one water stop on the way. In all that distance, they had not seen a single oryx, or even so much as an oryx track.

This was grim news. There were no other places in the whole eastern Sahara from which we might hunt. Two of the Arabs with the caravan said they knew where oryx and addax could be found. With Jean interpreting, I asked these two men where this was. One of the fellows, a lanky hook-nosed rascal with a walleye, knelt before us and smoothed the sand with one hand. On the smooth surface he made forty little depressions with the tip of his finger. Over this he made several passes with both hands. He spat between his palms and clapped his hands together. "The desert animals you seek are that way, master," he said, pointing to the northwest.

Very courteous of him, I thought, to invoke the blessings

of the gods of the desert before he answered my question. The man was obviously a crossbreed, mingling in his veins the blood of some Arab slaver of years ago with that of the desert tribes. Nominally such people are Mohammedans, but they still retain much of the ancient folk magic and witchcraft of the Nilotic natives.

Jean was shaking his head. "*Ce n'est-pas bon*, that one." I didn't know whether Jean was referring to the evil-looking Arab kneeling on the sand before us, or to his proposition that he could lead us to the country of the oryx and addax. As an afterthought I remarked to Jean, "Ask the fellow his name."

"*Ouwash*," the Arab replied. His name was also the Arabic word for white oryx. That's a good omen, I thought. And then aloud, "Let's give it a try," I said. I was beginning to believe the desert hocus-pocus myself. Ouwash insisted on taking a friend with him as an additional guide. The other Arab's name was Jebel, which means devil. I don't know what kind of omen that was.

Bright and cold the next morning, we instructed our wives to stay in the main camp near the fort, where they would be comparatively safe—except from any wandering lion, leopard, scorpions, Arab bandits, or vicious desert tribesmen. (*We* did not mention the possible dangers; our wives did.) We left the truck and a driver with the women. Tom and I cranked up the two command cars and swung aboard. We took two of our retinue of camp boys, and the two Arab guides, Ouwash and Jebel. Bepoix drove one car and Tom and I took turns driving the other. We rounded the Oum Chalouba fort and headed north along the faint camel track which leads to Fada. Some sixty miles north of Oum Chalouba, several hours later, we turned northwestward along the course of a large wadi, or wash. The hard-packed sand on the floor of the wadi made comparatively smooth going, which was just as well, as one of the old command cars began to cough and stutter. Late in the afternoon, it died completely.

Fortunately Tom had worked in the oil fields when he was younger. By the light of our one lantern, he dismantled certain parts of the viscera of the ailing car. "No matter what I look at, it all needs fixing," he observed philosophically.

We made a cold camp under a stunted little tree, which turned out to be the last piece of major vegetation we were to see for a long time. The next morning, Tom got the car started again and we continued west by northwest, down the floor of the big wadi. By noon we had made perhaps seventy-five miles or so. I couldn't tell for sure, as the speedometer on the car I was driving had stuck at 62,000 miles some time in 1944, when the American Army had abandoned the thing.

Our noon stop was difficult, as there was absolutely no shade. The burning ball of the sun hung straight overhead. The two Mohammedans squatted and scowled at us as we sipped some of Jean's bitter red wine with our heads stuck under the running board. Bepoix was questioning the two Arabs. Again the hawk-visaged Ouwash made the forty little pits in a smooth patch of sand, and then ran the tip of his finger among the depressions in a mysterious figure-eight pattern. He spat between his palms, and pointed straight west down the wadi.

Tom had been standing in the back of the car for elevation. He called down to us, "What do those white oryx look like?" Tom squinted through his binoculars in the direction Ouwash pointed. "There's something jumping around down there," he commented, as he looked again.

Both Jean and I climbed up on the bed of the car. The shimmering heat haze made the sand dunes on either side waver and swim before our eyes. There did seem to be a light-colored animal standing on the floor of the wadi, three or four hundred yards away. It was the waves of heat over the sand which made the animal seem to jump and move. Through the moving mirage, I could make out long curving horns and a light-colored body. *"Ouwash!"* grunted Jean.

We coaxed the two vehicles into reluctant life, and moved

on down the wadi. As we approached, the single oryx turned
and ran. Just ahead, we saw two more oryx. The animals
were moving across the sand dunes from our right. Just beyond was a small herd of eight or ten, also moving from right
to left.

"*C'est bon, c'est bon!*" Bepoix was mumbling. In another
mile, we were in the midst of oryx, all moving in a southwesterly direction. We had, by the magic of the forty pits
in the sand, found a migration of these desert animals. During
the next two days we saw several hundred oryx.

But seeing an oryx and bagging an oryx are two different
matters. We seldom got closer than three hundred yards to
any of the animals, and usually it was five hundred. Towards
evening, when the heat haze settled down, I jumped out of the
car and ran to the top of a sand dune to try a long shot. Five
or six oryx that we had been glassing immediately started off
at a dead run. On the top of the sand dune, I had a good prone
rest. The oryx were angling away. The last one in line looked
the biggest. I settled the scope of the Weatherby .300 well
ahead of the animal's nose, and touched it off. The bullet hit
the oryx right through the middle. He dropped out of line,
faltered a few steps, and then lay down. As we came up to
administer the coup de grâce, Ouwash and Jebel turned to us,
pleading and kneading their hands. Ouwash held a wicked
curved knife he had jerked out of his belt. I grinned at them
and shook my head.

The camp was in the middle of the oryx migration. That
night, at dark, we could still see animals moving by us, always
in a southerly direction. At daylight the next morning, oryx
were still drifting past. By this time we were becoming very
choosey about oryx. The horns of the first animal I had
downed were forty inches long. This is very good for the
scimitar-horned oryx, but we thought we could do better.
Tom made a spectacular long shot on a single male oryx which
was running straight away from us. The horns of Tom's

oryx measured 44½ inches, about equal to the existing world's record.

The next afternoon, we found a large herd of about fifteen animals, moving across the wadi perhaps ten miles below camp. One of the oryx had horns which curved back and down almost to his rump. He was a monster. It was my turn to shoot. Feeling confident, I elected to try a very long one. The oryx were moving almost at right angles across our path, perhaps four hundred yards away. Settling the Weatherby very carefully, with my elbow resting on a hummock of sand on the edge of the wash, I pulled the crosshairs of the scope well ahead of the big oryx which was running in the middle of the herd, and carefully squeezed off the shot. The oryx just behind the big one dropped, as though jerked down from below. The shot had broken his neck cleanly just behind his ear. I groaned.

"Take the big one! Take the big one!" yelled Tom. I jumped back into the car. It was Tom's next shot but he insisted that I take it. Our game licenses called for three white oryx apiece. I had not intended to shoot three, but under Tom's urging I decided to try it again. Jean was pounding the accelerator with his boot, trying to urge the car to the top of a line of dunes. We stuck in the sand with the wheels churning. I jumped out and ran forward. The herd of oryx were again four hundred yards or so away, a very long shot. The big animal, with the enormous horns, was running second to last. I aimed at the rump of the oryx in front of him. I heard the clunk of the bullet hitting flesh. The big oryx dropped out of line, circled a moment, and then rolled on his side. Again Ouwash and Jebel came up with their knives in their hands pleading to "*hallel.*" "Not this one," I said grimly.

The big oryx was a male, his horns measuring 51¼ inches, some six inches over the existing world record. Ouwash and Jebel were not at all pleased. Unless a true believer faces east and cuts the throat of an animal to kill him, a Mohammedan cannot eat the meat. Late that evening Tom shot a smaller

male oryx, and let the two Moslems hallel its throat just before
the animal died. They made a bloody business of it, but they
were happy as two clams. Now everybody had meat.

Flushed with confidence after bagging the record oryx, we
did not even hesitate when Ouwash made his pits in the sand
the next morning, and indicated that the gods of the hunt directed us farther west to where the addax live. Farther west
we went, straight into the heart of the Sahara. In that direction
there was not a fort, a town, or a source of water for a thousand miles. The big wadi, which we had been following so
long, gradually disappeared in a series of minor rivulets and
sand dunes. Still, Ouwash directed us westward.

By the time we had gone another fifty miles from our oryx
camp, the desert floor was as bare as Mother Hubbard's cup-
board. I didn't understand it. Addax are animals, and animals
have to eat. Still, when we asked him where the addax were,
Ouwash spread his hand and pointed westward.

Our misgivings grew when both of the cars began to falter.
With the increased heat around noon, vapor locks in the gas
lines were a matter of course. We cooled the locks by pouring
water on a rag, but the water was running low. We used Jean's
red wine to cool the gas lines. Jean was not at all enthusiastic
about this. Quite unnecessarily, he pointed out that if we
stalled, we would have over two hundred miles to walk to the
nearest French fort. No human could make it that far over
this blistering desert, even if he could carry enough water for
the trip. To make matters worse, the going through the sand
dunes degenerated from difficult to impossible. When a car
became mired in loose sand, we fed a couple of sections of
perforated air strip surfacing, which the thrifty French had
taken from some desert air field of World War II, under the
churning wheels. This system worked fine, and when the car
had gained momentum enough on the two strips to advance a
few yards, we had no difficulty picking up the steel sections,
running forward in front of the car, and placing them in position again. By noon, however, the steel strips had become so

hot in the sun that we could not handle them without blistering our hands, and the pulling along in low gear had overheated the already overtaxed internals of the dying engines. The one I was driving suddenly emitted a death rattle, and quit.

"It's that fuel pump," Bolack said with the air of a professional diagnostician. He was already getting out the tools. Tom dismantled the fuel pump, and we took it underneath the car, as there was no other shade. From a section of a coffee can lid, a flattened out brass cartridge case, and some scrap metal which we found under the seat, Tom sawed, hammered, and filed a new fuel pump into being. I did not dare to contemplate, during these preparations, what the outcome would be if Tom's makeshift contrivance didn't work. But, fortunately, it did.

During the hours that Tom and I had spent underneath the car building the fuel pump, Ouwash and Jebel had squatted in the sand with their burnooses over their heads. Half a dozen times Ouwash had made the forty pits with his finger. After the mysterious passes with his hands, he indicated that the addax were still farther west.

The breakdown of the car had considerably diminished our enthusiasm for addax. At that time, we would have settled for any plan which would have gotten us out of the desert. When the engine of the car wheezed into life again, we motioned Ouwash and Jebel into the back, and I swung the car around to go back. Already the tracks we had made in the sand dunes were beginning to drift over from the constant wind that moved across the desert floor.

Tom, who was standing in the back of the car, pounded on the top of my hat. He was looking west, directly behind us. I stopped. As we lost momentum, the wheels sank deep in the sand dune we were crossing. It would take us an hour to dig out even if we got the engine started again.

"Addax!" yelled Tom. "Addax! A whole herd of them!" I jumped up on top of the car and focused my binoculars in the direction Tom pointed. Through the heat waves, I could see moving animals. They were crossing the sand dunes, perhaps a mile west of where we had stopped to rebuild the fuel pump. The crazy heat waves made the animals seem to separate, so that their heads and legs moved independently.

Jean was looking too. *"Mon dieu! Beaucoup de choconas!"* I moved my glasses to the left. There were more addax to the southwest, and yet another bunch farther beyond. The whole western horizon seemed to be addax, all of them moving. Even if this mirage multiplied their numbers, there certainly were a lot of "choconas."

Bepoix had told us that we would be very fortunate if we found three or four addax. Half a dozen addax made a big herd. The mysterious addax is not a common animal by any standard, and never so easily found as the white oryx. Through the heat waves I had seen what seemed to be forty or fifty of the animals. They moved along easily over the sand, which, to my certain knowledge, was so hot that it would blister a man through the soles of his shoes.

My car was stuck, so we left it there. With the metal tracks we managed to back Bepoix's vehicle onto a hard area between two dunes, and turn in the direction of the migrating addax. I signaled Jean to drive, and got my Weatherby ready. We drove between lines of dunes on hard, gravelly soil for perhaps a mile. Tom, standing in the back of the lurching command car, could no longer see the addax. We signaled Jean to stop. Tom and I ran together to the top of a crested dune. At its summit we took a second to brush aside the superheated surface sand, so that we could rest our elbows and look over.

The addax were perhaps three hundred yards away. Fifteen or twenty of the animals moved in front of us. Their bodies were white, their horns black. Their splayed-out hooves, adapted to the desert environment, scarcely sank into the sand. The addax had already seen us. They wheeled away at a dead run. Off to my right, another group of addax appeared over

ate 38. Andrew Holmberg was very proud of my record Cape eland. Tanganyika.

Plate 39. The greater kudu has perhaps the most spectacular horns. Mozambiqu

Plate 40. Sable antelope in a savanna in Mozambique. The dark-colored bull her his females ahead of him.

Plate 41. The sable antelope is considered by many hunters to be Africa's hand-omest game animal.

Plate 42. A very large nyala from the coastal jungle of Mozambique.

Plate 43. A record im
pala (horn length, 32
inches) bagged in t
Ikoma country
northern Tanganyik

Plate 44. The oribi is one of the smaller game.

Plate 45. The witch doctor locates game by throwing down a collection of *ju jus.* Mozambique.

Plate 46. The lesser kudu grow large in the sansevieria thickets of the Samburu country in Kenya.

Plate 47. Gerenuk or giraffe gazelle, a common but beautiful animal of the desert areas of East Africa.

late 48. Andrew Holmberg and Ngoro admire my world's record fringed-ear ryx. Its horn length, 37½ inches.

Plate 49. A good oryx. This is the common beisa oryx, which ranges the arid terrain)f northern Kenya or Somalia.

Plate 50. Tom Bolack and the dui ker in French Africa. The duiker is one of the smaller antelope and extremely difficult to bag.

Plate 51. Brownie and a Robert's gazelle. The Robert's gazelle is the southern variety of the Grant's gazelle.

Plate 52. It was in this Emboni village in northwestern Kenya that we learned of the large Emboni elephant.

Plate 53. Mohammed, our first tracker, cuts the throat of a topi while it is still alive. The four Mohammedans who were among our safari boys could only eat meat from an animal whose throat had been cut (and therefore killed) by a true believer.

Plate 54. Two large water buck heads from Mozambique.

Plate 55. The northern or Grevy's zebra. This variety of zebra, as large as a mule, has much finer stripes than the common zebra and lives in arid country.

Plate 56. Not a sporting shot of a waterbuck bull, but ideal if you want to mount the head for a trophy.

Plate 57. A kob in the Rift valley .The kob looks like a heavy-set impala.

Plate 58. Our pygmy guides, Hota and Borgu, at little Baranda.

Plate 59. The forest sitatunga, called "the ghost of the forest" by the pygmies, is perhaps the rarest of all African antelope.

Plate 60. The hooves of the sitatunga are shaped like skis for running on swamp vegetation and for swimming.

Plate 61. Andrew Holmberg and crew in dugout canoes returning from sitatunga hunt. Note the sitatunga in the stern. Western Tanganyika.

Plate 62. Naked Dinkas "Hey You" and "You There," bring in my Nile lechwe. "You There" has fish oil and wood ashes on his head

Plate 63. The rare Soemmering's gazelle. Northern Somalia.

Plate 64.
Speke's gazelle. Somalia.

Plate 65. The dibatag is perhaps the wildest and rarest of all the African gazelle. He inhabits the arid stretches of northern Somalia.

Plate 66. Bongo head and skin. The stripes on the bongo's hide are protective coloration in the bamboo thickets.

Plate 67. Bongo hunting in the bamboo thickets of the Aberdare Mountains in Kenya, with Theo Potgieter, white hunter, and gun-bearer.

the top of a dune. Then another group moved into sight, and another. I stretched forward with the Weatherby, and selected a heavy-horned addax in the middle of the right hand bunch.

Just behind us, Jean ran up and began to yell. *"Le troisième!* The third one!" I didn't know which the third one was, from what end or what side, but I thought I saw the addax Jean meant. He was a magnificent animal, running in about the middle of one of the groups. I shifted the sight ahead of his nose and pulled off the shot.

"Got him!" yelled Tom and I together. Bolack and I grinned sheepishly at each other. We had both downed the same animal.

Jean now began to yell in French and Arabic together. Apparently, he was trying to point out another trophy-sized addax. The addax now ran at all angles, one bunch cutting diagonally through another. Two more herds of addax had appeared to add to the melee. The range had opened considerably. I quickly picked out another heavy-horned animal on the far right. I squeezed off a shot at him just as he disappeared over a sand dune. I thought I heard the whump of the bullet. Tom had fired at another addax somewhere on his side.

Within a few seconds, there was not a living thing in that stretch of desert. Before us, in the little valley between the sand dunes, lay three dead addax. We ran forward together, shook hands all around, and thumped each other on the back. Bepoix was still exclaiming at the number of the animals. He said that in his whole lifetime he had never seen so many addax in one area. The first addax which Tom and I had shot together turned out to be the number two addax in the world's records, with a horn length of 41⅜ inches.

As we searched for the second animal I had shot, we saw other herds of addax in the distance, always to the west. We also saw vultures beginning to appear in the late afternoon sky. My second addax had gone about half a mile before he dropped. When we got to him, the vultures had already eaten his eyes and part of his face.

On the way back to the fort, the other car conked out, and Tom built most of a new carburetor out of bits and pieces. So we brought a record oryx, a record addax, and two motorized relics out of the Sahara Desert. If I ever go to the Beau Geste country again, I want Bolack to be the mechanic of the expedition. And someday I plan to learn how forty pits in the sand can locate game.

14 · Big As a Rhino, Fast As a Rabbit

"*Voilà!*" yelled Mamadu. A brown body the size of a Brahma bull crashed through the scrubby trees. Limbs and branches splintered and cracked, as the monster plowed through the growth, in a banking turn, and the black horns jerked to the side. A long tail, with a mop of fur at its tip, swung high. Then, animal and tail disappeared together. In another two seconds, all was silent, except for the buzzing of the eye bees. The path where the brown-bodied giant had fled was marked by churned-up earth and broken trees. A berserk bulldozer with a maniac driver could not have produced more damage or moved as quickly.

"Great blue-eyed blazes!" said Tom Bolack at my elbow. "Did you see that thing go!"

"Well, no, I didn't," I remarked as calmly as I could. I realized that I had gotten my rifle only half way to my shoulder when the quarry had bolted. I also realized that I had muffed my first chance at the giant eland of Central Africa.

Actually it wasn't my first chance. I had already botched two weeks of giant eland hunting in the Sudan, prior to this hunt with Tom Bolack in French Equatorial Africa. I felt like the acrobat in the circus who has just missed the flying trapeze for the second time.

I first heard of the giant eland, or Lord Derby's eland, from literary sources. On a safari into the Sudan in 1959, I had read carefully the account of hunting there written by Lt. Colonel W. Forbes, who was for many years Director of Game and Fisheries in the Sudan. Forbes, one of the old school of British sportsmen who had shot all over the world, described the giant eland as the greatest single prize of Central Africa. Forbes wrote in his account that the giant eland was the third largest land mammal of Africa, yielding rank only to the elephant and the rhino. Furthermore, Forbes stated, the giant eland is the shyest and hardest to see of all antelope.

I was intrigued by the thought of an antelope bigger than the African buffalo. I found an account by a French hunter who had weighed a giant eland and found that the carcass pushed down the scales to the 2,700 pound mark. Frankly, I couldn't believe that an animal of that size could be difficult to see. I remembered remarking to my wife Brownie, who usually accompanies me as photographer, that if any African animal is as hard to find as a Pennsylvania whitetailed deer in heavy cover, I would be happy to eat him, horn, hoof, and tail.

In the Sudan, I didn't have to eat a giant eland with his various accouterments for the simple reason that I didn't get one to eat. I spent two weeks in the western Sudan, with a game scout furnished by the new Sudanese government. This game scout and I followed various giant eland tracks for upwards of two hundred fifty miles, as near as I could figure. We walked on tiptoe for about one hundred miles of that distance, and that's a lot of tiptoe. During all of this scientific hunting, I saw the vanishing rump of one giant eland for one second. My snap shot was a clean miss. Years ago, a certain uncomplimentary friend of mine had said that I couldn't hit a bull in the posterior with a particular variety of stringed musical instrument. That fellow must have been right, I now thought ruefully, but it's a shame I had to come all the way to Africa to find out.

The sting of failure with the giant eland in the Sudan was somewhat mollified by a correspondence which I held with

Lt. Colonel Peter Molloy, recently Director of the National Parks of Tanganyika, and formerly Commissioner of Game in the Sudan. In his six years in the Sudan, Colonel Molloy and his wife had seen giant eland on only three or four occasions. On one of these, they had managed to photograph a bull eland. This picture is the only known photograph in existence of a live giant eland.

Hunters being what they are, if something is impossible to get, they want to get it. A friend of mine, Colonel Askins, had managed to bag two giant eland in French Equatorial Africa, just across the boundary from the eland country in the Sudan. We had already arranged a hunt in French Equatorial Africa with some friends of ours, Tom Bolack and his beautiful wife.

After hunting with Bepoix in the northern part of French Africa for oryx and addax, we worked our way south from the desert country into the brushlands near Fort Archambault. Bepoix had told us that he had found one remote area while he was hunting elephants, in which he had seen the tracks of a very large number of giant eland, although he had not seen any of the elusive animals themselves. Jean said that the giant eland, or *tandala* (he used the Sangoan word), was "very suspicious." I knew exactly what Jean meant. Suspicious skepticism regarding the human race was an outstanding characteristic of Lord Derby's eland, as I could testify at some length.

After a two day trip through low rolling quartzite hills covered with scraggly brush, we approached the village of Koundi. At the outskirts of the dozen or so scattered huts of Koundi, we were greeted by the chief, dressed in a long blue nightgown and a white turban. The chief of Koundi, who called himself Batal, picked out eight "volunteers" from among his villagers, to act as our porters and guides. He also furnished us with a game scout who was the only man within one hundred fifty miles who owned a gun. The game scout's normal duty was to kill cattle and wild animals affected by rinderpest. He also protected travelers who might be walking through the district. How he accomplished these onerous tasks with the gun he carried is beyond comprehension. His rifle was a 7 mm. relic, with a piece of boxwood for a stock. The barrel was corroded with several years' accumulation of rust and African spiders.

But the game scout did know the country, and that, we soon discovered, was a prime recommendation in that area. There were no streams, washes, or other major landmarks within many miles of Koundi. The low rolling ridges, and the brush-like trees with their glossy green leaves, were monotonously alike in all directions. Furthermore, the African sun, here almost on the equator, seemed to jump up into the sky early in the morning, hang at the zenith all day, and then plunge quickly into a twilightless sunset. With the sun acting in this peculiar manner, it was practically impossible to keep track of direction. Most of the time I could not have told within a quarter of the compass where Koundi or our camp might be. However, the game scout, and Bepoix's tracker, Mamadu, seemed to carry compasses in their heads, like migrating carrier pigeons.

As we set out southwestward from Koundi on our first morning of the hunt, the country was all the same. The only source of water in that whole area was a small pond, near the village, which was filled in the rainy season. A few buffalo and an elephant herd hung around here. In the low rolling hills several miles away, however, there was no sign of an animal track. The country was lifeless. We walked across fields of grotesque termite hills, each shaped like a toadstool. There were areas of bare earth, where the volcanic bedrock came so close to the surface that even the scraggly brush could not grow. But these barren patches were unmarked by the tracks of any animals.

Abruptly, some four or five miles from the village, we came upon the tracks of giant eland. We had crossed some invisible line, which I suspected marked a zone close to the village and its activities, which the shy eland never crossed. There were the tracks of small herds of females and young bulls. There were the tracks of groups of bulls, and lone bulls. Some of the signs were old, some very fresh. We found a place where a single bull had nibbled on some of the leaves of the stunted trees. The broken stalks of the leaves he had dropped still oozed sticky sap, indicating that the giant eland had been chewing there some time during the night.

Mamadu took to the track like a bird dog after a jackrabbit. He followed the single eland, as the bull had fed in a meandering course, nibbling leaves from the trees as he passed. I noticed that some of the leaves which the eland had bitten off were higher than I could reach with the barrel of my rifle. "Must have walked on stilts," I mused.

Unerringly, Mamadu led us mile after mile across the tracks of other eland, some fresh and some old. Finally, the trail seemed to straighten out for a few hundred yards. Then we jumped him. He got away like a rabbit stepped on by an airedale. There was a rush of sound, and the pounding of heavy hoofs. We saw several trees jerk violently sideways. That was all. The wind was right. We had been moving like shadows over the hard ground. If we couldn't see the eland, how could he see us? "Radar!" I remarked to Tom Bolack. "These animals use radar."

Tom did not smile. Wiping the sweat out of his eyes with his loose sleeve, he signaled up the porters and took a long drink of tepid water from the cloth-covered bottle. I noticed that Tom's shirt was drenched with sweat. His pants hung at half-mast. The temperature at that time must have been well over a hundred.

At my insistence, Bepoix told Mamadu to get on the track of the fleeing eland again. I had been through this before. We told the gunbearers and porters to stay well behind, and trail us at a distance. With our rifles ready, we crouched behind Mamadu and walked ahead. As we moved forward, we could see where the bull had been lying beneath a small tree. His hoofs had dug deep into the gravelly ground as he jumped

from his bed, and he had snapped off a tree as thick as my
leg as he ran. After three or four hundred yards, the bull had
slowed to a walk. About a mile farther on, he had stopped
once, turned, and looked back along his track.

We stopped at this place, too, and tried to wipe the eye
bees away from our faces. These contemptible little insects
are undoubtedly the most irritating forms of life in all of
Africa. The fact that the eye bees do not sting is beside the
point. Some thousands of them were constantly crawling into
our eyes to get the moisture, so our vision was continually
blurred by the dancing dots of eye bees.

It was Mamadu who first sighted the bull. Late in the afternoon, Tom and I had relaxed our vigilance in spite of ourselves. The bull eland had gone on and on. The eye bees had
buzzed on and on. Suddenly Mamadu crouched and pointed.
A brownish body with white stripes materialized out of the
green foliage. A long tail, with a knot of hairs at its tip,
whipped high. A tree snapped off. I raised my rifle blindly
and fired. Tom also shot at the same instant, leveling his gun
and pulling his trigger like a shotgunner swinging at a flushing
pheasant. I saw a bright splinter of wood jump into the air
where Tom's bullet hit. Two black twisted horns galloped off
through the trees, and were gone before I could crank in another shell.

"*Touché?*" asked Bepoix behind us. Tom and I shook our
heads together, and sagged down onto the ground. We called
up the porters with the water. They indicated that the water
was gone by turning the bottles upside down. "Maybe I can
wring out my shirt and drink that," I remarked to Tom.
Bolack just glared at me as we turned toward camp, eight or
ten miles away.

Back at our camp near Koundi, we revived ourselves with
what hunters usually revive themselves with when they come
dragging back from a disastrous hunt. The next morning, in
the comparative cool of the dawn, we were out in the giant
eland country again, with the game scout and Mamadu.

As we crossed the mysterious line which marked the edge of the giant eland country, the game scout remarked that only the month before he had discovered a giant eland which had died from rinderpest. The highly infectious rinderpest, that scourge of all hoofed animals, would wipe out all the giant eland in this whole area within a year. The game scout said he would take us to the dead carcass, as the animal had been a big bull.

Tom and I thought it would be nice to actually lay our hands on a giant eland, even if the thing had been dead for six months. But we never got there.

On the way to the deceased animal, we crossed a fresh set of tracks, a very fresh set. Mamadu mumbled in Sangoan that the tracks of this eland were so fresh that the animal had been standing in them only seconds before. A limb which the eland had ripped off still dripped sap from its broken end.

Again, Tom and I crouched on either side of Mamadu with our guns ready. Mamadu kept his eyes on the fresh tracks where the eland had been feeding among the trees. We inched forward slowly, like a bunch of marines about to flush a sniper. I tripped over one of the toadstool anthills. There was a movement ahead. A massive neck with a swinging dewlap beneath swung around. I could see white stripes, a white-marked face. I swung the Weatherby to my shoulder and fired blindly. The eland bellowed like a Brahma bull raked with a spur. He ran in a hacking gallop diagonally on my side. I cranked in another shell. I could see the great body flashing between the trees. I pulled just ahead of the chest and touched it off. I heard the plunk of the bullet. The bull bellowed and went down, sliding on his chin. We had our first eland.

My bull turned out to be a comparatively young one, with wide-spreading horns. The horns measured 43⅞ inches long, which is second or third in the record book. But no matter what the length of his horns, a giant eland is a giant in fact. For pure bulk he seems more impressive lying on the ground than a dead rhino.

Our bagging of the first giant eland had broken the spell. In the next ten days, Tom managed to get two very large old bulls to fill out his license, and I got another one, also a young bull. With all of these we found that we had to jump them, and then trail them again, two, three, or four times. The shooting is about the sportiest I have ever experienced. If you want to try something as big as a rhino and fast as a rabbit, try the Lord Derby's eland in Central Africa.

15 · Africa's Rarest and Most Beautiful Animal

A GRIM-FACED figure stood among the close-growing papyrus stems before me, his spear arm raised. The serrated barbs on the spear point were a foot from my chest. The man himself was one of the most magnificent physical specimens I had ever seen. He was close to seven feet tall, the bulging muscles of his ebony body accentuated by his nakedness. He wore only an elephant-tusk bracelet around his upper arm, and a string of beads as a crown on top of his head.

The giant, standing in the papyrus before me, might have been the cannibal king in some movie extravaganza, except that his nakedness would not get by the Hollywood censors. Certainly he would be an asset to several local basketball teams I could name. But if this was a scene from a scenario thriller, I was about to be the first victim of the plot. Curiously enough, I didn't particularly care at the moment. Fetid water reached above my waist. I couldn't possibly turn and run. To my knowledge at that time, I was surrounded by at least ten miles of unbroken swamp. I carried a .300 Weatherby by its sling on the back of my shoulder, but I made no attempt to swing the rifle under my arm into shooting position. I simply stood there in the stinking water. A flight of spurwing geese swished past over the papyrus crests above us. The dark face of the warrior before me cracked into a wide grin. He thrust forward with the barbed spear.

Why would anyone, even a dedicated hunter, get himself
into a situation like this? If the mosquitoes, crocodiles, hippos,
liver flukes, and belhartzia bugs didn't get you, the Dinkas
certainly would. The answer to this seemingly unanswerable
question is Mrs. Gray.

Hunters, at all times and in many places, have risked life
and reputation in the pursuit of something rare. When that
something rare is at the same time breath-takingly beautiful,
the pursuit of this trophy becomes an intoxicating addiction.
Such a trophy is that which is called, by both the hunters and
the Dinka tribesmen who know the animal best, "Mrs. Gray's
lechwe."

It was many years after the British army took over the
Sudan that British sportsmen discovered this animal. Hunters
from England who, in the early part of the century, had shot
everything from Marco Polo sheep in central Asia to bongo in
the most remote forests of Africa, still did not know of the
rare and beautiful animal that lived in the Nile swamps. Even
sportsmen with a penchant for seeking out difficult animals
in difficult places would never find Mrs. Gray in the "Sudd."
The Sudd, the place where the main or White Nile spreads
out into gigantic swamps covering hundreds of square miles,
is the reason that the ancient Egyptians never got through to
discover the sources of the Nile. Nobody—I repeat, nobody,
hunter or desperate fugitive—would ever enter those awful
swamps, unless he thought there was a gold mine there.

When the British administrators managed to punch a few
sketchy roads through the middle of the Anglo-Egyptian
Sudan, they discovered among other things the tribe known
as the Dinkas. Actually, there are several kinds of Dinkas, most
of them very tall, a physical attribute which they share with
several cousin Nilotic tribes. Some Dinkas keep cattle, some
hunt, and some live on fish. The Bahr el Ghazal Dinkas live
mostly on fish, which they catch around the edge of the Sudd
swamps. It was the Bahr el Ghazal Dinkas who brought in the
first Nile lechwe. The British administrators, knowing that

here was a new animal, sent the head and skin to London for observation. This magnificent antelope was named for the wife of Dr. Gray, then head of the British Museum Zoological Department. The Nile lechwe has been known as Mrs. Gray ever since.

But even the British hunters, who combed the Sudan from one end to the other to fill out their trophy collections, seldom bagged a Mrs. Gray. For one thing, Mrs. Gray is a lechwe, and lechwe are antelope that live in swamps. The red lechwe and black lechwe found in Bechuanaland and Northern Rhodesia also are swamp dwellers, but these southern relatives of the lechwe clan inhabit swamps which are pocket-handkerchief in size compared to the Sudd. The red lechwe and the black lechwe had been largely killed off before the Nile lechwe was even discovered.

If any hunter was intrepid enough to push his way into the swamps to find Mrs. Gray, the chances are that still he wouldn't see one. The Sudd swamps are probably the most impenetrable swamps in the world, in that you can't boat, swim, or walk through them. That is, no one can but a Dinka. Furthermore, even in his Nile swamp homeland, Mrs. Gray is mighty rare. The Dinkas say that the crocodiles eat the young, which reduces their number. The Dinkas themselves spear them when they can, and they are excellent spearmen. The British passed a law in the Sudan that any hunter could take but two Nile lechwe in his lifetime. Later on, they amended the law to read that a hunter could shoot only one Mrs. Gray during his entire hunting career. Few sportsmen ever had even that one chance.

Like the sitatunga and the southern lechwe tribe, the Nile lechwe has very elongated hoofs for walking or swimming in his swamp homeland. During his entire lifetime, the lechwe never comes to dry land. He escapes his enemies by running or swimming in the swamps. If necessary, he submerges all except the tip of his muzzle.

With all of these difficulties, (and probably because I had no foggy notion of what the Sudd was like) I determined to bag a Mrs. Gray lechwe. As my wife Brownie and I were in the central Sudan for several weeks in 1959, we would be close to the Sudd swamps; the rest, I imagined, should be easy. As a matter of actual record, nothing was easy. For one thing, the Sudan, at that time a new republic of but two years, presented physical difficulties of well-nigh insurmountable magnitude. As a military dictatorship overlies the republic form of government, it is virtually impossible to obtain permits, and the Sudanese are "permit happy." It is necessary, for example, to have a permit to bring a camera into the country; another is required to possess a camera; and a third permit is required for taking a picture. The procurement of hunting permits is a nightmare. Any one less dedicated than a hunter determined to get a Mrs. Gray would chuck the whole business long before the last illegible permit was in his possession. Fortunately, the Sudanese government has since straightened out a number of these difficulties; but at the time of our junket, the situation was maddening.

Half the headache of bagging a Mrs. Gray is getting on the ground, or rather the mud, of the situation; and the other half of the headache (the migraine part) is getting a look at a square inch of Mrs. Gray's hide after you get there.

Fortunately, we had the help of a Greek trader in Juba, in the southern Sudan. This man, Costi Yiaimanis, had spent most of his life in the Sudan, and had survived the changeover from the Anglo-Egyptian government of former times to the modern, hectic, and enthusiastic government of today. In those long years of ivory trading, meat hunting, and travel, Costi Yiaimanis had made friends in every tribe in the Sudan. He had learned the country, the customs, the languages, and the trails. Furthermore, Costi had a "box car." (In our native heath, in America, we would call this box car a beat-up, hand-me-down, abused, haywire, hung-together pickup truck.) In addition to the box car, Costi furnished us with a couple of camp beds, Sudanese camping equipment, a few cans of preserved food left over from the British army invasion of 1898, and four native boys, including one called the "driver." It must be confessed that the latter did indeed sit behind the wheel of the box car. Outside of this position, any resemblance to a driver was purely illusory. I have seen locoed mustangs who had better sense, better timing, and a better idea of speed and direction than this Sudanese maniac. The only reason that we weren't killed in the first miles of our journey after Mrs. Gray is that you simply can't go that fast on a Sudanese road. Fortunately, Costi had furnished us with a government game scout, who was a Zande. Zandes used to be cannibals, and some still are. This game scout, Rihani by name, came from the southern Sudan, and previously had visited the edge of the Sudd swamps with some British, although he had never seen a Mrs. Gray lechwe. At least, Rihani knew trails in that direction, although usually the driver paid little attention.

We headed northwestward from Juba, toward a fringe of the Sudd swamps called Lake Nyubor. Lake Nyubor is actually an old bed of the Nile, where the annual overflow fills a vast depression. As the Nile recedes, its tributary, the Lau River, gradually dries to a trickle, which leaves Nyubor a lake of sorts, with vast stretches of papyrus swamp round about. Between Nyubor and the main Nile, the swamp never dries out, though it does recede to about waist depth in the driest season. One of the British game commissioners had discovered that a herd of lechwe stayed in the Nyubor swamps even after the flood season. Lake Nyubor, therefore, is the best bet—if there can be any best bet—to get a glimpse of Mrs. Gray.

The British commissioner who was head of game supervision in the Sudan, Lt. Colonel Peter Molloy, spent some ten years in the area. Only twice during this time did he and his photographer wife manage to get pictures of Mrs. Gray. We had read Colonel Molloy's account of the matter, and also corresponded with him, but even his admonitions of "ravenous mosquitoes" and "endless miles of waist deep water" did not prepare us for what we found.

Frankly, we were apprehensive about the Dinka tribesmen. We met our first group of Agar Dinkas a few miles (and a whole day's travel) from Lake Nyubor. We had just been arrested by a Sudanese military patrol. We had forty permits in our possession, but it developed we should have had forty-one. It didn't restore our confidence when the native sergeant soldier held our travel permit upside down as he squinted at it with a blank expression. Several of the soldiers were Dinkas. They were the fiercest, biggest, most muscular men we had ever seen. Fortunately, we managed to get out of arrest by acting stupid, which was no great effort. I am sure that the native sergeant thought that we were Britishers who had somehow been left over from the former regime.

When we stopped at our first Dinka village, people crowded around us as though we were a new species of animal. Most of the men towered over us, and even the women were close to six feet in height. They giggled, pinched our clothes, and went through the box car to see what the ridiculous foreigners had with them. We found it a bit difficult to act nonchalant in the middle of a herd of male and female giants, every one of whom was stark, staring naked. It was days before we got used to it. Once we did get acquainted with the Dinkas, however, we liked them tremendously. We found them intelligent, inquisitive, proud, and with an excellent sense of humor. I might add that the jokes were mostly on us. As Rihani, our game scout, could not talk the Dinka language, we had little verbal communication. The Dinkas only understood one word. This was "Missygray," which they pronounced as one word.

As we approached the great depression which is Lake Nyubor, the brushland began to fall away and finally became open toich. The toich is the flat plain which surrounds the Sudd swamps. During the period of high water, even the toich is flooded, but at that time, late in February, it was dry. A few herds of Dinka cattle grazed on the toich. As we bounced laboriously over the dry hippo tracks which pockmarked the toich, we headed toward a Dinka village perched on a knoll at the very edge of the main swamps. Here, countless generations of Dinkas had built up a low mound of fish bones, garbage, and dirt, so that the swamp ground was only spongy, instead of being downright soupy. On this precarious hummock perched the little, round, grass-topped houses of perhaps a hundred Dinkas. There was also a somewhat larger "rest house," which had been built there years before by the intrepid British. The rest house had been taken over by the Dinkas, but they cheerfully moved out to accommodate us when we arrived. Unfortunately, a large flock of outsize bats, hanging in the thatch under the roof, stayed on. It was hard to tell, during our brief stay in the rest house, whether the noise of the mosquitoes or the noise of guano dropping from the roof was more disturbing. Colonel Molloy, who had stayed here on several occasions to observe Mrs. Grays, received our highest words of praise.

Only one of our boys could talk a bare smattering of English, and the others represented four different Sudanese tribes, mostly from the southernmost Sudan. Somehow, during the first evening of conviviality with the Dinkas at the village, translated through half a dozen intermediate tongues, our boys managed to get some information for us about Mrs. Gray. The information was not good.

The Dinkas said there were very few Mrs. Grays left in the Nyubor part of the Sudd. "Someone has killed them," they said guilelessly. As I found some lechwe horns on the stinking refuse piles at the edge of the village, I had little doubt who the killers were. After the British government left, the Dinkas had speared lechwe whenever they caught the animals at a disadvantage. As meat was hard to come by, they could not be blamed too much.

The Dinkas had a flotilla of dugout canoes pulled up in front of the village. These canoes are made of the hollowed-out trunks of the doleib palm. With them, the Dinka fishermen pole up and down the semi-open water of the lake, in that

part which was the old river channel. Beyond the open channel, where the papyrus begins, even the dugout canoes cannot get through.

The first day after our arrival we paid a couple of Dinka
fishermen to take us in one of these treacherous dugouts to
the end of the open water, where we might begin to look for
lechwe. Almost immediately we regretted this plan. For one
thing, if you hiccup in a palm log dugout, you overturn it. As
far as the Dinkas were concerned, this was great fun. For a
batch of cameras and a gun, I didn't think it funny at all.
Furthermore, the treacherous little craft did not seem to get
us to the heart of the business anyway. When we poled as
far as we could eastward into the main swamp, the canoe
could only go a short distance up the hippo paths from the
open water. Then, when we stepped out of the dugout, which
was an acrobatic feat in itself, we were standing up to our
waists in stinking, weed-infested water. During two days of
this kind of frustrating going, we got only a glimpse of a
single female lechwe at the edge of the papyrus. In the same
time, however, we learned a lot about Dinkas, even if our
knowledge of the Nile lechwe was not increased at all.

Because of these difficulties, and also because of the bats in
the belfry of the Dinka rest house, we determined to move
down the edge of the toich, four or five miles eastward. From
this vantage point, I expected I would be able to walk into the
swamps where the lechwes were. The major difficulty in moving camp was that our Sudanese boys didn't want to leave the
Dinkas. As each of our lads possessed some remnant of store
clothing, or a pair of out-at-the-heel tennis shoes, this made
them city slickers in the eyes of the Dinka maidens. Kamun,
the driver, was even more difficult than usual, which is mighty
difficult. He thought of a thousand reasons why we should
stay in the bat-infested, stinking Dinka village. I drove the box
car myself, along the edge of the toich where the ground was
dry. As soon as we got out of sight of the thatched huts of
our Dinka friends, we began to pass through small herds of

tiang coming down to the edge of the swamp to drink. As we jounced along over the awful pockmarks left by wallowing hippos when the toich was mud, herds of reed buck and beautiful kob skittered off before us into the high grass along the edge of the water. We made camp under the last tree, which marked the periphery of what is laughingly called "dry ground" in this part of the Sudan. That evening I shot a couple of kob so we would have meat during the serious business of finding a Mrs. Gray.

The echo of the shot had not died away before fifteen Dinkas appeared to help us. They had, with commendable courtesy, dressed themselves in suits—a process which consisted of smearing fish oil on their bodies, and then sprinkling the stinking mess with cow dung ash. Designs were smeared in the ashes with their finger tips, in the mode of the day. Three or four Dinka women insisted on helping Brownie as she skinned out the capes of a kob and a reed buck. By this time, both of us were so inured to nakedness that we would have started up in amazement if any one had shown up at our camp wearing so much as a Bikini.

Fortunately, in the contingent of Dinkas were two stalwart fellows who, I gathered, were the hunters of the village. I never did learn their names, so I gave them a couple of titles. The shorter one, a stocky lad of about six feet two, I called "Hey You." His taller companion I gave the title of "You There." Both of my guides were very much pleased with their elegant names, and I have no doubt that they are still using them. These two guides, as well as most of the Dinka population, simply moved with us to our new encampment, and stayed there. Camping arrangements were comparatively simple. At night they fell back into the dry grass and were asleep when they hit the ground. Apparently the voracious Nile mosquitoes don't like Dinka blood; but they sure do enjoy a tender American. Even with the well-constructed mosquito net which Costi had loaned us, four or five of the brutes always managed to get inside somehow, and they made the night hideous with their droning and whining.

I must confess that, even with all of these drawbacks, the edge of the Sudd is a thrilling place. In the early morning, scattered herds of tiang, kob, wart hogs, and baboons filtered past our camp to drink. Hippos, moving into the swamp from their night feeding on the toich, disturbed thousands of ducks and geese. The knob-nosed Nile and spurwing geese circled back and forth over the tips of the papyrus in screaming masses. Especially numerous were flocks of whistling teal, which alighted and then circled nervously over the small ponds of open water, where the tiang and kob disturbed them. Colonel Molloy had described this as the best duck and goose shooting country in Africa. But there were no such pleasures for us. I was somewhat apprehensive that the three or four rifle shots of the evening before might have driven any Mrs. Gray in the vicinity even deeper into the swamps. I need not have worried.

With my two guides, Hey You and You There, I started off at dawn into the Sudd. Rihani, the game scout, insisted upon going along, in spite of the fact that I could see with half an eye that his enthusiasm for the problem was at an all-time low. Being a Zande, he had no use for swamps; but he considered that his mission was to guard me from the dangers of the Sudd, and I am sure he considered the Dinkas themselves the major hazard.

We started off down a cattle and game trail across the toich. For perhaps a mile, we walked through grasslands with the water gradually getting deeper around our ankles. Fires started by the Dinkas had burned great patches of the dry grass above the water. In the mud I could see the tracks of tiang and hippo, but no sign of the elongated hoofprints of Mrs. Gray.

By the time we reached the papyrus, we were walking in water just above our knees. The papyrus was a sign that the ground here never dries, even in the long-enduring drought season. Papyrus is a beautiful plant. It feathers out, perhaps twelve feet tall, in a burst of fine spiderweb fronds which glint in the early morning sunlight, like thousands of soap bubbles throwing the spectrum of the sun in all directions. After a few hours of slogging through papyrus stems, the illusion of beauty is gone. The papyrus becomes a green hell of harsh rasping stalks, tripping nodes beneath the water, and an impenetrable, endless mass of stems before the eye. I soon found why Dinkas grow so tall. They have to. The short ones were drowned long ago, or eaten off above the water line by mosquitoes. My Dinka guides, with their long legs, slipped along like storks. Rihani and I were half swimming most of the time.

Worst of all were the hippo trails. The bulky bodies of the river pigs had plowed great furrows through the papyrus. Their pudgy feet had tramped out the mud beneath to a depth of five or six feet, and crossing these hippo canals became a major feat, as I was trying to keep my rifle and camera reasonably dry. I didn't succeed. Even at that, we might have followed the hippo trails, if they had led in the right direction. The hippos moved during the day into the middle of the lake, several miles to the west, near the Dinka village. We were heading northeastward, crossing all the hippo channels at right angles. Insomuch as Hey You and You There were very purposeful about their direction, I hoped that they were taking me to some place in the heart of the Sudd, where Mrs. Gray would abound.

As it was, the two Dinkas spent most of their time pulling Rihani and me out of hippo mudholes. Fortunately, they thought this was very funny. As I wiped green slime from my camera, or poured water out of my gun barrel, their good humor rose to new heights.

I had been doing a good deal of walking after buffalo and other kinds of game, even before we came to Lake Nyubor. I thought I was in fairly good shape. But even before noon of the first day in the swamps, I was tiring fast. We ate a romantic little picnic lunch of cold kob meat, while we stood up in the water. While Rihani and I munched glumly, and slapped at mosquitoes, the two Dinkas frisked around like a couple of kids. To use up part of their excess energy, they speared fish in a hippo channel just ahead. As the water is murky, the spearmen cannot see the quarry. The Dinkas pranced up and down the hippo canal, disturbing the matted papyrus roots with their feet. When they saw a swirl in the dark water, they made a stab at it with their barbed spear. Hey You soon transfixed a large tilapia, which looks like a bass. He made a sling of papyrus fiber, and hung the fish over his back. Apparently this was to be their meal when we camped that night in the swamp.

Camped in the swamp! I had heard of people sleeping standing up, but never in three feet of water. The thought of my little camp bed back there on the toich, with only four or five voracious mosquitoes inside the netting, made me wriggle with delightful anticipation.

Early in the afternoon, we burst through the endless papyrus into an open, swampy meadow. Here the water was only a foot or so in depth, and ambatch grass stood above the water here and there in soggy hummocks. I gathered from the action of the Dinkas that this was the place where Mrs. Gray came to feed. As we walked around the edge of the swampy clearing, I saw dollops of dung on the matted grass. No other animal but a lechwe could exist in such a place.

For perhaps two hours, we circled around the edge of the swamp meadow in the midst of the Sudd. Although the whole area was only half a mile across, we could see very little of it at a time. Our vantage point was so low that we could not look over even the scattered clumps of ambatch grass, a hundred yards or so distant. My two Dinka friends, with their eyes a foot or so above my own, could see a lot more.

You There suddenly grabbed my arm and pointed with his spear. I could see nothing. We moved forward at a crouch. I stepped on top of a grass hummock. In the distance, I could see a flick of motion. I focused the binoculars on it. It was a brownish animal, with a white tail that jerked back and forth with windshield-wiper regularity. The animal had no horns. Hey You nudged me, and held up one hand with his fingers widespread. I looked again. I could see another, and then another animal. Hey You was better with his unaided eyesight than I was with a pair of 8 x 30 binoculars. There were indeed five Mrs. Grays. There wasn't a horn in the bunch. (The female Mrs. Gray is hornless.) But even with this disappointment, I thrilled at the movement of the animals as they walked out of the green wall of papyrus, and began to feed on the tender shoots of ambatch grass. I could see in the glass, as the lechwe raised their feet, that their hoofs were elongated like sled-runners. One of the larger lechwe playfully ran forward a few steps. She looked like she was walking on the tips of the grass stems. To my certain knowledge, the water at the edge of the papyrus was two or three feet deep.

We watched the herd of female lechwe for perhaps ten minutes. I was amazed at the grace of the animals: the way they held their heads, and handled their slim feet with quick running steps as they moved out into the meadow. Only Hey You and You There seemed to be downhearted. This was unusual, as all day long they had been as happy as a couple of lobsters in mating season. Now they shook their heads sadly, and turned to go. I could only deduce that if female Mrs. Grays were in the meadow, then there would be no bulls. The only good thing I could see about the business was that my two Dinka friends had apparently given up the idea of camping in the swamp and dining in a regal manner off raw fish while we stood up all night in the water.

How we ever got out of the swamp I will never know. It was dark, with the sudden African lack of twilight, long before we had slogged our way through the four or five miles of papyrus. I had ceased trying to keep the camera dry or my gun above water. The belt of half-rotten papyrus stems that collected in front of my thighs and waist grew bigger and bigger. I didn't even jerk it away. Somehow, by starlight, we came out on the toich. The pinpoint of light which was our campfire looked like a beacon of hope. I don't even remember eating or rolling onto my cot.

It was no surprise then, in the morning, when I couldn't remember getting dressed. I found that my legs were badly swollen, and my shins cut in a hundred places by the saw-tooth edge of the ambatch grass. But no matter. With a hearty breakfast and a rising sun, what hunter loses hope? I gathered that my two Dinka friends had another idea for Mrs. Gray. Hey You and You There were as fresh as two daisies covered with morning dew. I gathered from their grins, and their slapping each other on the back, that they were reenacting for their friends' benefit the trip of the afternoon before, when the white man had gone head first into a hippo channel, and come up blowing muddy water from every opening.

Somehow we started off. The only one less enthusiastic than myself was Rihani. (At least we knew what to expect.) We headed easterly, along the edge of the toich, for perhaps three or four miles, and then plunged into the papyrus. We continued to head eastward, apparently to strike a spot six or eight miles distant from where we had been the day before. Long before noon, I had become tired, hot, and dry. I had a small canteen, and this was already empty. I noticed that the Dinkas drank water in the swamp only in the places where lotus lillies grew. Here and there, apparently, springs or seeps welled up from the bottom, and kept the water com-paratively fresh. I knew that the Nile, and all of its tributaries, are full of liver flukes, belhartzia bugs, and heaven knows what else. But the dangers of these things are notions of civilized man. Besides, you can't even see them—unless you look closely. So, at the next lotus-marked pool, I drank with the Dinkas.

Some time along in the morning, Hey You and You There had dropped off to the side to spear a fish they had seen swirl. Splashing ahead, I happened to look up. There stood a giant of a man. He was motionless facing me. He raised his right arm. He cocked his elbow. The barbed spear in his hand was level at my chest. This was it! I was going to be spitted by a Dinka, and I didn't even care.

The strange Dinka spearman apparently thought the look of woe on my face was the aspect of a confirmed coward. He thrust forward with his spear, and stuck it into the water between my feet. He broke into gales of laughter. He would have rolled on the ground, only there was no ground. So he hung onto the papyrus stems. Soon Hey You and You There joined in the general fun. It was a good joke, being in the middle of an endless swamp, dying of exhaustion, and undoubtedly being eaten from the inside by liver flukes and loathsome parasites, and being scared to death by a strange giant with a spear.

A few hundred yards farther on, we came to a muddy hummock in the swamp. Four Dinka families were perched on this hump of mud, in four little grass huts. Racks of dried fish were half-obscured by the smoke of wet wood fires. Three women and half a dozen scraggly children stared at us in amazement. The whole village and its dozen or so occupants, were on a piece of ground not fifty feet across. How the hummock came to be there in the first place, or how the Dinkas had ever found it, I'll never know.

The joker who was going to spear me apparently told Hey You and You There where Mrs. Gray lurked in the swamps beyond the little village. We soon started off again. Early in the afternoon, we came out into another ambatch meadow, somewhat smaller than the one we had seen before. Again the faint trails in the grass and the dollops of dung showed that the swamp-dwelling antelope had been there. But the dung was old, the trails were unused.

We waited until late evening, on the off-chance that a Mrs. Gray would appear. Even Hey You and You There seemed dispirited. They made motions above their heads, in the outline of the lyre-shaped horns of the bull lechwe. Then they

looked down at their feet, and made long faces. They were
trying to tell me that Mrs. Gray would not come there.

So be it! The hunt was a bust. I knew that I did not have
another day's hunting left in me—not in that swamp. My
legs were cut to ribbons by the sawgrass, but as they were
numb with weariness anyway, I didn't even notice. I moved
mechanically as we turned back towards the little fishing village in the middle of the swamp. Lifting each sodden foot up
and over the clods of papyrus became an impossible feat. I
stumbled frequently, but no matter. Drowning would be a
welcome end.

We passed the little village. Again the women and children
eyed us solemnly. I scarcely noticed the clouds of mosquitoes,
as thick as smoke around the piles of fish guts and fish bones
at the edge of the water. We splashed on. Just beyond the
village, I tripped, and fell into a hippo channel. Hey You
had to pull me out by the seat of my pants. Had it not been
for him, I think I would have floated face down, and just
stayed there. Hey You grinned at me as I blew water out of
my mouth. The stuff tasted like hippopotamus dung.

As I got the water out of my ears, I heard some one yelling.
The voice was off in the distance. Hey You and You There
whistled in reply. We splashed on. I wasn't interested. If
the Dinkas wanted to meet friends in the middle of the swamp,
they could meet friends and be damned to them. I didn't even
care if I got lost. I just plain didn't care.

Running towards us was the joker I had encountered earlier,
the head of the Dinka fishing village. I scarcely noticed that
he was running through papyrus and water where I could
scarcely move my legs. "I wonder how they bury their dead
under these circumstances," I muttered to myself. "Would
it be burial at sea technique, or a simple civil ceremony?"

The newcomer was talking in low tones to Hey You. He
made the sign of horns over his head, and pointed back behind him. Hey You turned to me, and made the sign of horns
again. He pointed to my gun. They had seen a lechwe. Well,

what if they had? I couldn't get to the place if the lechwe was covered with hundred dollar bills.

They pointed roughly in the direction of camp, to the west. That was the only reason that I went along with the idea. The three Dinkas frolicked along in front of us, as though we had not already come fifteen miles through the awfullest going in the whole of Africa. The Dinkas were obviously irked by my slow progress; even Rihani looked as though he would never make it. It appeared there was going to be a double burial somewhere in that endless papyrus.

By twilight, we had made only a couple of miles. At least it was cooler. Funnyface had waltzed off into the papyrus, and disappeared for ten minutes. He came back grinning broadly, again pointing behind him. I was a little excited by his infectious enthusiasm. I quickened my pace from the gait of a string-haltered sloth to a snail's gallop. The three Dinkas disappeared again, and then came back to get me. With a Dinka at each elbow, we somehow moved forward. The water was still waist deep. We broke through a fringe of papyrus.

There was a small opening. It was an ambatch meadow, perhaps a hundred yards across. On the far side, I saw the outline of an animal's head. At the sound of our splashing steps, the head moved upward. Two long, double-curved horns arched back over his withers. He turned and looked full at us. To both sides were other animals and other horns. Half a dozen Mrs. Grays stood at the edge of the papyrus. Most of the animals were half invisible. The one in the center had the longest horns. I threw the Weatherby to my shoulder. There was water on the telescopic sight. I blew off the drops. It was still dreamy, and the light was poor. The crosshairs settled on the base of the bull's throat, then jerked away to the side. My exhausted arms could not hold the rifle still. As the crosshairs moved past the bull's chest I jerked off the shot. I did not even bolt in another shell. I was done.

At the clap of the shot every lechwe disappeared, as though jerked into the papyrus from behind. The Dinkas raced forward a few steps, then stood glumly. I had missed. I had seen my first and last Mrs. Gray.

I sat down heavily in the water. I heard Rihani sink down behind me. There was a splash over across the clearing. A plume of water shot up above the tips of the papyrus. Some frantic animal had made a gigantic leap there. The three Dinkas ran forward and disappeared. There was a shout, and then another. They came through the papyrus, carrying the bull on their shoulders.

It was a triumphant procession that came out of the papyrus onto the toich, just at dark. One of the Dinkas had raced ahead to carry the news to camp. Brownie had driven the box car along the edge of the toich, to save us a mile or two walk. When we got back to camp, I remember only measuring the horns of the lechwe. Thirty two and a half inches.

Colonel Molloy tells me that at certain dry seasons, when the swamp water is low, Mrs. Grays come out to the edge of the toich, and may occasionally be seen there. Several British sportsmen have bagged a Mrs. Gray in this way. As far as I am concerned, the law which states that a hunter may take only one Mrs. Gray during his lifetime, is entirely unnecessary. One Mrs. Gray is enough.

16 · *Rare African Trophy*

THE LWANGWA SWAMP stretched before us to the horizon. Our frail, palm-log dugout nosed along a watery trail, through the giant lotus leaves. Only minutes before, a bull hippo had made this swath through the swamp vegetation, as he crashed away before us. But it was impossible to move in this morass without following hippo trails. Just ahead, the greenish-yellow snout of a large crocodile surfaced on the murky water. The croc looked at us with a cold eye, then sank without a ripple.

Find game in this stinking swamp? Andrew Holmberg, our white hunter, must have been crazy. More likely we'd find a watery grave. We'd come close to it already. If hippos or crocs didn't get us, malaria undoubtedly would. Even the natives were unfriendly.

Holmberg had promised us a sporting chance to bag one of the rarest trophies in Africa. In fairness, I must say I'd asked him, "What game in East Africa is hardest to get, and how do we go about getting it?"

At the time, we were sitting on the shady veranda of the Norfolk Hotel in Nairobi, planning our two months' safari. It was to be an ordinary safari in most respects but, since I had waited twenty years for the chance to hunt in Africa, I felt I should get at least one unusual trophy.

"The bongo is considered the rarest by some," Andrew replied, having toyed with his glass for some moments before answering. "The bongo lives in the heavy forests of the Congo, and in the bamboo belt high on these East African mountains. Mighty few bongo have been taken."

"Let's try for a bongo," I said quickly.

Andrew smiled in his usual quiet way. "So far as I am concerned, I know one that will beat the bongo. Not more than ten or a dozen specimens have been taken by sportsmen in the past twenty-five years. If you're so eager, let's get a sitatunga."

So it was decided. I confess I had never even heard of a sitatunga, so I sneaked over to the library near the hotel and looked it up. "Handsome, swamp-dwelling antelope with spiral horns," the book said. Even some of the sportsmen who hang around the bar in the New Stanley Hotel in Nairobi had never heard of a sitatunga. Most of my friends there thought I was crazy, and said so frankly. They were right.

Brownie and I, with a modest-size outfit, consisting of a safari car and a truck, started off in a southwesterly direction from Nairobi. We then swung south to Tabora in western Tanganyika.

At Tabora we added another native to our group of twelve safari boys. This man, a Bantu, had come from the great swamp area of western Tanganyika. Here the Lwangwa and Mkombo rivers unite to form a swampland of five thousand square miles. Andrew had once hunted elephants on the fringe of this country, and he had made a few friends there. We found out from the commissioner of the Tabora District that, since this was the dry season of late August, our safari car could probably make it as far as the Bantu village on the edge of the swamp.

Beyond Tabora, we passed through a tsetse-fly control station, then were on our own. A fairly passable elephant trail had been partially cleared by a Hindu who hauled supplies to his small store, which administered to the wants of the natives.

Our sitatunga search almost ended before it began. As we rounded a bend in the trail, we found ourselves in the middle of a raging forest fire. The scattered trees and the waist-high grass burned like gasoline. We quickly stopped the car and truck, and cleared a space around them. As we worked frantically to keep the fire from the vehicles, duikers, reedbucks, and other smaller antelope rushed past us. A terrified mongoose crouched near our feet.

Eventually, the fire burned its way past us, and we resumed our trek. Farther on, elephants had blocked our progress by pulling down trees across the trail. Several times we could hear herds of the beasts, crashing and trumpeting in the distance.

Finally, we arrived at the Bantu village, a squalid, fly-buzzing place. The Bantus raise rice along the margin of the swamp, and also fish in the deeper water. The fish are much like our black bass, and weigh about two or three pounds. They will rise to a fly, and are delicious eating.

For their fishing, the natives make canoes by hollowing out trunks of palm trees. They do the hollowing with the iron tools that the Bantus have made since prehistoric times. Since the palms have pithy interiors, the ends of the dugouts aren't solid, and have to be plugged with wood and resinous pitch. The plugs are constantly on the verge of coming out.

Normally the Bantus stand in these treacherous craft, and push them along with an eighteen-foot pole. Even when we sat down in one of the dugouts, and held on with both hands, we found it about as stable as balancing on one foot on the top of a flagpole. When we actually went out for our hunt, we could man only four of these dugouts, and they were the four best ones.

But the stability of the canoes became an academic matter. The Bantus weren't going to take us far out into the great swamp, they said.

"The devil people, bwana, the devil people live out there," one of the natives said, pointing a dirty finger out over the swamp.

"He means the natives who live on the island in the swamp," Andrew explained. "The Bantus are scared to death of them, since they used to raid this village, and kill and eat the people."

After a day of haranguing, we finally persuaded a group of Bantu men to take the four serviceable dugouts along the edge of the swamp, to a small point of land about a mile from the village. Since it was the only approximately dry ground in the vicinity, we pitched our tents there. Hippos had been accustomed to come out of the swamp at this point, and the trails they left created a mooring area for the canoes.

We devoted the next three days to careful preparations for our invasion of the swamp. We took inner tubes from the safari car's wheels, and put them in each of the canoes, so that if the tippy things capsized, we would at least have a fighting chance.

We prepared large pieces of canvas to use as a floor for the camp we intended to make deep in the swamp. There are islands of vegetation at many places in the swamp. They are not solid ground, but interlaced masses of papyrus, lotus, and other plants, so thickly grown together that they form floating islands. We planned to use one of these as a base from which to bag a sitatunga.

The only catch was that we couldn't get native boatmen to go that far out in the swamp. Only one, Hamisi, was willing. He was the one we'd brought from Tabora. Hamisi had such confidence in us that he agreed to act as guide, although he had never been as far in the swamp as we hoped to go.

While the canoes were being prepared, we hunted near camp. The country teemed with game. In several savannas, along the edge of the swamp grass, reedbucks were common. These graceful little animals normally will not stand when danger is near; they squat in the grass, like crouching pheasants. We found the best way to locate them was to climb trees at the edges of open, grassy places. From such vantage points, it was easy to spot bucks with good horns.

The glades were also full of wart hogs, duikers, bushbucks, waterbucks, and greater and lesser kudu. We saw a very fine greater kudu bull just back of our camp.

But our sights were set for a sitatunga, which Andrew said lived out beyond the papyrus clumps where the hippos boomed and splashed at night.

Andrew had given us a description of this rare antelope, a close relative of the bushbuck and the kudu, and also told us something of its habits. Of medium size—standing about forty inches at the withers and weighing two hundred to two hundred fifty pounds, it is especially distinguished by its extremely elongated hoofs, which are well adapted to swimming, and to running over spongy swamp vegetation. The animal is a powerful swimmer. When pursued, it often will submerge itself up to the nostrils in water. The male sitatunga has spiral horns, while the females are hornless. The record horn length for East Africa is twenty-seven inches. The animal is covered with long, coarse hair, usually dark yellowish-brown in color, which protects it against insects.

The Bantu villagers showed us the skull and horns of a sitatunga which had been caught in one of their fishnets and drowned. It seemed likely that this was as close as we would ever get to one, for my resolution was weakening. In the daytime, it was the flies; at night, the mosquitoes. My wife and I had the usual mosquito bars fastened to the inside of our tent, forming something which resembled a tent within a tent. But seemingly tens of thousands of the droning insects, moving in off the swamp, would get between the wall of the tent and the mosquito netting. In this confined space, their humming chorus sounded like a formation of bombing planes overhead. We couldn't sleep for it. We used insect repellent constantly, and took antimalaria pills once a day. But our safari boys were being chewed alive.

The problem raised by the refusal of the Bantu boatmen—other than Hamisi—to man our canoes was a grave one. Andrew and I visited the Bantu village, and gave a pound note to the Hindu who ran the squalid little store, hoping he would wield enough influence to get boatmen for us. It was money wasted. Some natives said there were bull hippos in the swamp that would attack any canoe that came near them. Others complained that crocodiles came out on the floating islands at night, and no man would be safe there after dark. But mainly they were afraid of the inhabitants of the island.

In desperation, Andrew called for "volunteers" from our own safari group. He did it by simply pointing to four of the boys. And that was that.

Most of our boys were Masais. A few were Wakambas, and some Somalis. In their native areas, none ever got closer to water than when they stretched out on their bellies to drink from some slime-covered waterhole. They were appalled at the idea of going out in a frail canoe, on a swamp so vast they couldn't see the other side of it. Even Ngoro, our head gun-bearer, who had killed a lion single-handed with his long-bladed spear, seemed to turn pale at the prospect.

It was a sorry company that started out into the swamp early the next morning. Hamisi tried to instruct the others in poling the craft through the narrow hippo paths, between the walls of rank-growing vegetation. We were able to take very little equipment with us. I could see that Andrew was worried.

"It will be a thin camp," he muttered, as he settled in the bow of one of the dugouts. "That is, if we ever get far enough to camp."

I saw what he meant. By the time we had loaded a little food and the canvas strips we intended to use as a floor for the camp, we could carry little else. No beds. No comfortable tents. I thought of what the mosquitoes would do to us as soon as the first shadows of evening stretched across the swamp, and shuddered. No wonder the sitatunga is rarely taken by sportsmen!

We clutched the inner tubes as we pushed into the first lakelike pool in the swamp. The safari boys seemed to gain a little confidence. No one had capsized. I remember thinking that if we did, it would be almost as unpleasant having a crocodile chew off our legs as we dangled helplessly in the tubes, as it would to be bitten in half immediately, *without* the tubes. Nobody could swim more than a few strokes through that yellowish, plant-choked water.

But there were compensations. Lotus, with leaves a yard across, covered places where the water was comparatively open, and their blossoms made every patch a flowering garden. Orchidlike blossoms clung to the dark masses of entwined papyrus and feathery-topped reeds. Water birds were everywhere. In the distance, thousands of knob-nosed geese glinted their metallic gleam, and Egyptian geese circled in cackling masses over the tops of the papyrus. There were a dozen kinds of ducks. Other water birds, with spiderlike feet, trotted over the tops of the lotus leaves. These were jacanas, much like our rails of North America, and just as good eating.

By late afternoon, Brownie had grown tired of photographing flowers and geese, and all of us were wondering how we were going to pass the night in this strange place. Long before dark, clouds of mosquitoes began to appear, all undoubtedly loaded with malaria. I'm sure each one of us wanted to turn back and give the whole thing up, but none wanted to be the first to chicken out.

Finally, Andrew signaled to Hamisi, in whose canoe I was riding, to bring the other dugouts alongside. It was no go. We were licked.

Hamisi skillfully pulled the dugout forward, into a pond-like opening. Just ahead lay one of the matted islands, which had become more frequent the deeper we went into the swamp. In the comparatively open water in front of the island, we could maneuver our canoes around, and turn back through the narrow hippo trail along which we'd just come. Andrew signaled Hamisi to come closer.

Hamisi was standing in the stern, using his pole to push us forward from clump to clump of vegetation. But the dugout had stopped its forward motion and was drifting slowly. We were not going toward where Andrew still beckoned us.

"*Bwana,*" Hamisi said to me softly. "*Bwana, bunduki.*"

From my seat in the bow, I turned my head cautiously to look over my shoulder. There was Hamisi, standing in the stern, still as a statue, pointing with desperate urgency. I turned quickly. I could see nothing but a wall of branching papyrus stems. Two twisted sticks moved above the papyrus tops, and the late sun glinted white on their tips. Sticks? But there were no sticks here. They must be horns! Hamisi gently poled the dugout a few feet nearer, and then I saw what he was pointing at.

My first view of live sitatungas was sudden and unbelievable. There were three of them, two females and a bull. The bull stared straight at me, his head erect, and a female stood on either side, also staring.

"*Bunduki,*" Hamisi whispered again. "The gun." The Weatherby .300 lay in the canoe, on top of a pile of food just behind me. I twisted around, and the dugout rocked dangerously. My feet and legs had long ago gone to sleep from being in such a cramped position in the bottom of the boat. My fingers touched the rifle, and I grabbed it, swung it around, and bolted a shell into the chamber.

One of the female sitatungas turned, and trotted across the swamp on fantastically long hoofs. The other turned to run, but the bull stood and stared. I couldn't get the scope on him. The rifle stuck out at an awkward angle. Frantically, I motioned to Hamisi to twist the canoe a little, since I couldn't turn my body. At that, the bull flipped his tail and whirled around, and I saw his moving shoulder in the scope. I fired. As the rifle kicked back hard, the dugout rocked, and Hamisi thrust out his pole to keep us from capsizing. The sitatunga disappeared through the papyrus. I had made a clean miss, and I slumped forward against the bow in bitter disappointment.

But there was a movement beyond the papyrus stems, and through a narrow opening I saw one of the female sitatungas splashing along. She seemed to be running on the surface of the water. The other female appeared for an instant, and then the bull. I pulled the crosshairs of the sight just forward of his shoulders, and pressed the trigger. The bull disappeared in a splash of yellow water.

"*Mazuri, mazuri sana*," yelled Hamisi in a screeching shout. He was prancing up and down the length of the canoe, brandishing his pole like a tightrope walker.

Andrew came up in his canoe. He started to get to his knees, then thought better of it.

"Hamisi says the sitatunga is dead," he said.

The jubilant Hamisi had already poled our dugout alongside the floating island. He jumped out on the matted roots, and the whole mass sank and waved beneath his weight. He moved away rapidly, but reappeared in a moment, dragging the body of the bull sitatunga over the reeds.

The animal closely fitted the descriptions of sitatungas I'd heard and read about, except that its face was handsomer than I'd expected it to be. There were white markings on both cheeks, and on the bridge of the nose; the ears were rimmed with white; and there were also two prominent white patches on the chocolate-colored throat. The bull's horns, which we measured later, were nineteen inches long—far from a record, but that didn't bother me. I was delighted with the trophy, and so was Andrew.

It was nearly dark by the time our canoes pulled up the hippo trails which led to our camp. Even the mosquitoes didn't seem quite so bad, when other members of the safari crowded around to congratulate us on the sitatunga and to admire the animal.

That night, sitting by the fire, the safari boys played their homemade guitars, and made up a song about the great sita-

tunga hunt. They sang of the bwana and brave memsahib,
who had dared the hippo and the crocodile to shoot the sitatunga.

As the mosquitoes closed in later that night, I didn't feel
so brave. But I knew for a certainty why the sitatunga is considered to be one of Africa's rarest trophies.

17 · Ghost of the Forest

THE BABINGAS of the Bangui country called it a "boruya," and so it was. In the language of the Pygmy people of the Congo rain forest, boruya means ghost. This ghost, so the Pygmies told me, lived in the Big Forest and wore horns on his head. Furthermore, the Pygmies stated with conviction, the boruya could not be killed.

I reasoned that if the thing had horns, it was an animal and not a ghost. In the Congo rain forest it could only be a bongo. It took me two weeks and a walk of three hundred miles to find out that I was dead wrong.

Jean Bepoix, our French guide in Equatorial Africa, had promised to show us a bongo. The forest-dwelling bongo is perhaps the most difficult animal in all of Africa for a sportsman to bag. Besides, the bongo is the beau brummel of the animal world. But the dark red coloring and white stripes of the bongo blend in well with the shadows of the forest places where this rare antelope lives. There are few sportsmen who can boast of having a bongo in their trophy collection. I wanted to be one of those.

Furthermore, Bepoix told me as we drove southward from Fort Archambault in French equatorial Africa to the Bangui River, that he had found, on his last trip into the Big Forest, a village of Pygmies who knew all the game in the area. Bepoix had not actually seen the Pygmy village as it was a three-day walk from the nearest road, but he had talked to two of the Pygmies from the village. Pygmies are hunters and not farmers like the larger-bodied Forest Negroes of the same area. The Pygmies know the rain forest and the game within it like the palms of their wizened little hands.

It sounded like a good bet for bongo, especially as two of my friends had already bagged bongo along the Ubangi River. If we could persuade the Pygmies to go with us into the country of the boruya, finding a bongo would be a cinch.

Jean Bepoix and I gathered what equipment we needed for a two-week walking safari. In Jean's old power wagon we headed east from the town of Bangui along the road to Aguifendi. This area, now called the Central African Republic, was, before 1960, a part of southern French Equatorial Africa. The countryside is covered with dense jungle growth very much like the Belgian Congo, which lies just across the river. The road which we traveled, however, angled away from the river proper and headed easterly through the fringes of the rain forest towards the Ouarra River, where only the small side streams are flanked by belts of jungle growth. This kind of country is called Gallery Forest.

We stopped at the village of Baranda where the Forest Negroes, under French supervision, had planted large banana plantations. This was as far as we could go by car. We paid a citizen of Baranda to watch our vehicle and hired fifteen other Barandians to serve as porters for a march southward into the jungle country.

This time of year, the middle of April, was, as Jean called it, "zee dry season." It rained regularly every night and quite often during the day as well. The long palm-thatched houses of the Forest Negroes simply break up the larger drops of water and filter them in a fine, exasperating spray over the occupants within. After our first night in Baranda, we were never dry for the rest of the trip.

But wet as we were, it was exciting to start southward the next morning on a walking safari. As the line of porters with our loads of equipment on their heads straggled out behind us, I felt like Livingstone penetrating the inner recesses of the

Dark Continent. We followed a narrow trail through the wet grass of a big savanna between the arms of the gallery forest below Baranda. When we entered the jungle itself on the same narrow trail, the early morning sun was blotted out as though by an eclipse. We never crossed another savanna or saw the sun clearly again. Furthermore, my enthusiasm for the walking safari was considerably diminished by the time we had walked eight hours without stopping to eat or rest. As I was carrying nothing except my rifle, I could not complain. Most of our grinning porters were carrying fifty pounds or more apiece. It developed that our goal for our first day's march was a new plantation of the Forest Negroes some thirty-five miles within the rain forest. Here a few families from Baranda had begun to clear the trees and plant bananas. The major attraction, if there was any attraction in that dank and dark place, was a large grove of oil-nut palms. The Forest Negroes roast the datelike nuts of this palm to eat, and they also collect them for the oil which they contain.

As we arrived at this outpost of no civilization at all, I just had strength enough to ask Bepoix how we were going to meet our Pygmy guides. He had already explained that the Pygmy village was two days march beyond Little Baranda, as they called the clearing in the forest. "Zey send for zee Babingas when we leave zee road," Jean explained.

I went to sleep with the rain dripping in my face, trying to figure out how any human could go one hundred miles on foot through the forest trails while we were going thirty or so. Through the roar of the tropical rain on the thatched roof I heard the boom of thunder; it seemed to have a regular rhythm and cadance. "Zee drums," Jean mumbled in the dark beside me. "Zey tell that we come safe to Little Baranda."

Talking drums! So that was the way! In the morning I examined the telegraphic apparatus of the Forest Negroes. The drum, a large hollow log with a slit along its upper side, was suspended horizontally on two sharp stones. The telegraph operator sat astride the drum and beat it with a large stick wrapped with skin. That same morning the two Pygmy guides, Hota and Borgu, appeared. The message had been relayed to them by intermediate drums when we left the road.

First the porters held a ceremony over my Weatherby rifle to make sure that the bullet would be effective against a boruya. They danced around the gun, yelling "bump-bumpa," and pushing good luck into the barrel so that it could not miss. As I had made a couple of spectacular misses in the previous two-months' hunt in French Equatorial Africa, I was all for this.

While the porters were sorting loads and eliminating every unnecessary item, Bepoix was questioning the Pygmies through an interpreter. He asked them especially about the boruya, the ghost of the forest. The two Pygmies nodded solemnly as they heard the word "boruya," and pointed behind them towards the solid walls of trees. "Yes, the boruya lives there. He has twisted horns and cannot be killed. He has never been killed."

I saw one of the Pygmies carrying a knife suspended by a bandoleer of red hide marked with white stripes. That strip of skin could only have come from a bongo. And yet these two little fellows had just said that the ghost of the forest cannot be killed. Something was very wrong here. Perhaps the Pygmies were not telling all that they knew. Maybe they were treacherous and deceitful.

I could not have been more wrong about the two Pygmy guides, Hota and Borgu, who took us next morning into the great rain forest to the south. After several days, I found that these two diminutive men were quiet, soft-spoken, and capable. Although we could not speak a word of any mutual language, I grew to know them very well and to like them immensely. Our Pgymy guides were so thoroughly at home in the great rain forest that they seemed a part of the animal life there. Curiously enough, the six Forest Negroes who had somewhat reluctantly agreed to accompany us on the hunt as porters were lost once they left the clearings of their banana plantations and the trails between them.

The great rain forest is like a damp cellar. The ribbed trunks of the forest trees tower so far overhead that their tops are lost in the green gloom of the canopy of vegetation. Trailing lianas hang out of the semiobscurity from the tree limbs far above. The forest floor itself is in eternal darkness. Here and there younger trees and bushes struggle for a single spot of sunlight which might give them strength enough to compete with their neighbors. The silent twilight of the great forest is marked only by the steady drip of water and the occasional cry of a hornbill in the crowns of the trees above. One of the queerest effects of the forest is the loss of a sense direction. The faint light which filters down through the millions of glossy leaves overhead gives little indication of where the sun is. There are no landmarks. I was astounded to find that the Forest Negroes were as easily confused about directions as myself. But the Pygmies never were. Whether we were on elephant trails or walking through the forest with no sign of a trail, our two Pygmy guides took us unerringly and directly to any spot.

Curiously enough, one of our major problems was water in that dank forest. We were, so Bepoix told me, approximately fifty miles from the nearest stream. There were, however, shallow depressions in the forest floor which filled with water during the rainy season. As it continued to rain every night during our stay, I made a mental note that I never wanted to see the rainy season if this was their idea of a dry period. My thin bed soon was slimy with mildew. My mosquito netting fell apart in gray patches. The big brown-winged mosquitoes which appeared at nightfall could sail through without folding their wings. As usual, our two Pygmies were the only sensible ones. When we camped, they constructed a low platform of small branches on which they slept. Beneath, they put a smoldering punk log. The smoke kept the mosquitoes at bay. To keep off the rain, they pulled a covering of enormous green leaves over their faces and shoulders.

From Little Baranda, we marched for two days, in a generally southward direction, to a deserted Pygmy village in the forest. As we slogged into the little clearing beneath the trees, we could still see the decaying sleeping platforms which the Pygmies had built there and the framework of two domed huts which they had used for more permanent shelter. Near the old Pygmy camping place was a depression in the forest floor as big as a city lot and half filled with green, slime-coated water. As we approached the spot, a number of brown tree ducks flew up and perched on the limbs of the dead trees in the middle of the pond. We brushed the scum aside and filled our canteens.

There certainly were bongo in the vicinity of the old Pygmy village. If I needed any further proof, the moldering skull and horns of a bongo bull that I found in the Pygmy camp furnished it. Our two Pygmies were armed with tiny bows and arrows and long-shafted spears. If they could get a bongo with that equipment, I certainly ought to be able to shoot one with a rifle.

It was typical of the Pygmies that they did not argue when Bepoix said that the boruya was a bongo. When I told the interpreter to tell our two little guides that I wanted a bongo very badly, the interpreter did not use boruya. He used a different word which means bongo in the Babinga language. But no one seemed to wonder about this.

The first morning of hunting we found the tracks of a bongo bull two or three miles from the deserted Pygmy village. As it had rained the night before, the tracks in the mud were obviously burning fresh. With one of the Pygmies in front of me as a tracker, I tiptoed along on the sodden forest floor straining for the first view of the quarry. Four of the Forest Negroes, who had come along with us to carry water bottles and lunch, trailed behind. I was amazed at how much noise these porters made as they slogged through the mud.

I finally told Bepoix to order them to hang back a hundred yards so that we would have a thin chance of getting up to the bongo bull. I had learned before how keen-eared a bongo can be. Our second Pygmy guide simply faded off into the trees at the side of the trail and was gone.

We tracked the bongo where the animal had fed early that morning. He had nibbled on some pale green shoots of a three-leafed plant which grew in little clumps on the forest floor. Hota tested the juice from the severed stems. The fluid was still fresh and sticky. The bongo was just ahead. The tracks of the bongo bull straightened from his zigzag course. The imprints in the mud led toward a moss-covered log on the forest floor. Steping as daintily as pouter pigeons, Hota and I rounded the upturned roots of the dead forest giant. There was a sudden rush of sound in the stillness. A sapling snapped. Hoofs pounded on the mud. Then the silence closed in again. We found the bongo bed just on the other side of the log. We were no more than fifteen feet away when the animal jumped up and sprinted for safety. I grinned a sickly grin at Hota. He solemnly motioned me on. We would try again.

Late in the morning we stopped for a rest and an unappetizing lunch. In the last four hours of steady tracking, we had jumped the bongo three times. We had never so much as seen a patch of red hide in the gloom between the trees. I was wet and frankly discouraged. I had been through this kind of bongo hunting before.

While we ate our slimy sandwiches, the other Pygmy, Borgu, appeared among us. He came as silently as he had gone. He carried on his back a little knapsack made of leaves with carrying straps manufactured from vines. The package contained large land snails, some kind of bulb that he had dug up, and the carcass of a small squirrel-like rodent which I had never seen before. In all of the later days of the hunt, whenever one Pygmy guide was tracking for us, the other was off foraging. How the food gatherer could find us in that vast place was a continual mystery. I was constantly impressed by the differences between the Pygmies and the Forest Negroes: the Pygmies were completely at home in the forest; the agricultural Negroes were ill at ease as soon as they left their shambas.

In the afternoon we found the tracks of another lone bongo bull. We had already crossed the tracks of two or three groups of female bongo with young. There had been another single track of an animal with enormously elongated hoofs. I thought that it might be the track of the rare okapi, since I had never seen an okapi track. When Jean asked the Pygmies about this, they shook their heads and pointed southward. We decided to have one more try at a bongo, since the track looked very fresh, as if the animal had begun to feed early in the afternoon. The track led us in a few minutes into a half-open clearing. This was one of the depressions which hold water in the rainy season. Although it was now dry, we could see on the boles of the trees where the water had stood six or eight feet deep some months before. The standing water had killed a few trees so that a little sunlight filtered through. Where the pond had been, the ground was covered with the three-leafed plant which the bongo like. This bongo bull had apparently left his bed to feed in the clearing. His tracks were everywhere. Some of the pale green weeds growing in the pond bed had been nibbled off only minutes before. It took one of the Pygmies perhaps thirty minutes to find where the bongo had left the weed patch and returned to the forest. The tracks led straight to a blowdown of trees where some gale of long ago had uprooted four or five forest giants and laid them in a pile. Other trees and saplings had long since reached up to use the precious sunlight in the vacant place. Some large trees grew on the bodies of the fallen.

Hota, who was in the lead, held up his hand for me to stop. He looked at the fallen trees for five minutes. Then he cautiously moved a few steps to the side and stopped again. He held up his nose and sniffed the wind like a hunting hound. Hota was scenting like a wild animal for the body odor of the bongo. He looked back at me. I could not tell from his expression whether he had smelled the bongo or not, but he seemed confident. He crawled to the right and crouched again, testing the wind. Then he pointed with his hand held close to his body. There was a dark space between two of the fallen trees. A few ferns grew there. Behind the fallen trunks was dark shadow—nothing more. The Pygmy motioned me forward. I crawled behind him and looked over his shoulder. There was nothing.

Suddenly the shadows moved. There was a rush of motion behind the fallen trees. Frantically I threw the gun to my shoulder and shot at the movement. A bright splinter of wood jumped from the side of one of the trees. Even as the thing ran, I could not make out the form or the color of the animal. The bongo was gone.

After this bitter disappointment, it was too late to get back to our camp in the deserted Pygmy village. Bepoix and I split a can of sardines between us and slept sitting up against the bole of a tree. Our four porters were equally miserable as the big brown mosquitoes droned back and forth. The two Pygmies, as usual, dined well, and slept well on their little platforms which they constructed in a few minutes. I finally spent half the night making a sleeping platform for myself. I abandoned it after one try. Lying on those raw poles was like sleeping on a set of broken springs without any mattress.

Our first day of bongo hunting was a good sample of the week that followed. The bongo were present but elusive. Twice the Pygmies smelled or saw bongo ahead. I never so much as got a glimpse of a tail or a horn.

The continued dampness was making me sick. My skin be-ban to feel like the epidermis of a toad. I had never heard that mildew can grow on a human, but in the rain forest I think it is possible. Even Bepoix was silent and moody. He had lived a good part of his life on the edge of the great forest, although only once before had he penetrated so far to the southeast. Furthermore, Jean had run out of cigarettes and we were both just about out of food. Three of our porters had deserted us. We wondered if these Forest Negroes would be able to find their way back to Baranda. At the time, we didn't much care.

Only the two Pygmies, Hota and Borgu, seemed to be undiscouraged, and well fed. The clammy gloom of the rain forest seemed to be a natural background for their taciturn dispositions. Nor were they downhearted that we had not yet bagged a bongo, or even seen one, for that matter. We would try again, Hota said in his quiet way. He knew where there was another forest pond that was about a five-hours' walk to the southeast. We would try there in the morning. Neither Bepoix nor I was particularly enthusiastic. We were so leg weary that a five-hour march to this new spot appalled us. And what difference did direction make? The country was the same no matter where we went.

We started out on the next morning a dispirited and silent crew. As usual, Borgu disappeared into the forest at the side of the elephant trail an hour after we had started. Our three remaining porters carried what was left of our equipment; it amounted only to our moldering beds and what was left of our mildewed tent. Jean was down to his last jug of wine and there were two cans of bully beef remaining. We were going to have a thin and hungry time getting back to the road.

The two Pygmies took us unerringly through twelve or fifteen miles of forest without ever so much as following an elephant trail. We had started off as the first dim daylight filtered down through the great trees. About noon, we saw ahead a lighter patch of shadow which was the forest pond. The two Pygmies could not have taken us straighter to this remote spot if they had used radar. But the Pygmies and their forest ways seemed destined to failure anyhow. The pond itself was almost dry. What water there was looked like a bright green rug and was about the same size. As we stepped up to the edge, a half-dozen brown ducks spurted up from the slime-coated puddle and circled among the trees.

Around the edge of the scummy pond were a few old bongo tracks. There was nothing fresh enough to follow. A bongo bull had been nibbling on some weeds growing at the edge of the water a day or two before. We had come all of this distance for nothing.

Hota, as usual, was testing the wind with his nose. I was accustomed to the Pygmies' scenting like hunting hounds. It no longer seemed strange. This time Hota crouched and ran around the edge of the pond like a beagle. Borgu followed him closely. The two put their heads together but spoke no words. Both of them testing the wind. A very faint breeze blew through the dead trees in the middle of the clearing. The brown ducks sat above us on some bare limbs and looked down stupidly. Jean motioned the three porters to sit down. They collapsed. We followed the two Pygmies in a half circuit around the pond. Hota and Borgu were standing behind the bole of a gigantic tree. They looked around the curve of the trunk and then shrank back. "Boruya!" Hota whispered beneath his breath and pointed. I looked where he pointed. There was nothing. There were only the great trunks of the trees growing thicker on the far side of the pond. There was no bongo, no life, no thing.

"Jean," I said half aloud, "these damn Pygmies can see—

Over beyond the pond a brown something moved among the trees. There was another, and another. I could hear a rustling on the sodden leaves. Automatically I threw my rifle to my shoulder and followed the movement of the running forms. There was a pair of horns zigzagging through the shadows. Just behind was another set. I could see the ivory tips of the horns as they appeared and disappeared among the trees. Through the telescopic sight of the rifle I could see the brown shoulder of the biggest bull. I jerked the trigger savagely.

The clap of the shot sent the tree ducks spiraling into the air with unducklike shrieks. The two Pygmies disappeared as though an invisible force had jerked them from behind the big tree. Jean and I ran forward. He was muttering something in French and pounding me on the back. "C'est bon, ça. Vous avez tué un bongo."

There on the dry leaves lay an animal. But it was not a bongo. The lyrate horns might have fitted a bongo but the brown hide with the white-spotted markings was a far cry from the red white-striped bongo I had expected. The hoofs of this curious animal were shaped like skis and were almost as long.

"Why, it's a sitatunga!" I said incredulously. "A sitatunga in the big forest. It can't be."

It was indeed a sitatunga. But not an ordinary one, if any sitatunga can be described as ordinary. The African sitatunga lives in vast swamps such as papyrus-bordered lakes or the great Sudd swamp of the Upper Nile. I had already shot a sitatunga in the swamps of western Tanganyika. So the ghost animal of the Pygmies was a forest sitatunga. We had been after a rare bongo. This animal was rarer still.

We found out later that the British, fifty years before, had described a new species of forest sitatunga which lived in the southern Sudan, but that they had never been able to get a complete specimen. Certainly the one which we bagged so accidentally was not an isolated animal, since there were at least six sitatunga in the group which we had encountered by that remote pond.

We had some very bad moments during the rest of the day when we thought our two Pygmies had deserted us. We were extremely dubious if we could find our way out of the big forest without them. They joined us silently as ghosts late in the afternoon. They would not touch the animal which we carried, nor even look at it. I noticed also that they would not look at me nor come close to my gun. The ghost of the forest had been killed. This could only be done by very powerful magic. As for myself, I thought it was sheer unadulterated luck.

18 · Bingo on Bongo

THE RED ANIMAL was walking on mist. He humped his back and minced forward a few steps. Still, I could see no ground below or sky above. Just behind the first bongo, another appeared. The vapors swirled around their legs, and cleared for a moment. I saw white stripes against dark, chestnut red hide. Above were massive horns a yard long. Both animals were big bulls. I had waited two years and hunted nine weeks for this one shot.

In some things I am a hard-luck guy. If a pretty girl comes to our house, I'm the kind of fellow who ends up with the chaperone. The bongo is a mighty pretty girl. But male or female, the bongo antelope of Africa is shyer than the most blushing wallflower that ever refused a dance. I ought to know. I spent over nine weeks of hunting, on four separate African safaris, before I shot at one.

If the African bongo were as common as zebra, which it isn't, it still would be one of the favorite trophy animals in Africa. Lots of sportsmen like to go after something just because it is rare and hard to get. "Rare and hard to get" are gross understatements as far as the bongo is concerned. All hunters like to bag game which makes a good trophy. Of all of the trophies anywhere in the world, the bongo qualifies as one of the most beautiful. Even with the incentive of being rare, and at the same time a spectacular prize, there are very few hunters who have a bongo head over their fireplace.

The bongo is described as a beautiful member of the bushbuck and eland tribe, which inhabits the forest of Africa from the Congo to Mount Kenya. It is a large animal; the males weigh about six hundred pounds on the hoof, and both males and females are horned. The coloring of the bongo, however, is what makes the animal so especially beautiful. The body is a chestnut red, set off by parallel white stripes. The face, also, is marked with white, as is the throat. In spite of huge, oxlike ears, the bongo certainly rates as the pinup girl of all African game. But it is the bongo's retiring habits which make him so rare in game collections. The bongo has an innate shyness, which is not only agoraphobia, but a downright mania to avoid people. If humans show up in an area, the bongo move out. Bongo are never found close to a settlement, and the smell of human scent alone seems to throw them into hysteria. Habitually an animal of deep forests or heavy bamboo growth, the bongo is virtually impossible to approach in his native element.

I knew all this before I started. And yet, like many another hunter before me, I counted on luck and the gods of chance to deliver a bongo to me. It was the only major game animal of Africa which I had not yet taken. On safari into the southern Sudan in 1959, I had counted on getting a bongo. As a matter of fact, I was naive enough to think that it might be easy. At the very headwaters of the tributaries of the Nile, on the boundary between the Belgian Congo and the Sudan, the British, during their occupation of the country, had reported a number of bongo. Along the low divide which marks the boundary is a series of seeps, rich in minerals, which the bongo use as salt licks. The British government set aside a number of these salt licks as a bongo preserve. When the Sudan became independent in 1956, in a move to try to establish a tourist and safari business, the new Sudanese government gave me permission to take a bongo on this bongo preserve. What a cinch! It would be like shooting a pigeon in Central Park.

With my wife Brownie as photographer, and a game scout

furnished by the Sudanese government as guide, getting to
the bongo preserve was a series of adventures in itself.

Our first disappointment was to find everywhere the evidence of native poaching. Game pits were dug on all of the
trails which led into the salt licks. But even at that, there were
fresh bongo tracks at the main lick. Rihani (the game scout)
and I visited the major licks at dawn and at dusk for several
days. We stayed at one of the licks all night, for a series of
mosquito-infested vigils. On the first all-night stand, a young
bull bongo stepped daintily around the freshly-dug game
pits, and approached us. He stood and looked at us for five
minutes, with his ears cocked forward, while I admired his
beauty. I passed him up. His horns were perhaps twenty-five
inches long, and slender. I have thought about that young
bull bongo a thousand times since. There is a hunting adage to
the effect that if you see something you want, you'd better
take it. If you wait for a bigger one, the game bag will be
empty.

Three months later, in the jungles of French Equatorial
Africa, I went bongo hunting again. This time I went with
Jean Bepoix, who knew a strip of forest country along the
Ubangi River where the bongo are as thick as politicians in
Paris—but a lot harder to find. Two or three French guides,
of whom Bepoix is one, found some glades in the Ubangi
forest where the bongo come out at night to feed. The hunters
sit on a platform in a tree, and pot the bongo as they come
into the open. I had killed tigers this way in India, but somehow it didn't seem like a sporting way to get a bongo. I
needn't have been so puritanical in my sporting code. Before
I was finished more than a year later, I was ready to use anything from poison to hand grenades. As it was, Bepoix and I,
with a couple of Pygmy guides, staggered around in the semi-
twilight of the Ubangi rain forest following bongo tracks. By
accident, I managed to collect a forest sitatunga, which is the
only example of this animal ever brought in. Of bongo, I
didn't see so much as a square inch of red hide.

Hunters in the Belgian Congo occasionally hunt bongo, but in British Kenya they have been doing it for years. The eastern range of the bongo extends to the Aberdare Mountains and to Mount Kenya itself. Furthermore, the eastern variety of the bongo, which lives only in these mountain hideouts, is the heaviest kind, and has the largest horns in Africa. British safari companies for the past twenty years have taken a few misinformed clients up on the slopes of Mount Kenya to hunt bongo. Usually, a few days in the cold and rainy bamboo forest cured these intrepid adventurers of the bongo fever. Two weeks was the outside limit for a bongo hunt, and very few clients ever came back for a second try. An even smaller number ever managed to get a shot at a bongo. But a dozen or so bongo were brought in to Nairobi over a period of years. A real spurt was given the bongo business during the Mau Mau emergency. During this exciting time, most of the white hunters in Kenya were up on Mount Kenya chasing Mau Maus. Occasionally they saw a bongo and quite often they saw bongo tracks. Some of these hunters came back to Mount Kenya to have a crack at the bongo after the emergency was over.

I persuaded one such ex-Mau Mau scout to have a go at bongo in June of 1959. The white hunter concerned was David Ommanney, who had combed the ridges of Mount Kenya for the best part of two years with an outfit known as the Kenya Rifles. In some hundreds of patrols in the forests of Mount Kenya, Ommanney had bumped into bongo on three or four occasions. He had found several Mau Mau hangouts furnished with bongo skins. Apparently, at least some of the terrorists had worked out ways of getting these elusive animals.

David and I tiptoed through the bamboo jungles of Mount Kenya for two weeks. We followed a dozen fresh bongo tracks during this time. We bagged a rampaging mountain rhino. We avoided a herd of stampeding buffalo. But we never saw a bongo.

The bamboo belt on Mount Kenya is one of the most unpleasant places in the world to hunt. Even at midday it is as dark as a cellar and twice as damp. If it isn't raining, there is a cloying mist which hangs eternally on the flank of the mountain. The bamboo itself is monotonous. It is overhead, all around you, and underfoot. I had always thought bamboo was tropical. Not this kind. Mount Kenya bamboo was as cold as a forest of dry ice and twice as doleful. At its upper edge, where it merges into open moorland on the high flanks of the mountain, the weather freezes every night.

In spite of the forbidding country, somehow the bongo fever had me. After two weeks with David Ommanney on Mount Kenya, both of us were too tired to go out and fall into another muddy elephant track. But I determined to hunt bongo again.

The opportunity came with a trip to Somalia to check new hunting possibilities there in connection with the independence of the country on July 1, 1960. Before going to Somalia I stopped off in Kenya to have a last go at the bongo. Andrew Holmberg had said that he knew a piece of jungle country where bongo had never been hunted before and where we ought to get bongo and also the rare yellow-backed duiker. But when Brownie and I landed at the Nairobi airport, Andrew Holmberg, hobbling along on a pair of crutches, met us with a doleful face. He had been shot through the foot with a heavy double rifle while hunting elephants. It was obvious that he could not take us bongo hunting, but he would send a young member of his safari firm in his place.

We had heard of Theo Potgieter before. It was Potgieter who had finally killed the famous leopard of Manyara, which had mauled and almost killed two men. Potgieter also had been on Mau Mau patrol, especially in the Aberdare Mountains to the west of Mount Kenya. Backed by Andrew's bongo advice and with a small safari outfit furnished by him, we started out on what was to be my last bongo hunt. As there were three or four bongo safaris milling around Mount Kenya at the time, Theo decided to try the Aberdares. Few would-be bongo hunters have ever attempted the Aberdare area, chiefly because the jungle growth and bamboo forest there is thicker and more obscure than that on Mount Kenya. Holmberg had seen many signs of bongo in the south Aberdares while on Mau Mau patrol. Furthermore, Potgieter's brother-in-law ran a sawmill at South Kinangop at the south end of the Aberdare range. This seemed a good base of operations, especially since it was only a short eighty miles or so from Nairobi.

Holyoak's sawmill proved to be a fascinating place in itself. While a ranger for the British forty years ago, the father of Mrs. Potgieter and her brother, Eric Holyoak, had planted some thousands of acres of forest trees. The Holyoak sawmill, under license from the Kenya government, was cutting these same trees which had matured so soon into saw lumber in the ideal wet climate of the mountain. In their lumbering operations on the slopes of the Aberdares, the Holyoaks occasionally saw traces of bongo. Young Eric, as I found later, had been something of a one-man army against the Mau Maus during the emergency. He had been given three military decorations by the government for his activities against the terrorists. During Eric's forays on the Aberdare ridges, he had learned every elephant path and bamboo thicket in the whole area. Eric had never killed a bongo but he knew where they were.

Potgieter established our camp on the edge of a clearing near the sawmill. Even here at the foot of the mountain it was damp and cold with constant mist and rain like Mount Kenya. I had always thought of the bongo as a tropical animal. I should have known better by this time. We had one tremendous advantage, with Holyoak as a guide. Instead of searching for bongo all over the Aberdares, we went straight to them.

A steep canyon with two swift streams cuts the south end of the Aberdares. This is the Cherangani which flows past the Holyoak's sawmill. The Cherangani is an ideal trout stream and has been stocked by the British for the past several years.

In its upper headwaters, the Cherangani flows through steep-sided canyons. At its very head is a high hump of bare volcanic rock called the Elephant. On the first day, Holyoak, accompanied by one of his foresters, led us across the Cherangani canyon and up a grueling two-hour climb on the far side. Eric told us, as we stood panting on one of the frequent rests, that when he had surprised a bunch of Mau Mau in a cave on the side of the Elephant, he had seen bongo there. The Mau Maus had eighteen bongo skins inside their cave when he found the place.

The bamboo-covered spur just below the Elephant we dubbed "Bongo Point." The place was crawling with bongo. That first morning we trailed a lone bongo bull without seeing him. We crossed the fresh tracks of half a dozen other bongo at the same time. But the bamboo and other growth on Bongo Point was as thick as the hairs on a dog's back. There wasn't an opening the size of a card table in the whole place. And the bongo loved it.

For a week, Theo and I left camp every morning before daybreak and climbed up the slippery elephant trails to Bongo Point. We trailed bongo every day, usually trying to pick out a lone bull for our quarry. Twice we got within a few feet of a bull before he jumped and ran. We heard the bongo crashing through the bamboo, but we never got a single glimpse of red hide or white stripes. At the end of a week of tiptoeing, crawling, and sneaking, we were exhausted, and the bongo were spooked off Bongo Point.

At the suggestion of Eric, we attempted a flank attack on the situation. We were sure that the bongo had simply moved over to another bongo ridge, at the very head of the Cherangani. On two grueling days, we attempted to circle clear around the Cherangani basin. It was a six hour hike one way. We found bongo sign all right, but we also found a lot of other wild life. On the second expedition around the head of the Cherangani, we ran into a herd of fifteen forest elephants. The elephants were resting quietly, on the very crest of a knife edge ridge that would have been difficult going for a Rocky Mountain goat. To avoid any unpleasantness, we circled low on the flank of the ridge, to get around the elephants. In the middle of the steepest place, where even the bamboo had a hard time holding on to the vertical lava rock, we jumped a herd of buffalo. We were attempting a narrow game trail which followed a crack in the lava rock. Apparently this was the only way in or out of the place, and the buffalo were using it. Crackling bamboo stalks like jackstraws, the herd swept at and through us. We got out of the game trail by hanging on to rocky projections and swaying bamboo stems. The lead buffalo plunged down the trail ten feet from us. If a certain bamboo had pulled out of its none too secure hold on the base of a rock, I would have fallen right on top of the stampeding herd.

After the buffalo episode, we decided to give the Cherangani a rest. But we were the ones who needed it. A ten or twelve hour hike, day after day, up and down those slippery trails, will take the starch out of any bongo hunter. We took a swing north of Mount Kenya in the Northern Frontier, to look for a big elephant, and to let the hot desert sun dry some of the Aberdare mist out of our soggy bones. Two weeks later, we were back at the Holyoak sawmill, ready to try again. We had a plan.

It was obviously a poor idea to climb up in the morning and slide back in the evening. We gathered half a dozen reluctant safari boys, and put loads on their heads for a walking safari. We were going to establish a camp up on Bongo Point. Furthermore, we were not going to tiptoe after any more bongo. That stuff was for the bamboo birds. We were going to sit on a rocky spur, up on the side of the Elephant, and look for bongo with our binoculars, in a scientific manner. Eric had said that, during the emergency, on several occasions he had seen bongo come out of the bamboo just as the dawn mists began to rise. The animals fed on the edge of the moorlands for a few moments, and then melted back into the bamboo.

The new system worked perfectly. Not that our Siwash camp on Bongo Point was perfect. It was perhaps the steepest, most uncomfortable, sketchy, soggy, dripping camp that I have ever had the misfortune to be a part of. I have never seen a sorrier set of African natives than our safari boys in Camp Bongo. For three days, nobody could talk above a whisper, for fear of scaring the quarry, and nobody had a dry bed or a square meal. But it was worth it.

The first evening after we had set up our camp by a little dripping pool right at the foot of the Elephant, we saw a single bongo over across the Cherangani. Just at dusk, the animal came out of the upper fringes of the bamboo, and fed for a few moments at the edge of the moorlands. He looked like a spot of dark red blood in the distance.

The next morning at daybreak, we mounted the side of the Elephant to look again. At first light, ten bongo came out of the bamboo, and began to graze in the open. They were about a mile away, and by the time we had stalked them, they had returned to the bamboo, and we found only fresh tracks when we arrived at the spot. However, our plan was working. The next day we saw bongo again, both morning and evening. The only catch was that the unpredictable animals did not always come out of the bamboo in the same place.

The third morning, we covered the mile or so to the shallow valleys at the head of the Cherangani before daylight. Every elephant print in the trails which we followed was full of icy water. Every bamboo frond that brushed against us slapped us in the face as though with a wet towel. But we didn't even notice these discomforts. Just at daylight, we climbed on top of an isolated piece of rock at the base of the Elephant, four or five hundred yards from the place where we had seen bongo twice before. The morning wind blew up out of the Cherangani, drifting trailers of mist up the face of the Elephant. The first bongo appeared before the sun.

One animal, then another, stepped timidly from the dark arches of the bamboo, and walked forward into the open. The bongo trotted up the slope with curious hump-backed gait. As we focused our binoculars on them, we could plainly see the white stripes on their bodies.

"They're bulls—all bulls," Theo hissed in my ear, as five, and then six, animals stepped from the bamboo and began to feed. Kirimania, Theo's head tracker, was lying on his belly on the rock beside us. Kirimania had no binoculars, but he didn't need them. "*Ndume macuba, ndume macuba mingi,*" he mumbled.

Kirimania was right. All of the bongos were bulls, and big ones at that. Apparently this was the bull herd of all the bongo of the Cheranganis. Two more animals appeared at the edge of the bamboo. The head of the first one, as he stopped in the mouth of the game trail tunnel in the bamboo, looked like a beautiful trophy already mounted on somebody's wall. After looking around and fanning their ears, the last two bongo stepped forward. Theo and I stiffened together. The last two bulls were monsters.

"Those horns are over forty inches," Theo whispered. "And they're as big around as my leg." The last two bulls were bigger than any bongo I had ever seen, even in the museums. Their bodies were dark chestnut, several shades darker than the other bulls in the bunch.

But we didn't stay to admire the bongo, or to remark that we were probably the only hunters ever to see eight mature bongo bulls in broad daylight. Theo and I were already crawfishing off the wet rock. I picked up my Weatherby .300, cranked a shell up the spout, and checked the telescopic sight for drops of water. At a half run, Theo and I skirted the upper fringes of the bamboo to close the range. A few projecting and stunted bushes screened us from the feeding bongo. Within five minutes, we had crawled to a single bush which topped a low rise on the edge of the moorland. The bongo were just beyond.

I thrust the rifle forward and looked over. There were two bongo bulls, about one hundred fifty yards away. The mass of bamboo behind them had disappeared in white moisture. The mist was moving over the ground like fog in a horror film. The air behind was already filled with white vapor, moving up out of the canyon below. The bongo appeared for a few seconds, as though they were walking on clouds with no solid earth around them. I centered the crosshairs of the sight on the first bongo. He was a mature bull, but not one of the two dark-colored giants which trailed the herd. We waited tensely. A third bongo appeared in the swirling mist. Already the first streamers of vapor had reached us and passed over us. It was this way every morning. As the sun heated the air, the updrafts pulled the fog out of the canyons. Soon it would cover us.

Still I waited. A fourth bongo fed slowly forward, with hesitant steps. He was perhaps the biggest bull yet, but still not one of the trophy heads of the herd. If only we hadn't seen those two giants, I would have taken this one in a second. It was an easy shot.

The lead bull circled in his feeding, and turned down the slope. They were going back to the bamboo, as we had seen them do before. The timid animals never stayed in the open more than ten minutes at the most. Silently and swiftly, a mass of white fog swept up the slope. The bongo were gone.

I grabbed Theo by one shoulder and jerked him to his feet. We moved forward in a crouching run. The bongo would be lingering for a few nibbles at the very edge of the bamboo. I could get one of the bulls there, as the mist was not yet solid. As we topped the low rise where the bongo had gone, an opening appeared in the fog. I saw the outline of a back, and wide hooked horns. A black ear waved forward and back. A rift opened in the fog. There he was! I raised the rifle. Fifty feet away stood a buffalo. The white closed in again. For the first time I was grateful. Theo and I hastily backed up, and circled to the right. We had not seen the buffalo bull before. We must get to the edge of the bamboo before the bongo disappeared completely. A few yards away, we found a shallow swale in the moor grass, leading downward. We followed it at a half run. In the swale, the mist was thinner. As we trotted forward, the wind carried the fog above our heads, as though a white blanket had been raised. In the grass, a few feet from us, was another buffalo bull, this one lying down. He was faced away from us downhill, and was chewing his cud contentedly. Theo and I retreated back up the swale and circled again. We'd have to get around to the right farther to get a look at the bongo down below.

Suddenly we heard a snort, and a rush of sound behind us. One of the contemptible buffalo had caught our wind or had smelled where we had been crawling. The second buffalo jumped up out of his bed. With a pounding of hoofs, we heard the two gallop down the slope. There was the sound of other hoofs in the white mist. The bongo! We had spilled the whole business.

Through the white mists, Theo and I followed the retreating herd. We entered the bamboo tunnel. Perhaps the bongo would linger for a moment, once they reached the sanctuary of the bamboo. We trailed them downhill, but after fifteen minutes of silent advance, we had not seen them. The tracks on the trail were confused. Some hoof prints seemed to lead off to the left. We turned that way, and we went perhaps another hundred yards. Theo and I stopped together. Through the bamboo stems was a red outline. I could see the curve of a dark, rounded back. There were horns above the head. The animal turned towards us. There were the white markings of the face. Between the bamboo stems was the dark red outline of the bongo's chest. I raised the Weatherby, and fired in the same instant. The bongo staggered back and fell sideways against the bamboo stalks. We had him!

Theo and I ran forward. Even before we put our hands on the beautiful animal, Theo cursed.

"It's a female," he spat out. "An old female! How in the name of all the gods of bongo and man did we manage to stagger into a female?"

As for me, I was both delighted and disappointed. It was indeed an old female, so dark in color that we had mistaken her for a bull. But her horns were long and massive.

Have I got the bongo fever out of my bones? Not at all. Next year I'm going back to the Elephant, and watch for one of those two giant bulls that got away.